transvestism, masculinity, and latin american literature

transvestism, masculinity, and latin american literature

genders share flesh

ben. sifuentes-jáuregui

palgrave

TRANSVESTISM, MASCULINITY, AND LATIN AMERICAN LITERATURE
Copyright © Ben. Sifuentes-Jáuregui, 2002
All rights reserved. No part of this book may be used or reproduced in any manner whatsoever without written permission except in the case of brief quotations embodied in critical articles or reviews.

First published in 2002 by
PALGRAVE™
175 Fifth Avenue, New York, N.Y. 10010 and
Houndmills, Basingstoke, Hampshire, England RG21 6XS
Companies and representatives throughout the world.

PALGRAVE™ is the new global publishing imprint of St. Martin's Press LLC Scholarly and Reference Division and Palgrave Publishers Ltd. (formerly Macmillan Press Ltd.).

ISBN 0–312–29440–9 hardback
ISBN 0–312–29441–7 paperback

Library of Congress Cataloging-in-Publication Data
Sifuentes-Jáuregui, Ben..
　　Transvestism, masculinity, and Latin American literature: genders share flesh / Ben. Sifuentes-Jáuregui.
　　　p. cm.
　　Includes bibliographical references and index.
　　ISBN 0–312–29440–9 (hc.) — ISBN 0–312–29441–7 (pbk.)
　　1. Spanish American literature—20th century—History and criticism.
2. Transvestites in literature.　3. Transvestism—Latin America 4. Masculinity in literature. 5. Gender identity in literature.　I. Title.

PQ7081 .S56 2002
860.9'98'09045—dc21   2001044639

A catalogue record for this book is available from the British Library.

Design by Westchester Book Composition

First edition: February 2002
10 9 8 7 6 5 4 3 2 1

Printed in the United States of America

Contents

List of Illustrations vii
Acknowledgments ix

Introduction Chronicle of Gender Foretold: Transvestism 1
              and the Difficulty of Gender

Chapter 1   Nation and the Scandal of Effeminacy: 15
              Rereading *Los "41"*

Chapter 2   Fashion's Lost Word: Carpentier Writes Woman 53

Chapter 3   Gender without Limits: 87
              The Erotics of Masculinity in *El lugar sin límites*

Chapter 4   Transvestite and Homobaroque Twirls: 119
              Sarduy on the Verge of Reading Structuralism/
              Psychoanalysis/Deconstruction

Chapter 5   Kissing the Body Politic: 151
              Engendering Heterosexuality/
              Screening the Homosocial

Notes   193
Bibliography 223
Index   237

List of Illustrations

1.1. "¡Fuerza Nueva para Hombres!" ["New Strength for Men!]," *El Imparcial,* November 20, 1901.   27

1.2. José Guadalupe Posada's "Calavera Catrina," or "Calavera de la cucaracha."   29

1.3. José Guadalupe Posada's "Calavera de un lagartijo."   29

1.4. "Los Lagartijos," lithograph in *El Mundo,* July 27, 1897. Rpt. in Cosío Villegas.   30

1.5a. José Guadalupe Posada's "Los 41 maricones encontrados en un baile de la calle de la Paz el 20 de noviembre de 1901." [The 41 faggots found at a dance on Paz Street, November 20, 1901]. Front, loose pamphlet published by A. Vanegas Arroyo, 1901. Zinc etching.   32

1.5b. Continuation of *corrido* "Los 41 maricones . . ." Back. Description: Men sweeping street.   33

1.6. José Guadalupe Posada, "Los 41." Description: Calaveras [Skulls] dancing with orchestra. Zinc etching.   35

1.7. José Guadalupe Posada, "El gran viaje de los 41 maricones para Yucatán." [The great trip of the 41 faggots to Yucatan]. Loose leaf published by A. Vanegas Arroyo, 1901. Zinc etching.   36

1.8a.	Detail, "El feminismo se impone." [Feminism imposes itself]	39
1.8b.	José Guadalupe Posada, "El feminismo se impone." 1907. Zinc etching.	40
2.1.	Alejo Carpentier [Jacqueline, pseudonym], "S. M. La Moda," *Social* XI 2 (February 1926): 63–65.	77

Acknowledgments

Although I have spent my professional life using words and ideas, I find myself at a loss at this moment of acknowledging and giving thanks to so many people who have helped make this book possible. "Thank you" doesn't begin to express the overwhelming sense of gratitude that I feel for the ideas and time and friendship that many have shared over the last years. I hope everyone knows how important our conversations, debates, and humor have been to the development and completion of this book.

First of all, my greatest thanks go to Sylvia Molloy, who has acted as a teacher, an adviser, and a friend, patiently guiding me throughout this project with her brilliance and example. Without her support, I would not have been able to write it. I thank my teachers at Yale, where this project began. My teachers contributed enormously to my understanding of literature: Roberto González-Echevarría encouraged me to find the "Jacqueline" articles; Shoshana Felman and the late Hugo Rodríguez-Vecchini were important theoretical mentors. I am also thankful to Nicolas Shumway, James Fernández, and Josefina Ludmer for sharing their ideas and critiques of my work.

I am incredibly fortunate to be part of the Spanish and Portuguese Department at Rutgers, with wonderfully supportive colleagues. I thank them for providing a vibrant intellectual and professional space where I am able to rehearse my ideas. I thank Mary Lee Bretz, Mary Gossy, Jorge Marcone, Susan Martin-Márquez, Tomás Eloy Martínez, Dámaris Otero-Torres, Marcy Schwartz, Thomas Stephens, and Susana Rotker (who we miss so much), who shared their perspectives, read parts of the manuscript, and provided insightful criticism. Also, thanks to Lawrence LaFountain-Stokes, who has been a superb interlocutor on questions queer and Latino. Yolanda Martínez-San Miguel read the entire manuscript and made perspicacious suggestions and criticisms; I thank her for her generous and brilliant support. I am especially thankful to César Braga-Pinto for his knowledge of theory, our friendship, and "pizza."

During the 1998–1999 academic year, I was a faculty fellow of the Center for the Critical Analysis of Contemporary Culture at Rutgers. I am thankful to all the Fellows for helping me rethink questions of nation as they relate to sexuality. I particularly want to thank Susan Buck-Morss, Kim Butler, Pedro Caban, Bruce Robbins, and Carmen Whalen, who shared with me their work and criticism. I am grateful for the support of Rutgers, which granted me a sabbatical leave, allowing me to complete this project; I especially thank Barry Qualls for his support.

In the profession, I have met many enthusiastic and kind readers who have contributed greatly to the intellectual design of this book. I thank Henry Abelove, Jossianna Arroyo, Daniel Balderston, Will Corral, Martin B. Duberman, Rosemary Feal, Donna Guy, Myriam Jehenson, Oscar Montero, Ellen Nerenberg, Patrick O'Connor, Donald Pease, José Quiroga, Doris Sommer, and Diana Taylor. I also want to thank friends and colleagues in Mexico for their support: I thank Adriana Ortiz Ortega and Claudia Hinojosa for their friendship and hospitality, while I was in Mexico City; but above all for sharing with me their thoughts about gay and lesbian life in Mexico, which have informed my work in important ways. Special thanks to Noemí Ortega who was instrumental in my getting access to Castrejón's novel, *Los cuarenta y uno*. I thank Margo Glantz, Carlos Monsiváis, and Juan Villoro for reading parts of the manuscript, and for providing important cultural and historical details and criticism.

At Palgrave, I want to thank Gayatri Patnaik for her encouragement as well as her good-natured guidance through the editing process; also, thanks to Donna Cherry, Kasy Moon, and Jennifer Stais for ensuring that all materials were in order. My thanks to Meg Weaver and Amanda Fernández for their careful copyediting. I also thank the anonymous reviewers for their very useful comments.

I have been very fortunate to have wonderful friends who have touched my life in important ways. Michael Hollister was a source of inspiration and courage; his loss to AIDS left a great intellectual and emotional void, but his memory continues to give me grace and comfort. Bill Johnson-González has been an ideal reader and the kindest of friends; I am thankful for his intellect, and for his sharing his work and humor with me. Also, Monica S. Cyrino has been a true friend and supporter, who reminds me often that intelligence and pleasure are not mutually exclusive. I can't thank her enough for always being there. Finally, Mark Trautman has given me love, respect, and happiness. I hope that I can respond as eloquently. I thank him for being there, for thoughtfully reading the manuscript, and for so much more.

I thank everyone above, also my students, for the constant dialogue that influenced my work about gender and Latin American literature; and, I apologize for not being a better listener, and not always getting it right.

Lastly I want to thank my family for giving me so much. Without their patient love and understanding, I would have probably become a physician—and not a literary critic. My brother Juan and sister Carmen have always been good-spirited and supportive of my work, and have given me the enormous enjoyment of the avuncular role. My parents have taught me about respect and care, about learning, and about following my passions. To them, I dedicate this book.

Ben. Sifuentes-Jáuregui
July 2001

I am very grateful to the Museo Guadalupe Posada in Aguascalientes, Mexico for granting me permission to reproduce all of the Posada images on the "41." Above all, I thank the museum's director, José Luis Quiroz, for his assistance and support. Also, I would like to thank the Fundación Alejo Carpentier, especially its President, Andrea Esteban Carpentier, for permission to reproduce "S. M. La Moda" by Carpentier. I would like to acknowledge and thank Noé Hernández for allowing me to use his beautiful artwork as the cover art.

Portions of this book have been previously published in some form. Part of chapter 3 appeared in Balderston and Guy's *Sex and Sexuality in Latin America* (New York: New York University Press, 1997); a short section of chapter 4 appeared in Molloy and Irwin's *Hispanisms and Homosexualities* (Durham: Duke University Press, 1998); and a section of chapter 5 appeared in Duberman's *Queer Representations* (New York: New York University Press, 1997).

For my mother
and in memory of my father

transvestism, masculinity, and latin american literature

Introduction

Chronicle of Gender Foretold: Transvestism and the Difficulty of Gender

> Sucede que me canso de ser hombre.
> Sucede que entro en las sastrerías y en los cines
> marchito, impenetrable, como un cisne de fieltro
> navegando en un agua de origen y ceniza.
> —from "Walking Around," Pablo Neruda

> Si era hombre tenía que ser capaz de sentirlo todo, aún esto. . .
> —El lugar sin límites, José Donoso

> Y en el juego angustioso de un espejo frente a otro
> cae mi voz
> y mi voz que madura
> y mi voz quemadura
> y mi bosque madura
> y mi voz quema dura
> como el hielo de vidrio
> como el grito de hielo
> —from "Nocturno en que nada se oye," Xavier Villaurrutia

The Difficulty of Gender

Transvestism, Masculinity, and Latin American Literature: Genders Share Flesh began as a rather casual fascination with transvestism. Very soon after doing some preliminary work on the topic, I realized that, like with so many seemingly innocent acts of voyeurism, transvestism as an "event" contained and screened a deeper and more complex secret.

The figuration of transvestism would appear not just as an interesting idea to be grasped, but more as an imperative: understanding the very act of cross-dressing meant signifying and conceptualizing a dialectic, to which I had not been privy; however, once I began exploring and trying to decipher its mechanics, the very language and discourse about genders and sexualities with which I addressed questions of Latin American literature and culture would change dramatically.

Expanding on the question of the loss, actually, the nonexistence of an originary or virginal state, a critic once queried that, once you have been penetrated, what can you do? The specific context and details of this argument do not necessarily matter, for the question could easily be applied to a whole complex of social, historical, territorial, and, of course, sexual situations. After so many years, this remark on the challenges of penetration—with all its metaphorics from the romantic affects of seduction to its more explicit Romantic connotations of rape—still lingers in my mind. Echoes of a Mallarméan poetic declaration of independence, "*On a touché au vers*," of a de Manian theoretical cry, "*On a touché à la critique*,"[1] resonate clearly in the voice of a transvestite, whispering: "He trastocado el género" ("*On a touché au genre*"). Transvestism is an act that penetrates and tampers with those who witness it. This introjection of the transvestite into personal, social, and cultural psyches introduces a series of problems about uncertainty and authenticity, imposition, interiority and exteriority. Transvestism is about the raw touching, gentle tampering, and, literally, fucking up of any fixed notion of genders. Transvestism is the figure that describes in its own embodiment and realization the difficulty of gender.

Transvestism and Performance

It is useful to present a simple, working definition of "transvestism": *transvestism is a performance of gender*. Like "transvestism"—which lacks a concise and a theoretic definition (transvestism as a process is always evolving)—"performance" is also a complex term precisely because it has too many definitions.

So many times—and in as many ways—has that word "performance" been used, that it almost creates an effect of strangeness, of alienness.[2] What does performance signify? Or, better yet, *how* does performance signify?

While my intent is not to provide a genealogy of the term "performance" and its derivatives, namely "performativity," I would like to underline an *etymological* character of the idea: *per*-form. This is literally a doubling *on the side* of another form—also, a simulation of an "original" or a deformation of such. Performance ranges from the blind presumption of sameness to the grotesque and parodic. "Performance" is not a simple idea; it is a concept that has been laced with so many strands of the *theatrical* (How was Marilyn Monroe's performance in *Some Like It Hot?*), the *pedagogical* (How is your performance in school?), the *philosophical* (e.g., speech act theory) and the *sexual* (My, you were great!). These are just some of the connotations found in "performance."

Re-evaluating the question and structure of *sexual* performance is telling—perversely, all of the other "performances" can be found here. It does not require much imagination to locate the theatrical within sexual performance. Socrates's saying "no" to Alcibiades was as much a sexual act as it was a pedagogical one. And, of course, most of Freud's *oeuvre* coalesces and relates both philosophical and sexual performances. In short, sexual performance—as either a function or differential of sexuality—has been not just a means of identity but a means of knowledge(s).

The relationship between transvestism and sexual performance is a difficult relationship: there is so little known of transvestism as a sexual act because it evades prescribed sexual roles and our Imaginary fails to capture the sexual moment with or between transvestites. Therefore, while performance is theatrical or, perhaps, transvestitic, transvestism is not exactly a sexual performance. This is why I suggested the rudimentary hypothesis that transvestism is the performance of gender, a performance of what historically and culturally gets labeled "femininity" and "masculinity."

In a rather structuralist manner, insofar as gender—femininity or masculinity—is defined through the system of signs that the transvestite fixes and validates in his/her re-presentation, transvestism presents readers and viewers with a challenge. Let us think about what transvestism means *for an outside viewer*:

- Transvestism is about representing the other
- Transvestism is about occupying the place of the Other
- Transvestism is about (re)creating the figure of the (m)other (Sarduy).

I shall discuss each of these axioms in full detail throughout different chapters of the book. Now, what transvestism might mean *for the transvestitic subject* is something quite different:

- Transvestism is about representing the Self
- Transvestism is about becoming the Self
- Finally, transvestism is about (re)creating the Self.

In other words, transvestite subjects do not necessarily imagine themselves becoming some other subject, but rather they may conceive of transvestism as an act of self-realization. Transvestism inaugurates an epistemological shift that locates, defines, performs, and erases the fundamental dichotomy: Self/Other. This transvestitic erasure of the boundaries between the Self and the Other precipitates and manifests an anxiety that could be called "the denaturalization of genders." Transvestism is an operating strategy that deconstructs a specific "normality" in a gender binary and hierarchy. This deconstruction is peculiar because it takes place not only on the level of negation and *différance,* but, seemingly, of production and sameness.

The word "transvestism" itself contains an etymological conflict: on the one hand, "transvestism" comes directly from the Latin *trans-vestire,* to dress across; on the other hand, from the Latin through the French, *trans-vestire* becomes *travesti,* which later is "travesty" in English. So, on the one hand, transvestism signals a "crossing" from one gender space to another; on the other hand, it is a travesty or a lie. Consider that transvestism is obsessed with producing an effect of "realness." So, by juxtaposing transvestism's tendency toward the "real" with its etymological other, "travesty"/falseness, we can then begin to consider a fascinating dialectical movement: by showing the other's travesty through the denaturalization of genders, transvestism produces a "realness" for itself; and, by re-producing the other's "realness," by re-presenting the other, by constructing the other's "realness," transvestism also reveals the "falseness" (that is, the construction) of the other. Stated simply, transvestism makes something out of nothing, as well as nothing out of something. More specifically, transvestism recycles something out of nothing (production), as well as nothing out of something (consumption).

✦ ✦ ✦

This book is about reading the figure of the transvestite—principally, the performance and movement from "masculine" to "feminine"—in Spanish American literature; it also involves evaluating contemporary theories about gender in relation to Latin American cultural difference. Finally this book is about sexualities and queer subjectivities. When I use the term "transvestism," I am not talking about the blurring of genders (androgyny), rather I want to keep in mind the subject's desire to represent normative gender difference seamlessly. I have set it up a series of close readings that engage different moments in gender self-figuration in works by José Donoso, Severo Sarduy, Manuel Puig, and others. As a literary theorist, I am seduced by the radical power of literature. This may sound strange at a time when many literary scholars are becoming increasingly involved with cultural studies. I would not want to create a false dichotomy between both enterprises—literary and cultural studies—since both inform each other in complex ways. Importantly, critics cannot ignore the dramatic ways in which the thing we call literature—through its narrative and discursive complexities that exceed other textual forms—touches our lives. For instance, this book is about transvestism as a figure and metaphor, but it is also about an autobiographical moment, a moment of arrival and understanding. Coming to the United States from Mexico at age fourteen meant fashioning my life in new ways, learning and perfecting a new language, a new style of dress and address, a different education. The moment of crossing and understanding the new social, cultural, and political forces that informed my life in the United States can also be explained through and alongside the mechanics and process of subject formation, similar to transvestism's. Thus, reading about the unease felt by Donoso's La Manuela just before her performance brings about a moment of identification, of my own unease to express certain forms of cultural, social and sexual difference and identity. Or, witnessing Valentín in *El beso de la mujer araña* (*Kiss of the Spider Woman*) struggling to remain private in a place where privacy does not exist reminds me of those moments where I too could not be private, where my life was paradoxically trapped and on display.

Indeed, there is an even more important reason as to why I focus on literature: until recently, literature was one of the few remaining places where it was safe to write about sexuality and difference in Latin America. In the last few years, we have seen performances and writings that have brought discussions of marginal and contested sexualities to wider audiences—performances by "Las yeguas del apocalípsis," Pedro Lemebel's chronicles in Chile, Tito Vasconcelos's drag shows and Jesusa Rodríguez's all-women theater troupe in Mexico, Walter Mercado performing gender bending psychic readings in Puerto Rico and Miami. However, prior to these new expressions, it was within literary space where one would usually discover sexual difference, and it is precisely this space that I want to privilege. A scene from Gutiérrez Alea's 1993 film *Fresa y chocolate* (*Strawberry and Chocolate*)[3] demonstrates effectively the power of the literary: the gay protagonist, Diego, brings David, the naïve Communist student, to his apartment for the first time. Diego's apartment is covered with different cultural *objets,* highlighting two pictures: one of José Martí, and the other of the patriarch of contemporary Cuban letters, José Lezama Lima. There are also pictures of Marilyn Monroe, framed ballet shoes, and religious art. As part of his seduction, Diego promises David a book, not just any book, but

Mario Vargas Llosa's *Conversación en la Catedral*. That Diego gives David the book is significant in that the novel is the story of a man and his driver and their secret affair. I want to reflect on this scene as one where the homosocial story of the novel enables the gay man to speak, to give a gift, of what is "supposed" to remain silent, his gay desire. The gift of literature is also one of a space where Diego's gay desire may grow. Earlier, Diego had told David that, if he were interested, he would lend him his complete works of Sarduy and Goytisolo. Again, these authors' names point explicitly to gay male identities and desires. And later on, Diego asks David if he was familiar with Wilde, Gide, Lorca because they all had "something in common" with Diego himself. Again, the gay man uses literary figures to identify himself. We are brought to the idea that literature is a vested space where sexual and gender identifications happen. Because of the unique and protected space literature provides, we read literature and literary space, and write about it to reconcile those impossible narrative seams in our own lives. The efficacy of this critical act is one of insight and pleasure.

Sexualities and Nationalism

I begin with a brief reading of García Márquez's *Crónica de una muerte anunciada* (*Chronicle of a Death Foretold*). This canonical work immediately introduces the idea that the place of transvestism is not limited to marginal texts in Latin America. In these, my initial remarks about *Chronicle*, as well as throughout the book, I want to underline the different conceptualizations of the "body" as related in literature, politics, and theory, and outline the transformational vicissitudes that the body incurs once engaged within and outside the space of transvestism.

The overdetermined body of the protagonist (the death foretold) is characterized throughout the novel as Other—racially, spiritually, sexually, libidinally, and socially; in fact, from the beginning he is marked as outsider through his Moorish (read: Oriental) body. Santiago Nasar's body is one that submits to endless representations and displays. Just before the protagonist's death, we learn of his "talento casi mágico para los disfraces, y su diversión predilecta era trastocar la identidad de las mulatas" [almost magic talent with disguises, and his favorite entertainment of tampering with the identity of mulattas].[4] Nasar's fascination and skill with cosmetics and clothes to redraw identities cannot be read innocently. What I mean is that transvestism must be understood as a subversive practice that encompasses and goes beyond simple play. Specifically, transvestism takes on important cultural connotations in Latin America: in later discussions, I show that transvestism in Latin America is inseparable from the self-figuration of the male homosexual.[5]

Having said this, we must reread how, at the very least, his "magic talents" dramatize his position as Other; how García Márquez introduces and underscores the protagonist's difference by alluding to his "artificios de transformista,"[6] his skills as a transformer or transvestite. A closer reading of *Chronicle* teases out questions about body, gender, and nation that I address separately in a series of readings throughout this investigation.

It is useful to reiterate that the major difference between this project and that of other theorists of gender lies in the fact that, unlike Butler, Sedgwick, and others who stress the philosophical and political dimensions of gender performativity, I wish to emphasize specifically the place of the body and corporeality in Latin America, and the many ways to read its movements.[7] Given that the predominant models of (sexual) subject formation in Latin America result from corporeal positionings and readings (from Octavio Paz's "penetration model" to Sylvia Molloy's "politics of posing"),[8] analyzing sexual/gender figurations as well as nation formation reveals those corporeal attachments at their most physical level, not just their philosophical one. Once more, this study does not preclude discussing the philosophical underpinnings of subject formation; rather it asserts that there is a critical difference about the place of the body in Latin American cultures vis-à-vis the place of the body in contemporary gender theory in the United States. The subtitle of this book, *Genders Share Flesh,* highlights the place of the body in this analytic intervention and expresses the consititutive tension and battle seen in the articulation of gender in Latin American culture.

Besides the conceptualization of transvestism as a literary or critical body and figure, this project addresses questions about nationalism and literary history. Issues of nationalism cropped up at every turn: the relationship between the writing of a "national" subject and its similarities in the construction of a transvestite subjectivity was the most important.

The emergence of the relation between transvestism and nation could be explained as follows. Transvestism is about a peculiar act of self-figuration and disappearance. About this erasure and, sometimes, absolute dismissal of the transvestite *qua* subject in her own right, Marjorie Garber states in her important book, *Vested Interests,* that "[t]his tendency to erase the third term [a transvestite subject], to appropriate the cross-dresser 'as' one of the two sexes, is emblematic of a fairly consistent critical desire to look away from the transvestite as transvestite, not to see crossdressing except as male or female *manqué,* whether motivated by social, cultural, or aesthetic designs. And this tendency might be called an *underestimation* of the object."[9] Garber's highly suggestive "third term" is of interest to me because within its description we locate the importance and the relevance of transvestism as a sexual and political figure in and for Latin America; that is, how the invention of Latin America as a geographic and political construct mirrors the figuration of the transvestite. We cannot ignore the importance of context and referentiality. Each produces a subject—and the reverse is true. To this end, let us follow Garber's meditation on the "third." She notes that

> [t]he "third" is that which questions binary thinking and introduces crisis—a crisis which is symptomatized by *both* the overestimation *and* the underestimation of cross-dressing. But what is crucial here—and I can hardly underscore this strongly enough—is that the "third term" is *not a term*. Much less it is a *sex*, certainly not an instantiated "blurred" sex as signified by a term like "androgyne" or "hermaphrodite," although these words have culturally specific significance at certain historical moments. The third is a mode of articulation, a way of describing a space of possibility. Three puts in question the idea of one: of identity, self-sufficiency, self-knowledge.
>
> Let me offer three examples of that I mean by "third" here. They are: the Third World, the third actor, and the Lacanian Symbolic. The Third World is only a "third" in that it does not belong to one or another of two constructed regions, the developed West and what used to be described as the Communist Bloc. What the so-called Third World nations have in common is their post-colonial status, their relative poverty, their largely tropical locations, their largely non Caucasian populations, and the fact that they were once subjected to Western rule. Very little else makes the Third World an aggregation; the new nations that came into being as a result of decolonization have in other respects little similarity to one another. "Third World" is a political term, which simultaneously reifies and dismisses a complex collection of entities.[10]

I have quoted Garber at length because her insight and specific example coincide with my project. Indeed the "Third World" is the site for resistance against and questioning of the universality of the "First World" as it affirms itself through the act of decolonization. Nonetheless, we cannot ignore that "Third World" is a political term that takes on different and severe connotations when used primarily by industrialized, highly developed "First World" nations. In a passive and uncritical instance, "Third

World" is a term that is used to mark a hierarchy of "development," to express quantity and absence.

Sylvia Molloy expresses the problem of cultural imposition and hierarchy onto Latin America thus, "As North America's foremost Other—geographically and culturally—Latin America is constantly being asked, by the United States, to represent that Other along lines dictated by the United States' sameness. (That is, Latin America is being asked, or being pressed, to be other the way another would have it be, and not the way it sees itself.) [. . .] [T]his global, quasi-generic Other is less uniform than they (North Americans) would think; that in fact this Other is made up of many different idiosyncratic others . . ."[11] That Latin America resists the pressure to define itself always along the terms of the United States's critical discourse is an act of postcolonial resistance that has to be considered when writing a history of sexuality in any Latin American context.

It is not surprising then, that after describing this project to colleagues in other disciplines, a question that I often heard was: "Is there much cross-dressing in Latin America?" What raises this concern? Questioning about the prevalence of cross-dressing in Latin America is closely tied to the issue or, more precisely, the non-issue of sexuality, specifically marginalized sexualities, in Latin America, both misrepresented or underestimated outside and, all too often, within national boundaries.

When former Vice President Dan Quayle visited Latin America several years ago he discovered two things: first, that Latin is not spoken there; and, second, that dolls are well-endowed. Witnesses to this latter discovery laughed. But why did they laugh? Were people laughing about the doll with a big penis that Quayle allegedly bought at the marketplace? Or at Quayle's very fascination with the doll? In either respect, what is most interesting (and disturbing) is the laughter itself. I suggest that what informs and regulates this laughter has little to do with Quayle's stupidity and more to do with a U.S.-based erotic imagination and the fantastic, limited, and limiting stereotypes that those looking from the outside have created about the Latin American sexual persona. This event dramatizes that although the fields of feminism, gender, and queer studies have grown recently in the United States to think out the concepts of femininity and masculinity in the context of a postmodern debate; and, although this discussion disrupted—if not overhauled altogether—the neat, essentialist categories of gender formulated during the sexual revolution of the '60s and '70s in the United States, some U.S. readers and critics forget to ironize their positionality (whether national, social, economic, etc.) when looking at others outside the space of "America." So, it makes sense to talk about a "third" sexual or gender mode in the "Third" World because it reveals a sexual landscape scarred by different interventions, impositions, and metaphors.

Perhaps any elaboration on the question of colonialism is a possible inflection or reflection of metaphoric transvestism. If I have returned to—or, even, dwelled on—this question it is due to more than just my sensibility as a scholar of Latin American literature, for I argue throughout different chapters that the question of national identity has produced and continues to put forth (to dress up) a very "gendered" national subject—one that is almost always masculine, male, and heteronormative.

Quickly, I draw the following paradox. The figuration of Latin American national identity and of transvestism are analogic. One instance of figuring the national subject involves the selection of desirable fragments to compose "identity." Likewise, transvestism might involve picking and choosing desirable objects to create a gender effect. Often, queer bodies get marginalized by an official, "national" subject. Too often, in Latin America, the gay and the transvestite are synonymous. So, in effect, the national project casts out the very figure it reproduces. Or, as some would argue, the transvestite internalizes the strategies of authority, of power. Both gestures of national and transvestite identity formation happen simultaneously, creating interesting effects. This analogic relation signifies on identity formation.

My argument is that issues of gender identity, in general, and transvestism, specifically, have been made marginal in broad political and social discourses. This study brings them to the foreground.

❖ ❖ ❖

The motivating gesture of the book is to explore the figuration of the transvestite subject in Spanish American literature and culture. Each chapter proposes and conceptualizes a specific formulation of the "body"—the historical body, the textual and authorial body, the national and political body, and the theoretical body. What happens when each conceptualization enters the space and acts of transvestism? For example, two different men putting on a dress might not produce the same effect. For instance, in some contexts, for a man known to be gay to put on a dress might be thought of as "unoriginal" and disappointingly "expected," whereas a heterosexual man putting on that same dress might mean something completely different: that he is "daring" and "outrageous." It might mean that he is affirming his "openness" to gender, that he is "secure" in his masculinity. It might also mean that he is exercising his heterosexual privilege of doing anything he damn pleases because, after all, putting on a dress "means nothing." Thus one goal of this book is to understand the different forces that affect the meanings of transvestism.

The first chapter on *los cuarenta y uno*, the "41," deals with a sex scandal in Mexico in 1901, and it represents a kind of *summa*, where different critical forces join to reconstruct an "event." By looking at historical accounts, newspaper reports, Posada prints, a novel, chapter 1 retells the story of 41 men arrested in Mexico City for being involved in a queer dance where many of them were crossdressed. This chapter anticipates and takes into account different moments from throughout this work, how different theories inform our understanding of identities and identifications. Chapter 1 contributes to the growing interest and debates about the figuration of sexual difference in Latin America over a century ago. Specifically, it looks at sexualities in turn of the last century Mexico, in the context of ideas of posing and performativity. Chapter 1 problematizes the differences between homosexuality and effeminacy. Also, it looks at the construction of queer spaces wherein male heterosexuality may play, experiment, and expand its own desires. Finally, it introduces the problems of nation, nationalism, and sexuality into a Latin American context.

The second chapter of my project revisits—as far as I know, it examines for the first time—Alejo Carpentier's writing of/as "Jacqueline." Under the pseudonym of Jacqueline, a young Carpentier wrote fashion articles between 1925 and 1927 for the Cuban society magazine *Social*. Carpentier's Jacqueline writings are without a doubt a "minor" text, however, it is important to be included here because, as many know, Carpentier's work is considered central to the "Boom" novel in Latin America. He began experimenting early in his career with literary simulation, ventriloquizing the voices of others. The Jacqueline texts precede his first novel *Écue-Yamba-Ó* (1931), which shows his participation in the Afro-Antillean movement.

In discussing the "Jacqueline" texts, I analyze the rhetorical strategies Carpentier used to signify "feminine" qualities onto himself, to dress himself as a woman; that is, how does Carpentier write a narrative transvestism? What compromising poses does the author strike to be taken seriously as a woman? These questions open up an important critical space for feminist and gender studies research on the "body" of Carpentier scholarship: in other words, a critical imperative that operates here is understanding why his *oeuvre* is so resistant to feminist approaches.

The first and second chapters comprise examples of what could be broadly defined as "social texts," whereas the remaining three chapters focus on literary and theoretical works by canonical authors. Additionally, the first two chapters look very closely at the question of homosexual panic in the construction of gender and national identities. Hand-in-hand with the question of homosexual panic is the idea of homosexual fascination, which is explored throughout the book. How do certain relations of homosexual panic imply a certain fascination for the homosexual? How does fascination for the homosexual (read: desire) get masked by panic and homophobia?

In the next three chapters, which deal with literary and critical works by Donoso, Sarduy and Puig, I focus primarily on narrative as a genre. There is the interesting case of transvestite writing in the poetry of Clara Beter. Beter, really César Tiempo (i.e., Israel Zeitlin), was the famous prostitute, member of the Boedo group in Argentina. In 1926, Clara Beter published her "*Versos de una . . .*" (*Verses of a . . .*).[12] Unfortunately, since I was concerned exclusively with prose, I was unable to include her work in this project. One aspect about Clara that does survive in my discussion about transvestism is her poetry's relation to prostitution.

In the third chapter about Donoso's monumental novella, *El lugar sin límites* (*Hell Has No Limits*), I continue the discussion of transvestism and its endless figurations of the Eternal Feminine by looking at the question and dangers of performativity in the writing of gender. As such, transvestism is a powerful presence that constantly signifies on the "masculine," thus problematizing the axiomatics of *machismo*. Furthermore, chapter 3 analyzes the ways in which the transvestite's body is used as a textual space; a space that allows readers to dispense with the transvestite's subjectivity and to project and impose their own critical or sexual desires. Sexual difference and perversions—whether transvestism, prostitution, male homosexuality and lesbianism, even womanhood—are readily projected upon the transvestite's body. Here, I analyze in detail the idea that masculinity in its exaggerated form—in other words, *machismo*—doubles the project of transvestism. Hypermasculinity and the obsession "to act like a man" mirrors the very practices of transvestite subject formation. Finally, chapter 3 on Donoso defines the limits of creating a *corpus* of texts with "transvestism" as a regulating or central category, and explores narrativity itself as a transvestite practice.

The fourth chapter deals with the theoretical "body" in Severo Sarduy's critical work on transvestism. Chapter 4 is in some ways a continuation of the Donoso chapter; however, it delves into Sarduy's theoretical and novelistic texts. Sarduy's work evaluates the relation between his theories on transvestites and Derridean deconstruction and Lacanian psychoanalysis. Transvestism, for Sarduy, is a "metaphor for writing." It is a metaphor that gathers different literary forces (autobiography, language, literature, nationalism) and puts them into dialogue with each other. I am interested in understanding the ways Sarduy deploys the figure of the transvestite in his essays to create and situate in a critical space both Derrida and Lacan's work. Also, I discuss the ways in which Sarduy links the pulsion or drive of transvestism to the project of nation formation and *cubanidad,* a central theme in his narratives.

Chapter 5, Kissing the Body Politic, is in many ways the most ambitious: it is a reading of Puig's *El beso de la mujer araña* (*Kiss of the Spider Woman*), looking closely at the relationship between transvestism and the body politic. I understand body politic to be the ways in which a subject is clothed with particular political elements and how parts of the body (namely, the anus and the penis) are encoded to signal certain attitudes or pretenses. I have divided chapter 4 in roughly two parts: the first one deals with the ways in which heterosexuality is inscribed in any ideological political program; the second part examines how homosexuality is defined within and (possibly) without the Oedipal complex—and how this definition imposes certain demands of heteronormativity, the same demands experienced by transvestite characters.

About literary history, I hope that readers of this book do not look at the sequence of texts and surmise that I have planned a "development" of transvestism in Latin American literary history. Instead, I present examples of how transvestism might be read in a series of canonical works, taking into consideration cultural difference. I made this choice because I was interested more in exploring critical ways of approaching and reading the figure and figuration of transvestite subjectivity, than in creating a false canon of disparate texts, some brilliant, others mediocre. *Transvestism, Masculinity, and Latin American Literature: Genders Shares Flesh* shows a breadth of literary and critical approaches. Although I engage gender and queer theory, I try to maintain a critical distance from its universal claims. I also cast some doubt on the validity of Sarduy's reading of transvestism as a unique project of the Baroque; I am more interested in locating transvestism along a different genealogy with Rubén Darío and Latin American *modernismo.* These are some important issues about literary history that specialized readers should keep in mind as they move from one chapter to the next. For readers outside my field of inquiry, I hope I've been responsible enough to share my understanding of another way of seeing and appreciating the difficulty of gender. This difficulty stems from various and competing versions—the perversion—of gender narrative.

Transvestism, Masculinity, and Latin American Literature: Genders Share Flesh, then, is an inaugural reading of transvestism as a theory and practice in Latin American literature; others are welcomed to continue this discussion.

Chapter 1

Nation and the Scandal of Effeminacy: Rereading Los "41"

> *No soy yo la que pensáis,*
> *sino es que allá me habéis dado*
> *otro ser en vuestras plumas*
> *y otro aliento en vuestros labios*
>
> *y diversa de mí misma*
> *entre vuestras plumas ando,*
> *no como soy, sino como*
> *quisisteis imaginarlo.*
>
> —Sor Juana Inés de la Cruz[1]

> If the injury can be traced to a specifiable act, it qualifies as an object of persecution: it can be brought to court and held accountable. But this tracing of the injury to the act of a subject, and this privileging of the juridical domain as the site to negotiate social injury, does this not unwittingly stall the analysis of how precisely discourse produces injury by taking the subject and its spoken deed as the proper place of departure?
>
> —Judith Butler[2]

Prefacing Masculinity

The presence of an excessive and explosive masculinity in Latin American cultures bewilders observers and makes them ask whether there is a place for different and alternative conceptualizations of genders and sexualities. Indeed, what is most imposing about Latin American masculinity is that it is always, already heterosexual. Collapsing sex, sexuality, and gender into a metacultural phenomenon often called "machismo" pervades the ways in which the male subject in the lower part of this continent looks at himself—and how others look at him. But has that heightened notion of masculinity always been so understood and ever present? I would like to look at differing masculinities in the turn-of-the-last-century Mexico, focusing on a fascinating case known as *los cuarenta y uno* (the forty-one) that sheds some light on the complexity of the male gender and its subjectivity. In theory, this chapter is about the heterosexual male gaze onto the queer body, and about the complex and compromising ways heterosexuality needs, subordinates, and fetishizes the queer. Here I want to return to an earlier event in Mexican culture in order to understand the complexity of this specific, seminal moment in the history of sexuality. Let us then move from history to the "popular," and then to the literature that represents the first two "versions." The story of the "41" is, after all, a story that has been erased from empirical and literary histories; let us see why and how.

Historic "41"

November 20, 1901. Mexico City's citizens learn of the arrest of forty-one men at a private home on La Paz Street, where they were involved in a "scandalous" dance.[3] Some were dressed elegantly as women; others, in "masculine" suits. After the arrest and within a couple of days, they were tried and marched off to the Yucatán to work with the military. This event caused quite a commotion, unleashing more than a few publications of homophobic debate between liberal and conservative newspapers, Posada satires, and even a full-length novel, appropriately entitled, *Los cuarenta y uno. Novela crítico-social (The Forty-one. A Social-Critical Novel)*.

Scandal is a two-edged sword: it implicates and tears apart the reputation and status of a subject or subjects, and it also threatens the moral code of the communal space where the event takes place. Scandal sets up a relationship of difference, and it prompts the community to establish an imperative of discipline. More precisely, the notion of community becomes manifest and singular at the breakout of a scandal, and it demands that the scandalous subjects be normalized. How and when a subject produces a scandal are questions that relate to ontology; thus, it is difficult to gauge the "success" of scandalous performance.[4] However, reading and understanding how a scandal gets interpreted and understood "after the fact" teaches us about how a social space imagines its vulnerabilities and limits. Forty-one men in drag dancing at a West Village party nowadays would hardly cause a blip on the social scandal-meter; New York City would continue functioning, unfazed by this act. Yet, those 41 men who danced on November 17, 1901 in Mexico City caused quite a stir. As I will show in this chapter, the scandal of the "41" was more than a snag in the moral fiber of the city. It went so far as to represent a threat to questions of social and cultural status as well as of citizenship and national (well-)being.

Notice of the scandal of the "41" survives in the pages of Cosío Villegas's 1955 monumental history of modern Mexico:

> The truth is that modesty was going through a crisis. Before, artistic nudes were the stuff of the Inquisition; in the last third of the XIXth-century it was seen as natural that they were circulating among all types of people. Before, rarely one would find a trace of artistry in a nude; in the Porfiriato, the majority of nudes were considered artistic. [. . .] In the popular classes there were frequent blows to modesty and violations; in the middle and upper classes, rapes.
>
> Alongside all this, homosexualism began to grow: at the end of 1901, 41 "señoritos" dressed as women were surprised and caught at an *ad-hoc* dance; they were punished, being sent as soldiers to the Yucatán. Years later cases of this sort were repeated; even in the aristocratic streets one was warned of the presence of men in white suit . . . [5]

I would like to look closely at this quote from Cosío Villegas because it illustrates some important points and hints at traditional prejudices in reading the homosexual body in turn-of-the-last-century Mexico. What interests me here are the discursive flows and flaws of the text. First, Cosío Villegas notes that the moral fiber of *fin-de-siècle* Mexican society was in decay—strangely, the circulation of nudes is seen as an effective litmus test for social morals. Then, he comments on the frequency of shameful offenses among the lower classes and rape among the middle and upper classes as further signs of moral decay. Finally, homosexuality is listed along with these other faults. The topical progression in these two short paragraphs is thus: nudity—rape—homosexuality. The relationship between nudity and homosexuality is rather forced, especially considering what the author tells us about the men "in white suit." Homosexuality here is marked and read as a clothed body, often excessively so. So, whereas the larger heterosexual society sins by losing its clothes, the homosexual body sins by wearing all of them, displaying them. From a newspaper article of the time, Cosío Villegas draws the elements of style for those "men with white suit" with "shoes in the same color, a blue kerchief folded in the breast pocket in the American style, a red flower in the lapel, a little white Panama hat with a little colored ribbon, be it red or blue or both colors combined, and while walking trying to exhibit their shoes as much as possible."[6] The costume and its display remind us of what Sylvia Molloy calls "the politics of posing."[7] The costume has a double function: for the homosexual, to decorate and to identify himself, for the heterosexual, to imagine the homosexual body and presence as Other. This double-take of the homosexual making himself more visible, and of the heterosexual gazing at the homosexual seems to problematize Foucault's established relation between surveillance and discipline: Michel Foucault writes that "[t]he exercise of discipline presupposes a mechanism that coerces by means of observation; an apparatus in which the techniques that make it possible to see induce effects of power, and in which, conversely, the means of coercion make those on whom they are applied clearly visible."[8] For Foucault, discipline presupposes a gaze that makes those who are its object more visible. In other words, this gaze amplifies, extends, and over-determines the object prior to disciplining (or normalizing) him. But what happens when the "object" (in this case, the homosexual body) has already made himself more visible, more inviting by wearing certain codes, that is, when he has claimed a subjectivity? Then, the homosexual subject in rendering himself more visible—or just more beautiful—flirts with the heterosexual gaze, thereby signifying on the heterosexual gaze and calling into question his straight interests. In other words, it is important to question the claim of authority that the normalizing subject may have on the other, especially when that other produces a particular version of himself. It is too easy to accept the idea that the other is simply "playing" at being "other" the way a normalizing subject would have him be—that is, the homosexual is displaying and producing the stereotype imposed on him by heteronormative culture. Rather, I suggest that by co-opting the heterosexual gaze, a heteronormative Imaginary, the queer subject may perhaps challenge authority. On a less optimistic note, the homosexual often gets pictured as a rift or blur of the more natural or naked interests of the Nation.[9] Those interests are the erasure of sexuality from the official histories of the Nation and State. Homosexuality will always be something that happens elsewhere. It is quite telling that the costume to signify the homosexual body is a "white suit" with "a blue kerchief folded in the breast pocket in the American style, a red flower in the lapel, a little white Panama hat with a little colored ribbon, be it red or blue or both colors combined." The red, white, and blue fashion statement seems deliberately to point northward to the United States. Actually, *El Imparcial,* Mexico's then-official Liberal press, reported that "among the arrested were capitalists and others of high social class standing." So, we have here a situation of identifying and displacing homosexuality as something that is foreign, specifically as something that comes from the North—and, more importantly, as an invasion that disrupts or threatens the project of nation formation. This phenomenon of displacing homosexuality as something that happens elsewhere can be seen constantly throughout Latin America.

Further, Cosío Villegas's history of modern Mexico unwittingly participates in a homophobic tradition of distributing over-wrought images of the queer as unknown and unknowing. Again, Cosío Villegas's history offers not very particular information and a chatty moral exposé of the scandal, but rather a hermeneutic relation used to conjure up the homosexual as over-dressed, over-done, in effect, over-determined. In fact, the homosexual becomes a marked body, albeit one that is emptied of his critical and political impact.

So powerful was the historic event of the "41" that it should not surprise us to hear echoes of the legacy of those men in Francisco L. Urquizo's 1965 compendium, *Símbolos y números* (*Symbols and Numbers*):

> In Mexico, the number 41 has no validity and is offensive to Mexicans. The origin of this aversion comes from the *fin-de-siècle* or beginnings of the present century, when Mexico City extended no further than the Garita de Tlaxpana, La Piedad, San Lázaro y Peralvillo, and its inhabitants did not number 200 thousand; in everything there was peace and absolute tranquility. The metropolitan police surprised on a certain night a group of effeminates, of which there were 41, they danced joyously, modeling feminine garb. Great was the scandal in the press that it marked an epoch, the definite impact this event made seems undying.[10]

Urquizo's history of the number 41 does not quite add up. First, to say that "41" is "offensive" suggests that the number possess something more than "no validity"; it has, at the very least, an abject value. Also, Urquizo slips into a romanticized vision of Mexico as a quaint, peaceful city; he forgets to tell us that in 1901 Mexico is living at the height of the Porfiriato, one of the most repressive dictatorships the country has experienced. It is within this normalizing social and political context that the scandal of effeminacy breaks out—smack—the very political repression accounts for the "definite impact" that this event made. If we follow Carlos Monsiváis's observation that "[f]rom that moment [1901] up until recently, in popular culture, the gay is a transvestite and there is only one type of homosexual, the effeminate one,"[11] then that would mean that to some degree the homosexual is always being imagined otherwise. The homosexual as transvestite or effeminate is a product of a social and political Imaginary at work. How and why does a transvestite or effeminate man make the State so anxious as to repress with such force this "behavior"? This question is imperative when, in fact, the (effeminate and transvestite) homosexual is a construction of the very agencies of power that wish to exclude him. That this arresting incident "marked an epoch" leaves us wondering why it had so strong an effect. I would suggest that this event is more than just 41 "faggots" causing a commotion but rather a crisis of State authority. That is, the crime became magnified by the ever-increasingly conservative context in which these men were caught dancing. So begins the aversion to the number 41 as a cultural homophobia that reaches national proportions. I am tempted to (mis)read Urquizo's notion of "aversion" as more than simply "homophobia" but rather homosexuality itself. His line reads differently: "The origin of this aversion (homophobia or homosexuality?) comes from the *fin-de-siècle* . . . " Perversely, this would credit Urquizo with identifying the beginning of homosexuality as a public practice in Mexico. What his ambiguity as to which aversion he is writing about does do is to repeat the notion that the homosexual is trapped by definition by the strings of the homophobia. Urquizo goes on to outline some of the effects of the scandal:

> To say "41" to a man is to call him effeminate. To be under the auspices of that number is to be in a certain way effeminate. *The influence of this tradition is such, that even that which has an official bearing does not recognize the number 41.* There is no division, regiment, nor battalion in the Army that carries the number 41. They go up to 40 and from there jump to 42. There is no spreadsheet that has a line 41. There is no numbering in municipal houses that display the number 41. If by any chance there is no remedy, the number 40B is used. There is no hotel room or sanatorium that has the number 41. Nobody has a 41st birthday, from 40 you go up to 42. There is no automobile that has a license plate with 41, not a police or agent that will accept that badge number.[12]

If one ever doubted homosexual panic, now is the time to reconsider. Homosexual panic is the regulatory practice that seeks to distance or excise homosexuality from social spaces; it is an effort to dissimulate the existence of homosexuality. This dissimulation happens in a variety of ways—from "turning the other cheek," to the negation of homosexuality, to oppression and violence. It is mind-boggling that the number "41" caused citizens and

Nation and the Scandal of Effeminacy: Rereading Los "41"   21

officials so much stress. One reason for all this is that the number "41" does more than describe a subject or situation, it implicates others around it. Let me anticipate that the act of calling someone "41" is performative because it configures a new identity for the one at whom the finger is pointed. Also, as Urquizo points out, "41" is more than a number, it is a "tradition." Thus the weight of a homophobic history (a history of invectives) brands the subject a homosexual, and then wants to rid itself of him, at least rid Mexico of him. This idea that "tradition" regulates national subject formation as well as that it subtracts from the body politic what is undesirable dovetails with Molloy's argument on the anxiety that "posing" provokes in spectators:

> [p]osing makes evident the elusiveness of all constructions of identity, their fundamentally performative nature. It increasingly problematizes gender, its formulation and its divisions: it subverts categories . . . It also resorts to an exploitation of the public, in the form of self-advertisement and very visible self-fashioning, that appears to make the spectator very nervous about what goes on in private. [. . .] *In Latin America, this is particularly true in those cases in which posing—and decadence in general—are considered in relation to hypervirile constructions of nationhood.*[13]

Posing is an affect of gender that may destabilize the security of stereotypical masculinity; whereas transvestism is an effective debunking of gender codes. Posing often gets dismissed as "mere imitation," as Molloy argues; transvestism, as the figure of the homosexual, gets severed from the cultural fabric of the nation. I do not want to dichotomize transvestism as a more "radical" form of posing, rather I just want to understand both practices as being on a spectrum of practices that transgress gender normativity.[14] In the case of the "41," the transvestites or effeminates or *poseurs* or *maricones*—the names are many—are sent to the army to get "rehabilitated."

Another alarming aspect of this number is how non-discriminatory it is in its reach. We must note that not only are subjects marked otherwise, but places and objects are also. The efficacy of the number 41 is that it labels everything. Even official documents and the upholders of the law cannot escape the subversive power of the number. In other words, "41" is more than a performative iterated by those with official status, it is one that is available to a broader audience.

This peculiar quality of the number 41, that even the Law is no match for, radically calls into question the binarism of the (national) Self versus other. Since everything and everyone was at risk of being called and marked "41"—the homosexual panic is so extreme—the very difference that the number was to delimit seems inconsequential when the speaking subject evanesces without the grasp of a *sujet-supposé-savoir,* and strangely might become implicated by the very knowledge of the digits. That is, the voice of authority (the State) cannot authorize itself without being contaminated or marked by that which it wants to eject. I would like to submit that this difficulty follows a split between an "official" and a broader "social" performative act, one that is available to all subjects, not simply those privy to power. Following Foucault's definition of a relational conceptualization of power, I propose differentiating between the terms "official" vis-à-vis "social" performatives to explain what happens when a performative becomes disengaged from a structure or institution that has a special handle on it. With the term "social performative," I want to underline that the concentration of power becomes dispersed along broader cultural and social spectra, thus making the performative more unwieldy and difficult to describe. Here it is useful to think of Judith Butler's questioning of whether it is valid to limit the "tracing of the injury to the act of a subject, and [the] privileging of the juridical domain as the site to negotiate social injury." In other words, how do acts get negotiated within the realm of the Law as well as outside? Why privilege the juridical domain to determine the meaning of acts? The number 41 and, for that matter, any act that identifies the queer body and subject might be said to fall under the rubric of a social performative, again a kind of performative that extends beyond the reaches of official power. Aware of the numerous taxonomies that have been applied to performative utterances,[15] I would be cautious not to dichotomize this difference too severely. I find it useful to describe and understand how some performatives function differently depending on the subject who speaks, and the positionality that she or he occupies, that is, the space from where he or she speaks. When a performative is uttered, what is the referent that is being alluded to?

◆ ◆ ◆

I would like to turn to Shoshana Felman's discussion of the referent (the thing itself) in the context of performative theory, as articulated in the work of J. L. Austin. Let us trace the relationship between gender and the referent in performative speech act theory. "It seems," she writes, "that what it is important to see—what Austin's heirs have perhaps lost sight of—is not so much the reintroduction of the referent in the performative, but the *change of status* of the referent as such."[16] Felman attributes that change of status comparatively to psychoanalysis, and outlines three principle constitutive elements in that change. First, the referent "can only be approached or aimed at through the intermediary of language"[17]; that is, "the referent is itself produced by language as its own *effect*."[18] This insight is central to Butler's rethinking of gender (as) performativity. From this referential language effect, "[t]he referent is no longer simply a preexisting *substance,* but an *act,* that is, a dynamic movement of modification of reality."[19] Gender, likewise, obeys this relation: gender is not a body or substance, but a series of acts or movements. Second, Felman notes that the referent is dialogic: "The referent functions dynamically, in an intervening space; radically bound—in its analytic impact as well as in its performative impact—to a structure of effects, it can inscribe itself only as an effect of structure: as a relation to a relation."[20] This dialogic (and elastic) conceptualization of the referent gives way to understating the relation between language as *excessive* with respect to the referent, thereby creating an asymmetrical relation.[21] This asymmetry between language and the referent deconstructs the spectral correspondence of the Saussurian sign. Gender works in a similar fashion as does the referent: we can argue that gender "can inscribe itself only as an effect of structure." Masculinity and femininity are effects of a patriarchal structure. In Latin America where that patriarchal structure is omnipresent, those gender effects are radicalized and instituted as the phenomena of *machismo* and *marianismo* (the cult of the Virgin Mary as the standard for femininity). These gender figurations are not simply opposites; they are complementary, since they both nurture and promote each other's interests.

Finally, referentiality "can be reached and defined only through the dimension of failure: on the basis of the *act of failing.*"[22] Felman argues that "The act of failing thus opens up the space of referentiality—or of impossible reality—not because *something is missing,* but because *something else is done,* or because something else is said: the term "misfire" does not refer to an absence, but to the enactment of a difference."[23] Thus, echoing Felman, the act of failing to perform masculinity (as did the "41") opens up the space of referentiality, the space of gender. Transvestism as a misfire of "masculinity" does not exactly mean "castration" (something is not missing; it is hidden); transvestism signifies that "something else is done." The acts of the "41" cannot be simply understood as an absence, which is precisely the politically repressive formulation of their acts; rather, from a politically progressive stance, the "41" are an enactment of a gender difference. This is how the "41" should be recuperated in contemporary political, cultural, and social contexts. Also, what is the referent of the scandal of the "41"? What is the thing that the scandal wants to convey? A scandal is precisely about the proliferation of social and cultural expressions to a misfire. Scandalous narratives compact many conflicting versions of a story. This would make the scandal of the "41," the scandal of effeminacy, an elusive referent, within which many perspectives may be reflected.

Furthermore, calling someone or something "41" is a different kind of performative. Following Sedgwick's discussion of queer performativity, like "shame on you!", the authority of the performative no longer emanates from the Austinian formula: "first person, singular; present indicative; active." Like "shame on you!" the interjection "41!" is a performative elaboration that lacks the subject and verb, which in this case might be "I call, baptize, curse, or even, want you, '41' . . . " Thus the number 41 has the force of a performative to transform an identity; also, as Sedgwick suggests, "the verblessness of this particular performative ["shame on you!"], then, implies a first person whose singular/plural status, whose past/present/future status and indeed whose agency/passivity can only be questioned rather than presumed."[24] In other words, the subject named by the invective "41!" must be called into question because of his very indeterminacy. I return to my suggestion of approaching and gauging the performative along the spectrum of "official" versus "social" and not to reduce, but to begin to understand the multiple directions and forces that operate within and without language. To this end, the event of the "41" cannot simply be understood by just one text, its text. Cosío Villegas and Urquizo also give us only one part of the whole history of the "41." In general, this insight of how stories get told with different documents and methodologies has important implications for how critics deal with *questions of evidence,* and the slippage between universalism and particularisms in the realm of literary and cultural studies.

Popular "41"

As mentioned by Urquizo, the alacrity of the press gave this event quite a lot of currency. *El Imparcial* reported inconspicuously about the scandal:

> It has been running all over the press, a repulsive story about a scandalous dance of lonely men caught by the police. In this dance, individuals with bad habits [*de malas costumbres*] took part.
>
> Public curiosity and hidden or distorted references in the press have given reason for more or less fantastic versions [of the scandal] to circulate. There are those who assure us that among the men arrested were capitalists

and others of high social standing who belong to very distinguished families. Also it has been reported that the prisoners were assigned to the army.²⁵

Another paper reports that

> Sunday night, the capital's police came across a dance at La Paz Street #4 where 41 lonely men wore women's dress. Among those individuals recognized were *pollos* [fops] who are daily seen on Plateros [Avenue]. They wore very elegant ladies outfits, they had wigs, falsies, earrings, embroidered shoes, and their faces were painted with eye shadow and rouge. As soon as the news hit the boulevards, all kinds of commentaries have been made, and the conduct of said individuals is censured. We do not give our readers more details since they are highly gross.²⁶

These two reports give a cursory version of the story—and in both cases they suggest that rumors about the 41 men have already begun circulating in the city. The article in *El Imparcial* names the criminals as "individuals with bad habits," a synonym for homosexuals in Mexico. The other paper "protects" its readers from "highly gross" details—ironically, this coy gesture almost seems to encourage the rumors. Monsiváis argues that "popular scandal [was] the only road to acceptance for the existence of homosexuality."²⁷ I would like to suggest otherwise. For instance, what is interesting about *El Imparcial* is its effort to get the story straight (pun intended):

> We believe it is necessary to correct those [erroneous] opinions. The truth is that in that excessively immoral and scandalous get-together there was only a group of forty men, *very well-known* for their depraved behaviors [*muy conocidos por sus costumbres depravadas*], and *who more than once* have figured in this kind of scandal. The great majority of them changed their names when they were arrested. The police has been able to identify many of them, among whom was a young man by the name of Zozaya, an individual who worked as a dentist, and another who called himself a lawyer.
>
> All the prisoners have been sent to Yucatán, but not—as has been said—to join the ranks of the valiant soldiers, but rather they will be used to do excavating labor, like digging trenches, filling holes, etc. . . . ²⁸

El Imparcial reveals that this type of scandal has been seen before; there is a hint that among those arrested is a group "very well-known" for this kind of behavior. Another detail of note is the class status of the "41," some of whom were professionals. So besides the scandal of effeminacy being reported, there is some evidence—despite *El Imparcial*'s effort to displace class—to suggest that *bourgeois* excesses are up for criticism.

I cannot overemphasize that questions of gender—not just cross-dressing, but also notions of masculinity and femininity—have a lot to do with the scandal. Just a survey of articles and advertising from *El Imparcial* shows a deep concern for presenting traditional gender issues to its readers. An article entitled "Between Sisters: Fighting for a Boyfriend" (November 23, 1901) appears just above "The Scandalous Dance." In effect the caption for the sisters article is bigger.[29] This article tells the story of "Consuelo and María [who] are two girls from the provinces. . . . " The story continues that they both fell for the same man, a true neighborhood "Don Juan." The jealousy between them led María to stab her sister in the chest with a pair of scissors. There is not much else to the story except to give a didactic lesson. Days earlier (November 20, 1901), another article, "The Most Manly Man," reports the story of Lucio Suárez, a drunkard, who went to a *pulquería* looking to get free drinks. Wielding his knife, nobody paid any attention. To get attention, a furious Lucio then challenged "the most manly man" in the *pulquería* to a fight. Lucio was stabbed and died days later.[30] Again, the brief article presents little more than didacticism. That same day readers of *El Imparcial* could have learned in an advertisement about an electric belt that will deliver "New Strength for Men!" (figure 1.1).

The list of these didactic and positivist reports and advertisements—selling everything from syrups to help weak men to corsets to improve well-being and femininity for women—is endless. In the newspapers, the scandal of the 41 men was precisely what interested readers. I would emphasize that the stuff of scandal survives in the public imaginary precisely because homosexuality is already part of the everyday.

If the scandal of the "41" was resolved by the Porfiriato authorities by exiling those men in order to regain a sense of normalcy, then the "41" were embraced elsewhere in the popular imagination. It was important for the authorities to purge the Nation of queer bodies; after all, the very project of nation-formation has shown us time and again that the foreign, the sickly, the queer, and the poor cannot achieve the status of "real" citizens. Cast out, the "41" became the subject of another kind of representation found within the pinnacle of Mexican folklore at the turn-of-century: that characters in José Guadalupe Posada's engravings and etchings.

Posada ranks among Mexico's premier printmakers and artists. His work spans over four decades. In the early 1890s, Posada began a professional relationship with Antonio Vanegas Arroyo, an important publisher of

Figure 1.1 "¡Fuerza Nueva para Hombres!" ["New Strength for Men!"] in *El Imparcial*, November 20, 1901.

newspapers and periodicals. Posada designed thousands of broadsides, engravings, and etchings, which were available cheaply to the general public. Posada is perhaps best known for his representation of *calaveras* (skulls) (see figure 1.2). "Catrina Calavera" is one of Posada's most recognized images. These *calaveras* were folkloric representations of different types (literary, political, historical figures) and they abounded in his work. Often his engravings and etchings were accompanied by a news item, a rhyme, or a *corrido* (popular song); they were printed in many penny presses or as loose pamphlets.[31] "Calavera of a Lagartijo" (figure 1.3) appeared with the following caption: "I don't like those *lagartijos* [i.e., fops] who act so elegantly, who, without money in their pocket, walk with top hat and gloves. I won't want to leave a trace or a seed of them; I will make imperceptible dust of them 'til their last bone." The *lagartijos*, literally lizards, received their name because they spent the day in the sun; they were *flâneurs,* whose favorite practice was flirting with women who walked by. The most distinguished in the art of *"florear"* [to give flowers, that is, to give compliments—or in some extreme cases, to harass] were the *pollos* (young roosters) and the *lagartijos.* (figure 1.4).

According to Cosío Villegas, there was a "zoological scale" used to classify these "salacious boys": "león, *dandy,* catrín, lagartijo, serpentino, gomoso, y *sucré*" [lion, dandy, toff, lizard, serpentine, sticky and sugary.][32] Like he did before with the men "in white suit," Cosío Villegas goes to great lengths to describe their attire: "shark-skin tie or one with at least seven colors, yellow shoes with a pointy toe, narrow pants like umbrella sheaths, short jackets belted coquettishly to show off a flexible silhouette."[33] Additionally, he states that the problem of "giving flowers" had become so severe in Mexico City at the turn of the century that the city government increased its police force on its major avenues; so that by 1905 women were able to stroll around the downtown streets without much problem.[34] We can then begin to understand what motivated Posada's attitude toward the *lagartijos.* They represented social artificiality and pretentiousness; in other words, they dressed and posed across class lines. This act of crossing over becomes the regulating trope of scandal.

A signature of Posada's work was his almost obsessive representation of the ridiculous, the scandalous, and the macabre. Many examples of these scandals are published in sensationalist papers such as *El diablito rojo, La Tarántula, La Guacamaya, El Ahuizote,* just to name a few of the tens—or hundreds—of papers that captured Mexican audiences' attention in the late nineteenth and early twentieth centuries. The titles of the articles that

Figure 1.2 José Guadalupe Posada's "Calavera Catrina," or "Calavera de la cucaracha."

Figure 1.3 José Guadalupe Posada's "Calavera de un lagartijo"

Figure 1.4 "Los Lagartijos," lithograph in *El Mundo*, July 27, 1897. Rpt. in Cosío Villegas.

appeared in these papers are worthy of today's tabloid news headlines: "The Hanging in the Cathedral," "Lying Girl Taken Away by the Devil," "Son Poisons His Parents and Maid," "Two Children Strangled by Their Mother," and the list goes on and on. Posada never seemed to run out of exciting stories to illustrate, nor was his audiences' appetite for the lurid ever exhausted. So, it is hardly remarkable that when the scandal of the "41" erupted in the press, Posada would publish (at least) two different pamphlets describing and illustrating the events.

Some of the etchings appeared with *corridos* and others without.[35] The first one, entitled "Los 41 maricones encontrados en un baile de Calle de la Paz el 20 de Noviembre, 1901" ["The 41 Faggots found at a dance on La Paz Street, November 20, 1901"] (figure 1.5a), shows men in tuxedos dancing with other men wearing dresses. Below the drawing we find song, a *corrido,* that reads:

Aquí están los Maricones
Muy Chulos y Coquetones.

Hace aun muy pocos dias
Que en la calle de la Paz,
Los gendarmes atisbaron
Un gran baile singular.

Cuarenta y un lagartijos
Disfrazados la mitad
De simpáticas muchachas
Bailaban como el que más.

La otra mitad, con su traje,
Es decir de masculinos,
Gozaban al estrechar
A los *famosos jotitos.*

Vestidos de raso y seda
Al último figurín,
Con pelucas bien peinadas
Y moviéndose con *chic.*

[Here are the Faggots
Very Pretty and Coquettish.

Figure 1.5a "Los 41 maricones encontrados en un baile de la calle de la Paz el 20 de noviembre de 1901." ["The 41 faggots found at a dance on Paz Street, November 20, 1901"]. Front, loose pamplet published by A. Vanegas Arroyo, 1901. Zinc etching.

Abanicos elegantes
Portaban con gentileza,
Y aretes ó dormilonas
Pasados por las orejas.
  Sus caras muy repintadas
Con albayalde ó con cal,
Con ceniza ó velutina....
¡Pues vaya usté á adivinar!
  Llevaban buenos corsés
Con pechos bien abultados
Y caderitas y muslos......
Postizos....pues está claro.
  El caso es que se miraban
Salerosas, retrecheras
Danzando al compás seguido
De música ratonera.
  Se trataba, según dicen,
De efectuar alegre rifa
De un niño de catorce años,
Por colmo de picardías.

  Cuando más entusiasmados
Y quitados de la pena,
Se hallaban los mariquitos
Gozando de aquella fiesta
  ¡Púm! que los gendarmes entran
Sorprendiendo á los *jotones*!
Y aquello sí fué de verse....
¡Qué apuros y que aflixiones!
  Algunos quieren correr,
O echarse dentro el *común*
Otros quieren desnudarse
A otros les dá el patatús.
  Una alarma general....
Lloran, chillan, y hasta ladran,
¡Qué rebumbio! ¡Qué conflictos!
Pero ninguno se escapa.
  A todos, uno por uno
La policía los recoje,
Y á Tlapisquera derecho
Se los va llevando al trote.

Figure 1.5b Continuation of *corrido*, "Los 41 maricones..." Back. Description: Men sweeping street.

It has only been a few days that on La Paz Street, the Police came upon a grand and peculiar dance.

Forty-one lizards (*lagartijos*) half of whom were disguised as cute girls were dancing with much gusto.

The others with their suits, that is, masculine attire, enjoyed hugging the *famous little faggots*.

Dressed in taffeta and silk in the latest style, with well-coifed wigs and moving with *chic*.]

This first leaflet basically informs the reader of the events that occurred. Unlike reports in *El Imparcial*, which referred to the men's homosexuality in a roundabout way, as "individuals with bad habits" or "excessively immoral" men; or other papers that "did not give readers more details because they are highly gross," Posada, albeit homophobically, represents the queer body—"Los 41 maricones." But more than name them, he represents them visually: men in drag dancing joyously. It almost seems that the accompanying *corrido* gives movement to the dance steps. The opening line—"Here [they] are . . . "—suggests a sense of presence and witnessing of the event. Posada brings the crime to the reader, and brings the reader into the scene of the crime. In another print (figure 1.6) we find another presentation of this same dance.

This time we see an orchestra; the *corrido* and all the headlines are no longer part of the image. Moreover, we see a more remarkable image of *calaveras* dancing. Replacing the men with *calaveras* effectively shows the importance that Posada gave his skeletal friends: he used them to represent types, rather than real subjects. In effect, the *calaveras* have a universalizing aspect to them. Also, the absence of the text suggests that the image itself tells the story. Or, better, that the image accompanies the text of the public's imagination. The image illustrates the "rumors" circulating throughout the city, rumors such as that the son-in-law of Porfirio Diaz was at the dance,[36] that those arrested were "capitalists," "dentists," and "lawyers." By the time this Posada print hit the streets, everyone knew about the night dancers. Just as importantly, that they are represented shoeless is a clear recourse to a Hispanic attitude toward death; in this case, it signifies their condition (the homosexual as dead man), for all intents and purposes, in Mexican society.

On the back of "The 41 Faggots found at a dance" print, (figure 1.5b) the *corrido* continues to provide specific information about the scandal. First, it details the arrest and one of the principal motives behind it—the

Figure 1.6 José Guadalupe Posada, "Los 41." Description: Calaveras bailando con orquesta. [Skulls dancing with orchestra]. Zinc etching.

raffle of a fourteen-year-old boy among the men present. Castrejón's novel, *Los cuarenta y uno. Novela crítico-social*,[37] also brings up this fact. The image in figure 1.5b is so interesting because the men are shown wearing dresses, sweeping the street; also, all around them, the police and hundreds of spectators watch and laugh at them. As a matter of fact, though the *corrido* does not mention it, the novel tells that the 41 men were forced by the governor to dress as women and sweep a street. This scene is at once tragic and comic; it is emblematic of transvestism itself. If "[t]he speaking body is *scandalous* precisely to the extent that its *performance* is, necessarily, either *tragic* or *comic*,"[38] as Felman suggests, then transvestism is a scandalous speaking body to the extent that its performance gets construed as tragic *and* comic. The transvestite's body will be always misunderstood as saying something different. The 41 men were now a public, comic spectacle; homosexuality was now out in public as a laughing matter. Their "outing" is also supposed to mean personal "shame" and tragedy. Moreover, since the men were presumably from privileged classes, their public "shame" is doubled.

The second print of this series, "El gran viaje de los 41 maricones para Yucatán" (figure 1.7), tells the queer tale of the men's trip to the Yucatan. This print is usually collected together with the first one. Again, the *corrido* is central:

> Las impresiones del viaje—Resaladas cual no hay más—De todos los maricazos que mandan a Yucatán.

Figure 1.7 José Guadalupe Posada. "El gran viaje de los 41 maricones para Yucatán." ["The great trip of the 41 faggots to Yucatan"]. Loose leaf published by A. Vanegas Arroyo, 1901. Zinc etching.

Sin considerar tantito
A nuestro sexo tan casto,
Ni el estado interesante
Que casi todas guardamos.

Hechas horrible jigote
A todas nos encajaron
En un carro de tercera
Del trensote Mexicano.

Revueltas cual chilaquiles
Fuimos con jergas soldados
Que injuriaban leperotes
Nuestro pudor con descaro.

Al pobrecito Sofio
Le dieron muchos desmayos
Con los continuos meneos
De este tren tan remalvado.

[The great trip of the 41 faggots to Yucatan
 Naughty impressions of the trip of all the big fags that were sent to Yucatan.

Without much as to consider our most chaste sex, nor the interesting state in which we [girls] all kept ourselves.
 They boxed all of us like minced meat in a third class car of the big Mexican train.
 Mixed up like *chilaquiles,* we traveled with soldiers who injured our modesty shamelessly.
 Poor little Sofio had many fainting spells, because of the constant shakes (*continuos meneos*) of that very evil train.]

To our surprise, a feminized we, "nosotras," narrates the experience on the train. This telling of the events is quite surprising because it is the only presentation of what happened to the 41 men told in the first person, plural. There is a suggestion that the soldiers may have taken some liberties with them (the "*continuos meneos*" can be read both as the train's movements or penetration). In a strange way, this print gives Posada's work a complexity and a sensitivity to the men and their situation that the historical and literary texts lack. Furthermore, I would like to think about the image of the train, which has been classically assigned the meaning of "progress" and modernity, technological as well as cultural and national. In fact, it was Porfirio Diaz's major accomplishment as dictator to create a railroad infrastructure that modernized the country. This image of homosexuals on the train is quite interesting because, like the train, the construction of homosexuality is another articulation of modernity; whereas the train symbolizes an economic and political modernity, the homosexual appears in the language of cultural and social modernity. However, these articulations of the modern are incompatible: homosexuality represents a form of excess, which the political and economic modern cannot assimilate, and therefore needs to transport out and displace.

Paradoxically, what Posada's prints do is show that homosexuality is not something alien to the public. If it had been alien, he manages to bring it out. Homosexuality may not have been necessarily a "highly gross" detail, it was just something that was looked upon as a source of humor—*"puro relajo"* [loosely translated as, "just goofing off"] as Mexicans would say. These different reactions expressed by "high cultured, official" versus "popular" segments of the society toward homosexuality emerge continuously in Hispanic letters: from González Castillo's drama *Los invertidos* (1914)[39] where the upper classes use a technical, medico-legal language to talk about the homosexual, while the maid seems much more familiar and comfortable with the subject to Puig's footnotes in *Kiss of the Spider Woman* onward to Claudia Hinojosa's deconstructive readings of psychiatric texts about lesbianism.[40]

In a weird and unintentional way, the Posada prints seem to demystify the whole question of homosexuality, and place it on the level of the quotidian—something seen and experienced regularly, without much attention ever really paid to it otherwise. What would seem scandalous—or, at least, newsworthy—to Posada's public (and here I am assuming without much risk that the readers of the penny presses were primarily working class individuals) is that the men who were caught were *lagartijos* (fops, *poseurs*, homosexuals) in drag. This evaluation of the "41" would have us then look at the class and race distinctions that regulate the force of their performance; that is, the men were disobeying and not performing their class ranking.

The force of the scandal would linger in Posada's work beyond the days in November 1901 during which the scandal was hottest. Six years later, Posada designed a print entitled, "El feminismo se impone" ["Feminism imposes itself"]. But on what or whom? In a detail (figure 1.8a) of the print, we can see that feminism imposes itself on men, here wearing women's clothing and carrying out what is traditionally women's work: ironing, cooking,

Figure 1.8a José Guadalupe Posada, detail of "El feminismo se impone."

nursing, and the like. "Feminism" is here seen as a "feminization" or transvestism of the male body and persona. The brilliance of this print lies not in the detail, but in the whole picture (figure 1.8b). These men doing women's work surround the number "41," whose central presence may be submitted as evidence of the legacy of the scandal. Homosexuality or, really, effeminacy, is collapsed with feminism. "El feminismo" discloses that feminism (back then, meaning "woman-like") is seen as a threat, as an effeminization and sissification, as an emasculation. As such, it allows us a clearer view of the social and political understanding of such questions as feminism, homosexuality, masculinity and, even, pedagogy. To underline this point, let us return to Cosío Villegas. He ends his section on the scandal thus, "[t]here were not few who attributed these customs to the fact that education was in the hands of women."[41] In a more precise fashion, the scandal of the "41" is not simply a scandal of homosexuality, but one of effeminacy—and, by extension, its looming threat of castration. Conclusively, what the legacy of the "41" teaches us is to reconsider the origins and history of feminism (in a broad sense) in Mexico, to look at both misogynist as well as homophobic resistances that shaped it; to understand how those resistances are laced together by the empire of masculinity.

Figure 1.8b Posada, "El feminismo se impone," ["Feminism imposes itself"]. 1907. Zinc etching.

Literary "41": Writing and Effeminacy

Written in 1906, Eduardo A. Castrejón's *Los cuarenta y uno. Novela crítico-social* is the highest example of a bad novel. The *modernista* excesses, coupled with its positivist morality, are excruciatingly obvious to the reader.[42] But, why are these "bad" texts worth recovering and rescuing from oblivion? How does that recuperative process begin? It is best to value this category of "the bad" not for its aesthetic and literary weight, but for its social and historical content.

Actually, this strategy would be a felicitous one since the publishers of Castrejón's novel state that "the author has fulfilled a social duty" in the "faithful retelling of an event that produced quite a scandal."[43] This social duty had been previously explained by the publishers, "[W]hether one speaks of history or literature, all epochs are in agreement on the correction of customs, the condemnation of social vices, the abhorrence of all corruption, the exaltation of morality and the anathema of perversions of human feelings."[44] Really, Castrejón's mission is thoroughly accomplished: shunning homosexuality, alcoholism, prostitution, social climbing, drag, simulation, upper-class extravagances, and laziness. Let me give a quick synopsis.

The novel can be divided into two parts: The first half is the story of the men up to the arrest; the second half is a resolution of all the vices presented, and some new ones to boot. The scandal in the first half becomes a moral context against which other vices are measured. In other words, effeminacy and homosexuality become the mark of difference.

Ninón and Mimí are male lovers, though each has his own female partner, Judith and Estela, respectively. Judith, doubting Ninón's "unconditional" love for her, hires a private detective, "Manos de alacrán" [Scorpion hands] to spy on Ninón. The detective learns of the gay dance, and communicates this to Judith, who tells Estela. The women are furious. There being "no wrath like that of a woman scorned," they tell the police. The *fête* is interrupted by the police, who arrest the men. They are shipped to the Yucatán. Judith and Estela try to fend off the public humiliation of their association with Ninón and Mimí, so at a party they flirt shamelessly with two *lagartijos,* Antonio and Ricardo. Judith later agrees to run off with Antonio to Veracruz, where he then abandons her, forcing her to become a prostitute. She eventually gets pregnant, abandons her son, writes home asking for forgiveness, returns home, recuperates, and marries the loser Pánfilo for his money. This marriage quells all rumors of her past life and restores her dignity. Estela has different luck: one night her house burns down and she is rescued by a dashing mechanic, Alberto Bautista. They fall in love at first sight and agree to see each other secretly because of their class differences. She accepts his marriage proposal. Her parents consent to the marriage too, because this humble man has all the morals and values that will eventually get him out of poverty.

Of the "41," Ninón is the only one who repents for his "bohemian sins." He is released after 18 months. He works hard, earns money, and meets Josefina, a kind, sixteen-year-old girl from the country. They marry and live happily ever after in Yucatán. Never mind the pedophilia of the relationship between Ninón and Josefina; he alone is set up as an example of the triumphs of discipline and normalization. The other forty men and Judith's abandoned child, we are promised, will become the subject of Castrejón's next novel.

Besides the positivist tones of the novel, what makes it so unbearable is its *modernista* gushiness. From the beginning we read:

> La tarde iba muriendo! . . . . El Sol ocultaba su inmensa cabellera rubia, y en el horizonte las nubes amontonadas tomaban un tinte de bronce. . . . . .
>
> En la casa aristocrática de *Mimí*, adornada con exquisito gusto femenino y en la sala elegantemente amueblada, se esparcen ondas de perfume delicioso. *Mimí* está solo! . . . .[45]

> [The afternoon was dying! . . . . The Sun was hiding its immense blond hair, and in the horizon crowded clouded took on the shade of bronze. . . . . .
>
> In *Mimí*'s aristocratic house, adorned with exquisite feminine taste and in the elegantly furnished living room, waves of delicious perfume breeze throughout. *Mimí* is alone! . . . .]

Here, again, it is impossible not to notice the overdone language of the novel. Even though the publishers might have argued that the text is "positivist" (hence, scientific) in its message, these exaggerated linguistic formulations remind us of *modernismo,* the predominant literary current in Latin America at the *fin-de-siècle*. In brief, *modernista* language was concerned with surface and veneer as a way of suggesting and approximating an interiority; *modernismo* produced a split between exteriority and interiority, and meaning was the dialectical negotiation between these two spaces.[46] Further, I proposed before the idea that this was a "bad" novel; indeed, some contemporary readers of the text may choose to say it is "campy" or "queer." Both evaluations would be appropriate. In any case, there is a way in which the notion of the text's "badness" may be refunctioned and revalorized.⁴⁷ For example, if we consider that this "bad" text is necessarily written by a "weak" author—in the Bloomian sense—then we can begin realizing that the textual faults magnify certain literary tendencies and clichés of the genre. However, I would argue that here *modernista* excesses are meant parodically to represent the homosexual. The author uses these literary excesses to simulate the voice and gesture of the homosexual body, that is, to perform homosexuality.

Along these lines, the novel's opening offers an interesting context and tropes that are worth exploring closely. First, the dying afternoon is an important description of change, of decay. The sun as a "blond" is interesting as well. A common trope in *modernista* texts is the synecdoche, thus the sun's hair appears like that of a blond woman with beautiful, long locks. If this is how we read the image, it suggests the departure of a woman from the scene; a departure that leaves the place open for another woman to occupy. Also the reference to the feminine décor of the living room adds to the whole scene, and the wafts of perfume further feminize the interior space. The complete image is of decadence and femininity. Finally, the name of our protagonist, always in italics, *Mimí,* clearly makes reference to Giacomo Puccini's tragic heroine from *La bohème* (1896) who dies of consumption after having thrown herself into a bohemian life.⁴⁸ The protagonist has the name of a woman, but we discover that Mimí sits *solo* in his home. His appearance would seem predictable: "En su traje correcto, cortado á la 'Americana', se nota una elegancia exquisita; sus manos, blancas y tersas, juegan con los guantes, y su mirada impaciente mira el reloj, que le parece retarda mucho las horas." [In his correct suit, tailored in the "American" style, an exquisite elegance is noticeable; his hands, white and smooth, play with the gloves; and his impatient gaze looks at the clock that seems to him to slow down the hours.]⁴⁹ Again, the detail of the "correct" suit in the "American" style points to a bodily otherness. The suit's "correctness" is ironic because it is temporary, meaning that its being "American" undoes its sense of correctness; also because Mimí will later dress in women's clothing. Then, the author focuses on Mimí's fidgeting hands and his impatient gaze. Thus the tranquility of the ending day is contrasted with Mimí's movement and anxiety. This opening presentation of context and protagonist is emblematic of the entire novel's obsession with fetishistic details. Later on, when *Ninón,* also always in italics, and the other friends arrive, we can see further evidence of the text's excesses:

> La voz atiplada de los adolescentes, formando una inmensa algarabía, recorría todos los tonos de la dulzura; y sus modales afeminados daban á la

escena un tinte chocarrero y meloso, pareciendo la reunión más bien voces de señoritas discutiendo en el estrado, que de jóvenes barbilindos.
　—¿Me quieres?—decía *Ninón* a *Mimí*.
　Y *Mimí*, acariciando las mejillas de *Ninón*, se lo juraba entusiasmado.
　—¿Fuiste anoche á la ópera?—le decía *Estrella* à *Margarita*.
　—¡¡¡Ay . . . . sí, cómo no!!!
　—¿Y tú, *Blanca*, no fuiste?
　—¡¡¡No, tú!!! estuve un poco enfermo y no quise salir de casa.
　—¡Qué onditas tan preciosas tienes en tu peinado, *Margarita!* ¿qué, te las rizaste?
　—No, mi vida, si son naturales . . . . . .
　—¿Y tus choclitos, *Virtud*, son americanos? . . .
　—Sí, *Estrella*, están muy monos con mis calcetines calados, ¿verdad?. . . . . .⁵⁰

[The falsetto voice of the adolescents, forming an immense hullabaloo, ran up all the tones of sweetness; and their effeminate manners gave to the scene a vulgar and sweet tint. This seemed more like the voices of young ladies discussing at a ball, than of handsome bearded young men.
　"Do you love me?" *Ninón* asked *Mimí*.
　And *Mimí*, caressing *Ninón*'s cheeks, would swear it enthusiastically.
　"Did you go to the opera last night?" *Estrella* asked *Margarita*.
　"Oh!!! . . . but, of course!!!"
　"And you, *Blanca*, didn't you go?"
　"No, darling!!! I was a bit sick and didn't want to leave the house."
　"What precious waves you have in your *coiffure, Margarita!* What? did you roll them?"
　"No, love, they are natural . . . . . ."
　"And your shoes, *Virtud*, are they American? . . ."
　"Yes, *Estrella*, they are very cute with my patterned socks, aren't they? . . . . . ."]

Once more, the excessive language that the author uses to perform or parody the men's speech highlights the frivolous and the tacky. This particular linguistic representation is a performance of homosexuality—of the most homophobic kind, of course; not to mention, as a performance of femininity, it is quite sexist as well. We notice the men's obsession with their hair, their shoes (again, American-style), and, in general, their appearances. Another detail that is important is the overuse of exclamation marks to dramatize the men's language. Yet again, the multiple emphatic exclamations, along with the extensive use of ellipses, suggests that that which is thought of as the language of homosexuality, women, effeminacy, and transvestism requires a different grammar. (I will discuss this question in the next two chapters in fuller detail.) It is also worth noting references to the men's visit to the opera, as well as the high-pitched, falsetto tone with which the young men speak. This discussion about the opera signifies impressively on this scene. Opera is a staging of excess. Opera, as Wayne Koestenbaum has suggested, is also a particular space for the homosexual spectator.[51] Finally, the names of the men are all women's names—and perhaps, this is why they appear in italics throughout the novel, to highlight the travesty and transvestism of each name.

The men's operatic obsession with clothes and gesture culminates in a frenetic scene:

> La desbordante alegría originada por la posesión de los trajes femeninos en sus cuerpos, las posturas mujeriles, las voces carnavalescas, semejaban el retrete-tocador á una cámara fantástica; los perfumes esparcidos, los abrazos, los besos sonoros y febriles, representaban cuadros degenerados de aquellas escenas de Sodoma y Gomorra, de los festines orgiásticos de Tiberio, de Cómmodo y Calígula, donde el fuego explosivo de la pasión salvaje devoraba la carne consumiéndola en deseos de la más desenfrenada prostitución.[52]

> [The overwhelming joy caused by the possession of feminine clothes on their bodies, the womanly posturings, the carnivalesque voices, looked like a *toilette* to a fantastic chamber. The flowing perfumes, the embraces, the sonorous and feverish kisses acted out degenerate *tableaux* of those scenes from Sodom and Gomorrah, of Tiberius's orgiastic banquets, as well as Commodus's and Caligula's, where the explosive fire of a savage passion devoured the flesh, consuming it in the desires of the most unbridled hustling.]

This scene is important because it reveals the illogical way in which the author views effeminacy and homosexuality. Castrejón plays up the clichés of the effeminate man who accessorizes to become a woman as if it were his ultimate desire. Homosexual identity as a modern construction does not exist *per se* in this catalog of "posturings," but rather is alluded to through an amalgam of historical and Biblical references to criminalize the subject, while naming him indirectly. The reference to Sodom and Gomorrah readily names the crime, but not the subject. Also, Castrejón cites the three canonically decadent Roman emperors—Tiberius, the voyeur of sexual orgies among young men and boys; Caligula, the madman and outrageously perverse emperor; and Commodus, the practitioner of incest—to resignify homosexuality. The author conflates the sexual predilections of each emperor to classify homosexuality as the abject. It is really important to see here that Castrejón has identified the homosexual, only to deform his subjectivity. Then, he concludes the chapter by universalizing the dangers of the crime: "Y en esa insaciable vorágine de placeres brutales han caído, para no levantarse nunca, jóvenes que, en el colmo de la torpeza y de la degradación prostituida, contribuyen a bastardear la raza humana injuriando gravemente á la Naturaleza." [And into that insatiable vortex of brutal pleasures they have fallen, never to get up. The fallen young men, at the height of stupidity and prostituted degradation, contribute to the bastardization of the human race, committing grave harm against Nature.][53] Thus, the positivist project is reproduced effectively over and over again throughout the novel. *Los cuarenta y uno* is constructed as a morality tale that enumerates the alleged sins that plague not just Mexican culture in the early years of the twentieth century, but all of Nature itself. The text, rather than elucidate and give a "scientific" or "impartial" fictive account (worthy of the "positivists") of the events of the night of November 17, 1901, becomes an aggressive political diatribe against prostitution and homosexuality, seen in the text as synonymous.[54] In fact, the text serves as a premiere example of homosexual panic, similar to the one we saw in Posada's last print of his series on the 41 men, "El feminismo se impone" (1907). This panic relates closely to the project of nation formation seen during the conservatism of the Porfiriato, especially to its tenet of social order.[55] Also, this very strategy of homophobia as homosexual dis-figuration was seen in Cosío Villegas's historical narrative: first, claiming the homosexual body with all his excesses, only to then add new ones, and making the homosexual synonymous with prostitution, social climbing, and other unbecoming social vices.

Again, I want to take up Monsiváis's assertion that "in popular culture, the gay man is a transvestite and there is only one type of homosexual, the effeminate one." This cultural insight calls into question Butler's commentary that "[n]ot only are a vast number of drag performers straight, but it would be a mistake to think that homosexuality is best explained through the performativity that is drag."[56] Her argument prior to this statement is that "it is important to underscore that drag is an effort to negotiate cross-gendered identification, but that cross-gendered identification is not the exemplary paradigm for thinking about homosexuality, *although it may be one.*"[57] Butler's reading of *the limits of cross-dressing* to represent homosexuality is correct; there are many modes of social and cultural representation for the homosexual and cross-dressing may be just one such representation. However, when she pushes the point further to say that "a vast number of drag performers [are] straight," she nonetheless universalizes a fact that may be true in her cultural context, but not necessarily so elsewhere. In Latin America, for example, we could argue that a vast number of drag performers are gay—and the fact that the Latin American cultural Imaginary still reads the gay body as transvestite (a man who acts "like a woman") shows the need to theorize the paradigm of transvestism to understand homosexuality in that social and cultural context. In turn, this cultural difference and theorization exposes the cultural and historical limits in Butler's own theory of cross-gendered identification.

If Castrejón's version of homosexuality is an exaggerated effeminacy, what does his representation of femininity look like? Upon learning of her lover's "infidelity," Estela breaks down,

> ¡Cómo nos equivocamos las mujeres por coquetas! Admiramos el exterior, adoramos un rostro seductor, nos deslumbra el oropel, y caemos vencidas cuando debíamos ser las vencedoras.
>
> ¡Yo, la mujer eminentemente erótica; yo, que guardaba mis ilusiones amorosas para disfrutarlas á su lado, y que el mundo de mi ventura era para él . . . . . para un afeminado que desprecia mis ternuras supremas por las de esos repulsivos y vergonzantes![58]

> [What mistakes we women make for being coquettish! We admire the exterior, adore the seductive face—gold-leaf blinds us—and we fall defeated, when we should be the conquerors.
>
> I, the most eminently erotic woman, I, who kept my illusions of love to enjoy them at his side; my world of happiness was for him . . . . . for an effeminate who despises my supreme tenderness for the one given by those repulsive and shameful beings!]

Estela suggests that what is most becoming of a woman—her coquettishness, as well as her love for what is superficial and visible—is precisely her downfall. This downfall, of course, anticipates and resolves itself with her falling in love with the mechanic Alberto Bautista; meeting him is a rebirth and a "baptism" into a new life for her. In a text that is trying to do away with certain "excessive" sexualities and a particular concept of the perverse, it is intriguing to hear Estela refer to herself as an "eminently erotic woman." Why call herself "erotic"? Does this not undo the text's efforts to articulate an esteemed form of heteronormativity for the nation? I would suggest that Estela's self-portrayal as exceptionally erotic is meant to be read in contrast to Mimí's effeminacy, his unexceptional masculinity: "I, eminently erotic, I . . . was for him . . . for an effeminate." Estela's "I" luxuriates in the splendor of an Eternal Feminine that is supposed to placate the slightest homoerotic and queer desire in any man; however, there is a noncorrespondence that introduces a crisis of heterosexual desire. This crisis is what drives the women to give information to the police—that is, to "collaborate" with the police—so that the dance of the "41" is interrupted, thereby arresting any queer difference, and reiterating the place of heterosexuality and normalization.

Straight Interests

In the Introduction, I suggested that as with homosexual panic, it is necessary to account for homosexual fascination. There is a strange relationship of repulsion and attraction for the homosexual. In Mexico, Octavio Paz has noted that "[i]t is significant . . . that male homosexualism is considered *with certain indulgence or leniency (indulgencia)* as regards to the active agent."[59] This indulgence and restrained gratification is queer, since it allows heterosexual men the ability to experiment with other sexualities. In the context of this heterosexual privilege to look into a homosexual world, I would like to devote the final part of this chapter to the arrest of the 41 men and, particularly, to the presence of don Pedro Marruecos at the party. I am interested in this character because he, together with his personal servants, escaped the police raid. His story—and, of course, the entire second half of Castrejón's novel—would constitute the "literary" part of the text; the rest is more or less "historic." The author introduces him:

> ¡Don Pedro de Marruecos!
> Su solo nombre indica la magnitud de su popularidad.
> Alto, fornido, de tez blanca y bigote abundante y rubio, retorcido hacia arriba, era un tipo distinguido.[60]
>
> [Don Pedro de Marruecos!
> His name alone indicates the magnitude of his popularity.
> Tall, robust, of white skin and an abundant and blond mustache, twisted up, he was a distinguished fellow.]

The story continues. He has been to France, where he "learned much about prostitution"; in Italy, "he bought the caresses of famed actresses"; in Spain, he was just plain lascivious.[61] Let us not forget that he was married. Finally, a tired man, he ends up in Mexico:

Nation and the Scandal of Effeminacy: Rereading Los "41" 49

> La vida le era insoportable.
>
> Veía a las mujeres como un ser inútil y despreciable, incapaz de crear nuevos placeres para él, y maldecía la Naturaleza porque las delicias femeniles fueran tan cortas é insaciables.
>
> Su cuerpo impotente pedía a grandes gritos más placer, más ilusión, más deleites inconcebibles.[62]
>
> [Life was intolerable.
>
> He saw women as useless and detestable beings, incapable of creating new pleasures for him, and he cursed Nature because feminine delights were so short and insatiable.
>
> His impotent body cried out for more pleasure, more illusion, more inconceivable joys.]

This guy reeks of heterosexuality, of an *über*-heterosexuality, that cannot be contained, one that escapes all categorization. Fortunately for don Pedro, he learns of the gay dance. He feels that there he will get what he wants. He meets *Estrella*, one of several queens present. He flirts wildly and declares his love for her, fondling her body:

> Besaba los párpados temblorosos de *Estrella,* y en un arranque delirante acercó sus labios quemantes á su rostro y a sus mejillas, y su pasión, más vehemente, se confundió en un abrazo largo, muy largo, inefable, embriagador é histrionesco como la afectación de sus modales.[63]
>
> [He kissed *Estrella's* trembling eyelashes, and in a delirious impulse he brought his burning lips closer to her face, to her cheeks, and his passion, each time more vehement, became blurred in a long, long embrace, ineffable, intoxicating and histrionic like the affectation of his manners.]

What *is* he doing? What I want to focus on is this embrace between a presumed heterosexual and a queen, an embrace that is described as "ineffable, intoxicating and histrionic"—the very adjectives that we have heard before to describe the homosexual: unknowing, contaminating, and posing. That is, homosexuality is always being represented as something that is dark and mysterious, unknowing; representations of homosexuality as the infliction of disease, as a contaminant, have long circulated as *status quo* in Western culture; and, as we have seen in this chapter, homosexuality gets pictured as an affectation or pose. It is in this moment of passion between the "heterosexual" man and *Estrella,* that the police break in and arrest everyone—

except don Pedro, of course. He is spared the public humiliation. His perversion (his perverse heterosexuality) remains in the realm of the private. I end this chapter with the following questions, questions which I will take up again in later chapters: Why does such an insistent presence and indulgence of the heterosexual in queer space exist? Where does heterosexuality end and homosexuality begin? Homosexuality, though always embraced or engaged by its opposite, gets marked, yet heterosexuality manages in the end to escape being marked as difference; heterosexuality is unmarked, and this condition is its sign of privilege. Indeed, one could say that the real scandal of the "41" is not so much getting caught, but of don Pedro's getting away. For the fact remains that Castrejón's *Los cuarenta y uno* is also telling us that heterosexuality is somehow "insufficient," and that homosexuality, when "discreet," is the answer to uncontrolled desire, at least experimentally.

The scandal of the "41" gives us different circles of cultural representation—theory, history, art, and literature—which meld into a multiply faceted vision of a scandal whose impact has yet to be fully articulated and understood. Each cultural discipline contributes a small part to a larger story; in piecing together this event, certain social practices and prejudices become evident. In other words, what we need to understand and learn from this scandal is that, even though the "41" render homosexuality visible, critics, historians, and others have come along to redress homosexual presence as an obstacle to the project of nation formation. It is quite dramatic, then, to read Cosío Villegas's historical accounts, view Posada's images, or study Castrejón's novel, as each work identifies and criticizes the homosexual as excess. It is also quite dramatic then to see each man load the homosexual body with further, conflicting representations, thereby creating new "excesses." These new critical, literary, visual, and cultural "excesses" or impositions, rather than illuminate, blur and erase homosexuality.[64]

I want to finish this discussion with a rather simple question in an effort to reclaim the scandal of the "41" in the context of an antihomophobic discussion: why were these men partying? Certainly, this type of festivity was not the first of its kind: we remember from *El Imparcial* that these men "very well-known for their depraved behaviors, and who *more than once* have figured in this kind of scandal." Again, it was nothing unheard of or singular. I want to mention a small, but important, detail shared with me by performance artist and cultural critic Tito Vasconcelos.[65] He notes that just a couple of weeks before the party, world-renown "transformist" Leopoldo Fregoli performed in Mexico. Vasconcelos speculates that the excitement of his show was one of the motivating factors behind the conception of the "scandalous" dance. What seems most interesting is that Fregoli's performance—in which he became many characters in a single show, some of them in drag or transvestite—was accepted and celebrated by Mexico's theater-going elite; however, the "unprofessional" performances of the 41 men became the site for ridicule and homophobia. But more than a mere imitation of Fregoli, I would argue that the celebration itself was a building of community where homosexual subjectivity might be explored. Critic Michael Moon discusses "forms of resistance to homophobic oppression that gay men have developed and practiced." He identifies one such form, the "Scheherazade party": "—the conspicuous energies with which it is enacted as well as the phobic violence with which it is repressed . . . —as an emblematic expression of a perilously highly charged compromise, the energies of which both 'sides' in the ongoing war for and against gay visibility, homophilic and homophobic, have been effectively exploiting for most of this century."[66] The "ball" that the 41 men were having was very much like Moon's idea of a "Scheherazade party." And, therefore, the desire of Mexican authorities to suppress this "party," this scandal, was not so much to cover up the over-visibility of homosexuality as transvestism *per se*—although critics from Castrejón to Urquizo have done a damn good job at it—rather, what needed to be covered up was the sense of "community" with its potential for a gay politic, which could in turn question a heteronormative version of "progress and order." Again, homosexuality "bothered" the Law; it escaped its normalizing force and authority. Therefore, homosexuality needed to be silenced and erased from the confines of the Nation.

I have argued that the scandal of the "41" opens up an unprecedented chapter in the history of Mexican homosexuality—really, I venture to generalize, a history of Latin American sexuality—that has yet to be written. Recuperating the legacy of the "41" means peeling away the repressive historical writings of the event; recuperating means moving away from caricature and focusing on gay subjectivities, transvestite and otherwise; and rethinking the possibilities of narrative (melodrama and camp, in particular) to tell about queer lives and experiences; recuperating the legacy of the "41" also means joining their dance as an act of pleasure and resistance.

Chapter 2

Fashion's Lost Word: Carpentier Writes Woman

> *If I perceive my ignorance as a gap in knowledge instead of an imperative that changes the very nature of what I think I know, then I do not truly experience my ignorance. The surprise of otherness is that moment when a new form of ignorance is activated as an imperative.*
> —Barbara Johnson[1]

> *Art . . . posits man's physical and spiritual existence but none of its works is concerned with his response. No poem is intended for the reader, no picture for the beholder, no symphony for the listener.*
> —Walter Benjamin[2]

Reading Gender Signs

In the burgeoning fields of gender and queer studies, critics have begun discussing how transvestism functions as a phenomenon that conceptualizes and deconstructs the very nature of gender as a social construction.[3] As such, what defines gender most?

As mentioned in the Introduction, transvestism is the act of dressing with clothing that, according to societal rules, belongs to the opposite sex; it is an act of disguising oneself. A subject may define his or her femininity and masculinity—or that all-embracing axiomatic "gender"—through a system of signs, that is, clothing, cosmetics, behavior; the transvestite is a subject like any other, except that unlike other subjects, which have claimed themselves as "normal," the transvestite chooses to (ex)change or to confuse the "gender" signs. Within a normative context, this confusing of signs or "misreading" is a form of (il)literacy because transvestism is, as gay Cuban author Severo Sarduy[4] has said, "writing on the body." In his opening essay from *La simulación* (1982), Sarduy states that

> El travestí no imita a la mujer. Para él, *à la limite*, no hay mujer, sabe—y quizás, paradójicamente es [sic] el único en saberlo—, que ella es una apariencia, que su reino y la fuerza de su fetiche encubren un defecto.[5]
>
> [The transvestite does not imitate woman. For him, *à la limite*, there is no woman, he knows—and paradoxically perhaps, he is the only one in knowing—that she is an appearance, that the transvestite's kingdom and the strength of the transvestite's fetish hide a fault.]

Interestingly, in asserting that "there is no woman," Sarduy would suggest that gender is defined *a posteriori*, that somehow the body constitutes a (non)gendered screen onto which woman is projected as an appearance, a simulation. The transvestite, aware of this paradox, mounts on his body a series of cosmetic applications and performances that double the "artificiality" of gender.[6] The transvestite fetishizes the accessories and accoutrements associated with a particular notion of femininity, and then proceeds to display them to effect an illusion of otherness.

Sarduy's theory of transvestism is critically problematic: before clothing, the body has already been assigned a gender: "For *him*, there is no woman...." The subject of Sarduy's transvestite is always *a priori* "masculine." Additionally, the clothing itself is gendered or gender-coded. The Sarduyan articulation of transvestism is thus a tension or dialectic between a "masculine" body and "feminine" clothing to achieve a sense of "realness" on the part of the transvestite subject. However aware Sarduy is of the gendered body (in fact, he notes that the penis is "[m]ás presente cuanto más castrado" [more present when most castrated][7]), he links this provocative insight to an equally spectacular assertion that the transvestite becomes an idealized model of womanliness for women. It would be like saying that the transvestite is an "artificial woman"—and, furthermore, that his artificiality becomes a model for women. Sarduy does not ask what the politics of this relation might be or look like. This is a troublesome gap in Sarduy's work that cannot be ignored; let me advance that it is the result of an epistemological blindness. For the time being, what is most dramatic is seeing how Sarduy falls into the binary opposition, male/female, body/clothing, presence/décor, erect/castrated. I advance that the regulating idea that underlies Sarduy's conceptualization of transvestism is that the possibility of castration is the signifier of masculinity: what is most masculine for Sarduy is a man's ability to become "feminine." This is a theoretical refunctioning of the idea that masculinity is heightened through masochism. So what Sarduy articulates is not a theory of transvestism *per se*, but rather a theory of the possibilities of being "masculine." In chapter 4, I shall discuss further the problematics of and correctives to Sarduy's theory by suggesting that it is grounded in the epistemology of the heterosexual matrix. Sarduy's work is valuable because it gives an initial answer to the question: What defines (or becomes) gender most? Let us begin with the dress.

Jacqueline Writing . . .

Let us begin with a special case of a man writing (as) woman. In August 1925, a new column entitled "De la moda femenina" ["Of Feminine Fashion"] premiered in the Cuban magazine *Social*. As the title clearly says, it is about feminine fashion, specifically French fashions. The author of the column is the unknown Jacqueline. The author is the renowned Alejo Carpentier, who has been hailed one of Latin America's most provocative literary figures.[8] His experimentation with form was not only a bold, but also a seminal artistic contribution to what was to become the "Latin American novel" of today.[9]

In the enormous body of criticism that exists on the Carpenterian *oeuvre* there is absolutely nothing written about these articles, save references to them in some bibliographies. Perhaps, due to the nature of the topic—a man writing as a woman or, to put it in a more provocative manner, the author as transvestite—critics have avoided making statements about this text. To echo Sarduy, Carpentier was hiding a "fault." Perhaps the negative connotations of this word "fault" are responsible for the critical blindness enacted toward these articles; that this blindness exists is stunning because of the fact that Hispanists know that the representation of women in the work of Carpentier leads to great debates; and it would seem that through a critical analysis of the texts by Jacqueline, the dis-figuration of woman (or of the "feminine") in Carpentier could be better understood.

How can we talk about something that is not talked about? Where do we begin an exploration of a text that has remained hidden for over seven decades? I suggest that the author's and critics' desires to hide or forget these magazine articles represent a kind of displacement, which is a convenient point of departure since the very concept of displacement lies at the crossroads of this critical intervention. What happens to a theory or subject when it exits its "proper" place and enters another context? What changes? Does the subject suffer as part of this displacement and, importantly, how is the new context affected by the subject's new-found presence?

Writing (outside) the Literary

Each month when readers perused the pages of *Social*, they learned about important gossip, social events, fashions, and other tidbits that would instruct them about the "who's who" and the "what's what" of the upper echelons of Cuban society. The magazine's intention was social. In that vein, *Social* could be described as a text that disseminates the necessary information about a specific socioeconomic group. Though it is tempting to suggest that *Social* parallels the programs of so many publications—and especially those in Latin America (each work both defines and is defined by a class, whether of an intellectual or of a political order)—*Social* was, in actuality, addressing a different group, "the wannabes," those readers excluded from the cultural elite who, nonetheless, (if only vicariously) want to participate in the upper echelons of Cuban society. The very category of "wannabes" is important to us here because they "perform class" and, thus parallel and reproduce the same conceits about which Carpentier was writing.

In this manner, the magazine had a double readerly function: On the one hand, the wannabes used it to affiliate themselves—at least, superficially and cosmetically—with the wealthy, and, thereby almost incidentally, confirming and reinforcing the pretensions of upper Cuban society. On the other hand, the "real" reader of *Social*—that is, the reader for whom it was meant—not having to insist exclusively on the magazine's being a code and signifier of his/her class, regarded it for its entertainment value, devoid of any political or intellectual preoccupation. Re-reading the magazine today, it is most interesting to see how a new reader of *Social* might approach the magazine. Obviously, there are many interests that we may bring to the magazine's study: we can easily see that *Social* could be read for a sociological, a historical or even an anthropological analysis. All of these approaches are plausible and would depend on the particular interests and kinds of questions each contemporary critic may have in mind when examining the text.

Of specific concern to me as a literary critic is the degree to which I can read this magazine within the lines of the "literary." And, therefore, my particular interest and approach of the text go beyond the conceited value of the texts; I am interested in giving structure and locating most, if not all, of the articles found therein *outside* the literary. There are obvious exceptions to this generalization, such as the presence of poems, romances, and other short stories throughout the magazine. Nonetheless, *Social* was not a literary magazine; so, most of its writing stands outside the place of literature. I am also interested in the pedagogical value of the fashion articles—not so much in what they will teach about Parisian designs of the time, but rather how the fact that Carpentier used the language of fashion and pretended that this language was necessarily a "feminine voice," instructs us about his learning how to write for others, as well as an imagined Other. In other words, it is important to describe this extra-literary context because it dramatizes the transvestitic performance of the author writing; Carpentier is not simply writing a female character in one of his many novels, but rather he is pretending to be a woman, "writing like a woman," *outside* literature. The desired difference between the characterization between Jacqueline and Mouche of *Los pasos perdidos* [*The Lost Steps*], for example, is obvious: Jacqueline is a woman writing, Mouche is a woman written. "Jacqueline"[10] is a pretension of what can be called a gynographesis, writing inscribed with the inventions of "feminine" signifiers that address and inform questions for, by, and about women.[11] While it can be argued that Mouche as the *femme fatale* in *Los pasos perdidos* represents one stereotypical inscription of woman, nevertheless, that representation is clearly a design of a male fantasy; it could not ever be considered self-referential the way "Jacqueline" is meant to be. Carpentier's gynographesis, it should be understood, is a secret identification, in the psychoanalytic sense.

Uncovering the secret behind Jacqueline's articles will entail performing an in-depth reading of "Jacqueline"—the name of the writer, and the act of narrative transvestism. By performing this double reading, we can evaluate the text as one belonging to specific *Social* order; and, most importantly, as a pre-text or marginal space where Carpentier plays with the question of feminine subject formation.

Staging Jacqueline

Allow me to offer a brief outline concerning the organization of this chapter. First, I shall survey and organize Jacqueline's writing, all the while interrogating how Carpentier writes as a woman and what his representation of woman articulates. Looking at different statements in feminist and gender studies on the figuration of the "feminine" helps inaugurate a comparative discussion of the author's own rhetorical strategies. I will also discuss several stagings or approximations that the author makes in the writing itself on women and women's fashion. Turning the screw, I will re-phrase the question: What does Jacqueline's writing on women mean? This turn will take place by reformulating the question thus: what does Jacqueline's writing on women mean—*for women?*

Who is Jacqueline? Who are we referring to when we call out the name, Jacqueline? Who will answer?

Knowing that Jacqueline the woman did not exist, that she was the Imaginary creation of Carpentier, that she was a construction, it is logical to try to uncover those texts—in the broadest sense of the word—that Carpentier used in his creation and recreation of "woman." Furthermore, it is good to understand how Carpentier puts these texts in motion and at play to develop "Jacqueline." To accomplish this, I postulate for pragmatic reasons three approximations or narratological stagings in Jacqueline's text.[12] The three stages or tendencies, which are not meant to be developmental, are the following: first, the construction and figuration of Jacqueline—both as text and as author—as an aesthetic project will be analyzed and interpreted; a second literary tendency is that moment when the author struggles to appear most clearly as a woman through the citation of other women's voices, historical fragments, and through translation specifically; and, finally, in a third stage or tendency, Carpentier's unequivocal masculine voice returns to speak about and through Jacqueline. It is in this third moment when he makes certain claims and criticisms about feminine fashion.

"Of Feminine Fashion": Construction of Woman

Carpentier's first effort to initiate a "fashion statement" happens in the very formation or construction of Jacqueline, in the earliest articles, those written between August and December 1925; the column is entitled "De la moda femenina."

The desire for the definition and formation of the subject dramatically marks the initial moment of writing by Jacqueline (by Carpentier). From the first line of the first column, Carpentier names the scene of writing: Paris. The insights that the author makes about the French capital are fascinating, for within them he creates an eccentric center for Cuban fashion. Jacqueline writes that

> Paris, la Meca de la Moda, es la ciudad deliciosamente frívola por excelencia, pero es también el centro de las más profundas y ricas actividades creadoras. Cada año el caudal de energía que anima las menores gestas modísticas de arte, se desborda en alguna manifestación de gran interés para todo espíritu

refinado. Esta vez, la "Exposición de artes decorativas" ha constituido el máximo acontecimiento de la *saison* . . .[13]

[Paris, the Mecca of Fashion, is the deliciously frivolous city *par excellence*, as well as the center of the most profound and richest creative activities. Each year the generative energy that animates even the smallest triumphs of fashion and art flows over to some (artistic) manifestation, which could be of great interest to all refined spirits. This time, the "Exhibition of Decorative Arts" has constituted the maximum event of the *saison* . . .]

It is an unusual beginning that should make today's readers wonder if a woman really wrote such an introduction. Reading the very first sentence brings the idea of "excess" to mind. Jacqueline's writing is excessive in that it inordinately renames "Paris," calling it "Mecca," "deliciously frivolous," "center of profound . . . creative activities." Excessive writing has long been a cliché of masculine representations of women's voices; the use of such an "excessive" model to represent femininity or, moreover, women's subjectivity is commonplace, for example, the *modernistas* often oscillated between the contradictory representations of woman as either an empty receptacle for male subjectivity or woman as excess and frivolity[14]; this representation of the feminine as excess culminates in the West in Joyce's "Penelope" chapter of *Ulysses*, of course. Nonetheless for the transvestite writer, that excess, a kind of logorrhea, becomes the *materia prima* from which he will reconstruct himself as other. Carpentier recycles the excess to write femininity. We can think of Carpentier's project as a "writerly *performance*," that is, writing *through* a form. Really, Carpentier writes and speaks through an imagined form of femininity. Let us imagine that the author is speaking through some instrument. One of two things is happening: the sound that comes out the other end is amplified and changed in some way, or he has to blow differently to get a sound out of this horn. Put another way, either Carpentier's "real" voice changes when he speaks through this Imaginary instrument or he adapts his own voice (he blows differently) to make the musical instrument speak the way he wants it to. Or, the most likely scenario, both things happen at different moments in conjunction with each other. The author's voice is his and also not his. This contradiction is rendered visible in the very language of the fashion article: again, "Paris . . . is the deliciously *frivolous* city . . . , the center of the most *profound and richest* creative activities." Paris is frivolous and profound—this oppositional tension quivers throughout Carpentier's textuality as "Jacqueline."

For Carpentier, Paris specifically takes a prominent role in the construction of the scene of writing; it is eccentric in many ways. The author privileges Paris as the scene of writing for all the obvious reasons. He speaks as if he were writing from Paris; yet, at the time, he is living and writing in Cuba. Paris is the contextual space for writing (as) Jacqueline. In other words, Carpentier chose a foreign place, removed from the actual scene of writing, so he could speak as a woman. This geographic displacement puts into play another series of tropological changes, namely gender and class.

Carpentier looks to Paris to find a place that is both "exotic" and different from his own reality in which to create Jacqueline; but, mainly, he needs Paris as a symbol of centrality, of Westernness. We can see in Carpentier's initial move his struggle to mask—or, in this case, to "protect"—himself. Paris is a "safe" place for his transvestite writing; it is distant from the island and it provides that Europeanized and Europeanizing perspective that gives value and credibility to his words on fashion.

Insofar as Paris is that privileged position from which the author must speak and write, the constant re-naming of the French capital points toward a paradigm of "decolonization." González-Echevarría articulates this re-writing in Latin America:

> Colonialism not only destroys at the moment it is installed violently in dominated territories; but, for its own imperial enterprise, it also overturns and reinvents the previous histories of those territories. The mechanisms of that destruction and interested re-writing are visible, with such clarity, in the literature of colonial Spanish America, that it never stops surprising us. Therefore, the process of decolonization always implies a counteroffensive, by and in which it rescues not only geographic territories, but also mental ones; not only space, but time. That is: history.[15]

Following González-Echevarría's discussion, Carpentier would seem to be performing an act of decolonization: his production of signifiers for the French city reinterprets and proposes a radically new principle: Paris *is* Other. Paris is "deliciously frivolous"—in other words, artificial; the city has been imagined or constructed as the site of and for writing. Specifically, Paris becomes a necessarily artificial center because it serves two functions: the idea of "center" collaborates with the essential task of masking the author's performance as woman, while by showing the artificiality of the center through renaming (this is, by definition, an anti-essentialist act), Carpentier shows his role as a critic, as a man of letters.

Colonization happens when there is an asymmetrical relationship of power; this asymmetry invites decolonization. Writing about Cuba and fashion through Paris bares the structural similarities between Carpentier's writing and decolonization; that is, Carpentier as Jacqueline signifies on the decolonizing project.[16] How a French author might write about Cuba—or any other presently or "formerly" colonized space—would only underline that author's privilege to gaze at and to write that other space as the place of the Other; an author from a world power would probably orchestrate different critical strategies to articulate the subversive. For Carpentier and for authors writing after him, displacement and an embattled relation to approximate the Real[17] serve as master tropes and strategies of decolonization. It will be at the act of discovering and creating the scene of writing where Carpentier will invent a world that will appear almost chaotic, almost marvelous-real.

On the positioning of gender, however, Carpentier acts out a particular form of colonization. Subject formation on the level of gender is limited to a masculinist project; that is, questions of gender do not necessarily enter the discussion of a national identity *in relation to* or *in opposition to* other national subjects. Articulating a political ideology necessarily involves the not-so-subtle forms of engendering, indeed *masculinizing*, discourse. In other words, the national subject appears almost always as a "masculine" one. So, when Carpentier does not acknowledge his early writings as a woman, this non-action acts out the ways in which the denial of difference (whether gender, race, or class) articulates and regulates the figuration of a national(ist) subject. When the colonial subject denies gender—and the same could be said about, class, caste, and race—he reinvents the asymmetrical relations of colonization. So Carpentier's anonymous re-creation of the "feminine" participates in repeating the ploy of colonization. This repetition of colonial aggression gets played out not at the level of a body politic and the nation, but rather at the level of a gendered body. The writing of "woman" by a male subject is crucial to understand; it is why I have chosen only to discuss transvestism performed by men; transvestism performed by women entails other questions and issues of power and economics. The gender binarism implies a power asymmetry that takes on different meanings when transvestism is carried out by a man or a woman. Carpentier as a nameless author performs a "conquest": Alejo names Jacqueline. Carpentier as a transvestite means that he renames and reinvents himself. And this blurring or blanking out of his real identity is a sign of his privilege.

In his rewriting of "Paris" as an unstable site of privilege, Carpentier manages to decolonize his relationship with the nation; yet his attachment to gender binarisms and formation is suspect and colonial. Thus, Carpentier's (de)colonial move renders visible the oppositional and contrary tendency within transvestism.

Camp and Transvestism

"Many things in the world have not been named; and many things, even if they have been named, have never been described. One of these is the sensibility—unmistakably modern, a variant of sophistication but hardly identical with it—that goes by the cult name of 'Camp.'"[18] Thus writes Susan Sontag in her classic essay "Notes on 'Camp'," which has profoundly affected how literary critics understand the idea of "camp." Given this and other declarations, it is not surprising to see why some observers confuse transvestism with "camp"; one inevitably reads Carpentier's articles as such a phenomena. At random, here are some of Sontag's notes:

> [Camp] is one way of seeing the world as an aesthetic phenomenon.[19]
> [. . .]
> To emphasize style is to slight content, or to introduce an attitude which is neutral with respect to content. It goes without saying that Camp sensibility is disengaged, depoliticized—or at least apolitical.[20]
> [. . .]
> Random examples of items which are part of the canon of Camp: . . . *Swan Lake* . . . women's clothes of the twenties (feather boas, fringed and beaded dresses, etc.) . . . stag movies seen without lust.[21]
> [. . .]
> As a taste in persons, Camp responds particularly to *the markedly attenuated and to the strongly exaggerated*. The androgyne is certainly one of the great images of Camp sensibility. [. . .] Here Camp taste draws on mostly unacknowledged truth of taste: the most refined form of sexual attractiveness (as well as the most refined form of sexual pleasure) consists in going against the grain of one's sex. *What is most beautiful in virile men is something feminine; what is most beautiful in feminine women is something masculine* . . . Allied to Camp taste for the androgynous is something that seems quite different but isn't: a relish for the exaggeration of sexual characteristics and personality mannerisms.[22]

Again, following Sontag's rules of camp etiquette, transvestism can be described as camp. Yet, transvestism is not camp. Allow me to be mechanical.

Camp is a sensibility; it is conservative. Transvestism is radical because it breaks any fixed sensibilities; transvestism juxtaposes sensibilities and puts a dialectic into motion. Carpentier is "Jacqueline," the text; but he is not

Jacqueline, the author. This undecidibility raises the question of deciphering and defining the subject: is the subject a man or a woman?

Camp is about consumption; Sontag's examples of camp are things that cost (Tiffany lamps, the Brown Derby, operas, certain turn-of-the-century postcards), that are indulgences. While transvestism also consumes, it seems generally more about recycling excess and re-production. Carpentier's articles are re-writings (in the crudest sense of the word) of French articles; that he was writing them in Cuba as if he were in Paris means that he is reading French magazines and "borrowing" their ideas. Of course, he gets carried away.

Should camp seem sometimes apolitical, transvestism would sometimes be very much political. Had "Jacqueline" been a simple game, Carpentier would have revealed his name without prejudice. That he does not disclose his authorship underscores a political preoccupation.[23]

Camp is owning a feather boa; Transvestism is wearing that feather boa and standing up for its consequences. Carpentier (dis)simulates; he veils him/herself behind the feathers, and creates an illusion of Jacqueline who anonymously accepts the consequences.

Camp is a way of seeing the world. Transvestism is about being seen by the world. There is something strange about dressing up; that strangeness is linked with an exhibitionist impulse that transvestism paradoxically denies. In other words, some transvestites are preoccupied with the "realness" of their representation, so much so that their re-presenting (wo)man is full of an anxiety that must be veiled. The effect of "realness" is manifested most strongly through the aggressive denial of the masculine. Of course, some transvestites are more "real" than others: to see the "masculine" through the metaphors of femininity undoes the effect of "realness"; for some transvestites—and Jacqueline seems to be one of these—having a tainted "realness" is simply covered up with a stronger (fashion) statement asserting the Self as woman.

Camp is about placing "quotation marks" around certain words to ironize them; that is, Camp is about defining privilege. Transvestism is about showing that those quotation marks were placed there in the first place by the other and that transvestism works to remove them; transvestism is about exchanging privilege.

Camp is about "having." Transvestism is about "wanting." What does Carpentier want?

"Of Feminine Fashion": Construction of Woman (Part II)

One of the initially striking things that we notice about Jacqueline's text is her many commentaries that mention cities[24]: When she looks at a particular fashion or style, she asks whether fashion is transporting her and her readers, "nosotras" [a feminine "we"], to Calcutta or in any city in Europe, besides Paris. Jacqueline takes her readers to different places. Her definition of Paris as context not only shows the eccentric creation of Jacqueline, but it also shows that Fashion takes the viewer somewhere else; this "ecstasy" and continuous recontextualization suggested by Jacqueline becomes more problematic because "we" join her. "We" witness the fashions and the places along with the author; this use of this first-person plural defines an affiliation, political and along class lines. Sylvia Molloy discusses this use of "we" in the writing of Spanish American autobiographies to exemplify a class consciousness,[25] a class that "we" share at the moment of reading. Jacqueline dramatizes that moment of reading from the perspective of a particular social standing when she says that

> Nos hallamos ya en pleno invierno, y *bien sabéis* que el invierno parisiense equivale a decir: poco frío, continuas lloviznas, calles grises y luces que comienzan a aparecer mucho antes de muerta la tarde. Estas circunstancias, en otro lugar, en alguna austera ciudad báltica, por ejemplo, bastarían para sumirnos en la más temible melancolía, sin darnos más deseos que el de ver caer la lluvia plácidamente y recogernos por las noches ante la chimenea tradicional y llena de hermosas visiones *para quien sabe verlas.*
>
> Pero en Paris pasa todo lo contrario. Por voluntad de algún espíritu superior e irónico esta ciudad parece feudo de eternas paradojas. . . .[26]

> [We find ourselves already in the middle of winter, and *you* [readers] *well know* that the Parisian winter is like saying: mildly cold, continuous rain, gray streets and street-lights that appear much before the dying afternoon. Anywhere else, like in some austere Baltic city, for example, these circumstances would be enough to submerge us in a most frightening melancholy, without giving any more desires than just watching the rain falling placidly and gathering (ourselves) at nighttime by the traditional fireplace and full of beautiful visions *for those who know how to see them.*
>
> But in Paris we see the opposite happening. By the will of some superior and ironic spirit this city seems to be a center of eternal paradoxes. . . .]

Jacqueline brings her readers along with her in this excursion through the world of fashion. There is an intimacy that she shares with her readers. Furthermore, there is a pretension in her voice that reminds me of Rubén Darío.[27] Jacqueline is keenly aware of her readers' "familiarity" with the gray, mild, and rainy Parisian winters, and the melancholy such a winter brings, as well as in the "beautiful visions" that fireplaces hold, and the like[28]—all of these images must be read as echoes of Spanish American *modernismo* transformed now into "traditional" signs of a way of living. Yet, she continues to inform us about *how* her readers should read those images. I make a deliberate reference to Darío here to suggest that the project of transvestism is linked to *modernismo*, insofar as *modernismo* can be defined for its tendency to create a textual palimpsest that radically calls into question the notion of referentiality. In other words, transvestism (as theory and practice) follows the *modernista* project in assessing, constructing, and placing the figure(s) of the transvestite as part of a contextual operation or social construction. Transvestism read within such a literary history seems more productive than situating it within the *culture of the baroque,* which defines transvestism as necessarily an excess. Transvestism is an excess; however, I highlight the importance of how this excess is *deployed* to construct the subject. This reproduction of transvestism as only an excess (as Sarduy would suggest) must be regarded with caution because it hints at shades of a naturalism and essentialism of gender. The deployment of these excessive signs is a different question of epistemology that regulates subject formation. Likewise, Jacqueline writes a particular style. She then literally sees and reads for us; this reading, a kind of interpretative task, puts the signs into motion. Furthermore, by making us participants in the act of reading, she "reads" us.[29]

Jacqueline's prose is over-written, over-researched—in Spanish, *rebuscada*, or in good English, *recherchée*. Her guidance through the world of haute couture is thorough: we learn about a design, when to wear it, how to wear it, with which items to accessorize it, and so on. Furthermore, she introduces other details of the fashion industry: Carpentier tells us that fashion invents and reinvents itself in cycles. The months of August and September are what he calls "of elaboration": "Las actividades modísticas están sumidas ahora, como todos los años, en breve período de apatía, de tranquilidad, que resulta, en verdad, *más aparente que real*. Este es el momento que podríamos llamar 'de elaboración'." [Fashion activities are now submerged, like every year, in a brief period of apathy, of tranquility, that turns out to be, in truth, *more apparent than real*. This is the moment that we could call "of elaboration."]³⁰ Fashion must go through this period of elaboration during which designers are supposedly inventing or deciding what styles should dominate the following season. This didactic preoccupation about the cycles of the fashion world, on the one hand, is just another excess that the author brings to the text. Jacqueline points out, on the other hand, that the tranquility of this period is "more apparent than real"; that is, anyone would imagine that because so little is being divulged about *couture* during this period that little—if any—activity must be taking place in the houses of high fashion. In effect, this moment of elaboration is precisely Fashion's busiest.

This too is a period of elaboration for Jacqueline: she is now learning how to write as a "woman." A question remains regarding his/her success as a female or feminine writer. An issue that must be addressed is why Carpentier chose to sign these articles on feminine fashion with a woman's name; furthermore, yet another issue that needs attention is *why he withholds his real name and presents this particular appearance of otherness*. This essentialist gesture—one that says that only women can write for and as women—is fundamental to Carpentier's transvestitic act, and, perversely, it deploys arbitrary signs (in this case, clothing) for the reconstruction of gender subjectivity. This is all problematic. This essentialism is "more apparent than real," and, through transvestism, it contains a dialectic that motivates the creative act of writing.

Another question that needs to be asked as a corollary to the one of essentialism: perhaps it was Carpentier's fear of being identified *with or as a woman* while writing on feminine fashion that drove him to sign the articles under the name of the anonymous Jacqueline; to be sure, his fear of being identified *as a homosexual*[31] was greater than losing his name completely. Anonymity was safer than (the threat of) homosexuality for the Latin American master. Homosexual panic[32] thus lies underneath the mask of "Jacqueline," and it regulates the author's performance; homosexual panic drives Carpentier to become more and more "like a woman." So much like a woman that his (or her) excesses are noticed from the start: "Paris, the Mecca of Fashion, is the deliciously frivolous city *par excellence* . . . " It is important to notice that the place from which the homosexual panic emerges is quite different in Carpentier's text than the panic we saw in the previous chapter with the "41." The scandal of the "41" represented a homosexual panic produced on the level of a social group or groups as a means to define the Nation; in Carpentier, homosexual panic happens as an internal operation to define Self identity.

Again, the elaboration of Jacqueline as subject requires excessive writing. This excessive (compulsive) behavior reminds us of Sarduy's evaluation; that is to say, Jacqueline's writing as part of the "transvestite's kingdom and the strength of transvestite's fetish hide a fault." I would like to pause momentarily and examine Sarduy's statement. In giving us a "definition" of transvestism, he has simply shifted and problematized its meaning by introducing uncritically the term "fetish," thus further complicating our understanding of transvestism. I quickly begin by using Robert J. Stoller's definition of "fetish"[33]: a fetish is a story masquerading as an object. Stoller subscribes to a conservative definition of fetish, that is, repetition-compulsion activity, different from Roland Barthes who redefines a fetish as a drive or impulse. Therefore an unholy union of Sarduy and Stoller (with some Barthes) would suggest that a fetish is a body masquerading, performing, or speaking/narrating as another body. Or, transvestism is a drive or impulse that gathers and embodies changes of the body and represents them as the Other. In other words, transvestism functions as a discursive enterprise that transforms everything it touches. The transformative powers of transvestism inevitably suggest a performance and performativity.

Carpentier: "more apparent than real"

To be sure, Carpentier was *not* participating in the transvestitic experience of deconstructing gender hierarchy. He wrote articles on fashion for a more primal than for any particular philosophical reason: he wanted to eat and, along the way, acquire some class.[34] Writing as Jacqueline was a form of social and cultural survival. Though, as we shall see, Carpentier would never fully become Jacqueline, the woman. Desiring to pose fully as a woman inhibits the style of his writing.

After that "elaborative" moment of artistic creation, Jacqueline writes that

> Las mujeres, apenas suena la hora de la *rentrée*—de ese regreso tumultoso en que a una hora dada millares de temporadistas vuelven a Paris en banda—se precipitan a los grandes *ateliers* de la alta costura, donde las más maravillosas sorpresas las esperan, como la revelación de los nuevos modelos que habrán de ejercer una tiránica dictadura durante el espacio trascedental y efímero de una *saisón*.[35]

> [Women, as soon as the time of the *rentrée*—that tumultuous come-back when at a given time millions of fashion-conscious women return to Paris *en masse*—rings, run to the great *ateliers* of *haute couture*, where the most mar-

velous surprises await them, with the revealing of new styles that will exercise a most tyrannical dictatorship during the transcendental and ephemeral space of a *saison*.]

It is stunning to listen to Carpentier's assertiveness: "Women . . . run to the *ateliers* . . ." Carpentier as Jacqueline does not see himself implicated in this comment. Furthermore, the experience of shopping is presented as one of sadomasochism: "Her Majesty, Woman"—as Jacqueline often refers to her readers—now has the difficult task of choosing fashions or styles that are more appropriate to her taste and for her lifestyle. And, in choosing those fashions that a woman may deem appropriate, if not necessary, she is naming a tyrannical ruler to control her. The whole narrative with which Carpentier discusses the opening of the *saison* is fascinating; it may (hypothetically) sound like this: "first, you go to, say, Bergdorf's, and—surprise!—what pretty fashions you see there; finally, you buy a dress and you are caught wearing it all season." Or, it can also, and more likely, sound like this: "you go to buy that new Chanel dress but—damn!—you cannot afford it; this, of course, brings much stress to your life because all of your friends will be wearing something so 'in' that you will be 'out.'" Fashion is a space that converts everyone who touches it. In other words, Fashion signifies a Quevedian dilemma of wanting that which hurts the Self most. In effect, I would suggest that only a (heterosexual?) man could have articulated the tyranny of Fashion in such perverse or sadomasochistic terms, while not getting himself caught up in the trappings of consumption; that is, by assuming the position of an observer of fashion, the author stands outside the trap that he describes as Fashion.

So, what does it mean to be "in" or "out" of fashion? This spatial relationship requires a closer examination. To be "in-fashion/style" means to be contained within a discourse that controls the subject. Although to be "out of fashion" may refer to the old, the out-of-date, Carpentier has defined and valorized this pejorative as a tropological imperative such that to be literally "out of fashion" suggests the possibility of criticism. In other words, according to Carpentier, one needs be "out(side) of fashion" to write about fashion critically. Transvestism permits the young Alejo to write about feminine fashion in an essential—and, paradoxically, in an "objective" manner—while, at the same time, his exotic writing allows for a critical difference about the meaning of fashion.

This critical perspective that transvestism lends the writer is juxtaposed with an anxiety of authority. All along, Jacqueline refers to that "difficult task" of choosing the most becoming fashions to suit the taste and lifestyle of her readers. Ironically, what is presented is one taste, that of French designers, the "tyrannical dictatorship" of a "canon" headed by such masters as Coco Chanel and Jean Patou; there is also one lifestyle, that of the "elegant readers" of *Social*. On the question of the canon of fashion, who or what becomes most fashionable? The question will remain unanswered as it is difficult to gauge the degree to which a woman's response to the creative "triumphs" of a particular designer will define Fashion. Furthermore, it is wrong to engage in this question for it contains echoes of "blaming the victim" insofar as we attempt to decipher the active role that women play in canonizing fashion.

Carpentier's distancing himself from the project he is describing is a means of circumventing self-criticism; this takes us back to the moment of elaboration, which I introduced earlier. Again, the moment of fashion elaboration is also one of Jacqueline's elaboration. The cycles and stages that Jacqueline notes as part of creative production duplicate the formation of a subject. It is a moment "more apparent than real" since the author has not become that Other who he is trying to (in)form. The restlessness between Self and Other, the *unheimlichheit*, can be heard in the author's displaced voice as he refers to women in the not-fully-compromising first-person feminine plural (*nosotras*); or, in the strangely aggrandizing form of the royal second-person singular: "Your Majesty, Woman"; or, in the blatantly "objective"—if not, objectionable—feminine third-person singular, "she" (*ella*); also, he refers to women as "that prized jewel that is named feminine beauty." The author's restlessness echoes throughout the pages of Jacqueline's writing. This dissemination of naming women as the objects of Fashion is part of the unsettled nature of the writer, whose resistance in becoming a full-fledged woman, a transvestite subject, can be heard in his avoidance of feminine adjectives applied to himself, which contributes to the binary nature of his gender identification.

Let us say that Carpentier as Jacqueline "does not imitate woman"—to recap Sarduy's text. Actually, for Carpentier, "there is no woman, he knows—and paradoxically perhaps, he is the only one in knowing—that *she* is an appearance," a construction. He does not imitate women because he cannot make for a gender reconciliation between the Self and woman *qua* Other. The author's tyranny in pretending to know what it means to be a woman can be seen with such clarity *in the resistances* shown in naming himself as a female subject—Jacqueline almost never uses the pronoun "I." This pretension can be heard also in the inconsistencies of the author's addressing himself the way he would address women, for example, as "el sexo débil" (the weaker sex).

In the context of a gender binarism that structures Carpentier's notion of gender, the author seems to understand that to assume the role of woman would mean the negation of himself as a man, that woman is the negation or castration of man. Returning to Sarduy, he insists that, in the case of transvestism, the man, the penis, or the phallus is "more present when most castrated." Transvestism as performed by Carpentier and as defined by Sarduy signals a castration—woman is seen as the site of negation, of exclusion; transvestism for the Cuban authors dramatizes fundamental social dichotomies: male/female, masculine/feminine, presence/absence; in addition, their brand of transvestism promotes other dichotomies: sadism/masochism, structure/destruction, inside/outside, sanity/madness. This perspective of transvestism presents a double problem: that is, while it can perform a criticism of the theatricality of gender, transvestism can run the risk of misperformance, that is, of parodying women and, thereby, being reduced to a misogynist act. I am wary of this reduction, as well as of the danger of forgetting to talk about the misogyny involved. For that reason, it is important to consider the masks that transvestism *imposes* on the Eternal Feminine. How can one approach this "double" problem that the transvestite presents? In the process of writing, Carpentier projected some prejudices upon the transvestitic act, and, by extension, onto women. To insure that this violence is not repeated and that the subject is revealed, not evaded, it is important to "listen" to the transvestite speak; in other words, ask how transvestites generate a narrative, what different strategies they use to draw themselves—from their position as subjects.

If Carpentier is not imitating woman, what is he doing? What does he want? His most radical project is certainly not one of transvestitic performance and writing. I want to reread the question of Carpentier's *homosexual* panic as the panic of *being like a woman*. Carpentier does not perform homosexuality, but rather male hysteria. Hysteria is a crisis of identity. Out of this complex panic, a desperate reconstruction of subjectivity permeates the pages of Jacqueline's articles to control or normalize Carpentier's hysteria. The most blatant reconstruction of this loss of subjectivity lies in the historicizing of Fashion that Jacqueline describes. In other words, a hysterical Carpentier resorts to the dominion and structuralism of History to restore a sense of tradition to the Self. Carpentier will produce a history of Fashion in his articles. I am arguing that this historical element in his articles about women's fashion is a way for the male author to reassert his authority. History, after all, is valorized as a masculinist enterprise, whereas fashion writing is traditionally considered frivolous and superficial. To say then that Carpentier's most radical literary project is one of historical dimensions ironically becomes a problematic proposition. Jacqueline's articles are the origins of Carpentier's Latin American Novel as History.[36]

Madness and Transvestism

I want to undertake a parallel reading to the one that Shoshana Felman offers on madness in her *Writing and Madness*. She argues that

> The significance of madness as a crucial question in the current cultural scene is well known. Not only has madness preoccupied many different disciplines but has *caused them to converge*, thus *subverting their boundaries*.
> [. . .]
> The fact that madness has currently become a commonplace is, however, food for thought. And the fact that it has caused the verb "know" to be put in quotation marks is not the least of its consequences. In spite of its susceptibility to caricature, we begin to understand that if the issue of madness had been linked so insistently to the current upheaval in the status of knowledge, it is because madness poses in more than one way a question whose significance and meaning have not yet been fully assessed and whose self-evidence is no longer clear: not so much the question of "who 'knows' and who does not 'know,'" but *What does it mean to "know"*?[37]

What is most interesting about Felman's comments is the epistemological shift that she makes to discuss madness: no longer does our position as "healthy" and "sane" subjects matter in defining the madman. What does the madman say about us, our health and sanity? Also, Felman's insight that "[n]ot only has madness preoccupied many different disciplines but has *caused them to converge*, thus *subverting their boundaries*" takes on a particularly different meaning in Spanish. *Locura* means madness; *locura* also means queerness. And, in fact, queerness as a sign of radical difference causes disciplines and disciplined genders to converge, thus subverting their boundaries. Again, "translating" Felman's work, I am tempted to substitute "transvestism" for "madness." By doing so, later observations she makes sound like this, "The fact that madness [or transvestism] has currently become a *common* discursive *place* is not the least of its paradoxes. Madness [transvestism] usually occupies a position of *exclusion*; it is the *outside* of a culture. But madness [transvestism] that is a *common* place occupies a position of *inclusion* and becomes the *inside* of a culture."[38] It is important to distinguish between the "usual" ways madness and transvestism get read as positions of exclusion, versus the "subversive" ways of a "common place" madness or transvestism that occupies "the inside of a culture." In other words, when madness or transvestism are rarefied and used to mark the place of the Other, they get read as something outside culture; it is an act of objectification. However, when transvestism or madness are considered without prejudice, they become part of the interior of the culture. Rewriting Felman's passage allows me to account for transvestism as a "*common* discursive *place*," as a fad, as represented in contemporary American culture. In the case of Latin America and, until recently, in its major urban centers, transvestism has occupied that space of exclusion, although it has played a crucial discursive role. How transvestism functions as a discursive, literary space in Latin America is, indeed, the most important question that I am trying to gauge and open up in this project. Transvestism, like madness, signifies all around us; transvestism writes us. What is specific and subtle about reading madness and transvestism as subjective markers, rather than objective ones, is that it shows not only the interiors and exteriors of cultures but, crucially, the construction of these spaces. Addressing that construction helps us understand how and why a subject in a privileged position, one of centrality and hegemony, would resist the inclusion of the transvestite into his space.

Sarduy seems to evade this criticism when he asks "¿quién simula, desde dónde, por qué?" [who simulates, from where, why?][39] His Orientalist answer[40] will be that the transvestite's body may still serve to "occup[y] a position of *exclusion*; it is the *outside* of a culture"—to echo Felman. Likewise, Carpentier may have felt it was important to erase his presence from the transvestitic scene of writing. Revealing his narrative transvestism may have excluded him from a sense of authority. He did not want to be excluded from Culture. As we have seen, his own erasure, however, is not complete, thus accounting for the strong presence of other texts in the form of quotations of other fashion critics, photographs of fashions that do not correspond to the text, and even, as remarked above, discussions about the cycles of fashion, to name a couple of examples. In any event, Jacqueline represents that creation of a multiplicity of texts, textures, and insights; this creative impulse can be heard in the following discussion:

> Disponemos por lo visto de una infinita variedad de materiales que combinar y nuevas líneas que adaptar a nuestra personalidad y gusto. Las innovaciones presentadas este invierno nos plantarán, pues, una infinidad de pequeños problemas que se resolverán más o menos felizmente según nuestra comprensión o nuestras nociones estéticas. La implantación de una línea nueva nos crea siempre dificultades—¡las más encantadoras, ciertamente! . . .[41]

[As we can see, we have available an infinite variety of fabrics to combine and new lines to adapt to our personality and taste. The innovations presented this winter will pose for us an infinity of small problems that will resolve themselves more or less happily according to our understanding and our aesthetic notions. The coming of a new line will always create difficulties for us—the most charming difficulties, of course! . . .]

If we can read this statement not only as one that comments on the complexities that fabrics and styles bring, but also as a self-portraiture of the author writing, Jacqueline, then, appears as the metaphor of a *bricolage par excellence*. It is important to underscore that "Jacqueline" as a metaphor is a relevant description of her position since, while the text and persona produce a Bakhtinian *heteroglossia*, no dialogism is produced on the influence between context and subject. In other words, if we understand the Nietzschean concept of Art as the *thing* (or Felman's *chose littéraire*) that brings together culture (context) and individual (subject) into the same space, then, even given Carpentier's inability to transform himself into the Other as well as his failure to internalize other texts (this internalization could perhaps be best exemplified by removing the quotation marks, or by using pictures that refer to his articles[42]), we can say that Carpentier successfully manages this task. His excessive dependence of other texts to write himself as a woman may lead one to suggest that Carpentier, that prominent Latin American author, is already (?) too "strong" a male "author" for his own good—to recap (and problematize) Bloomian terminology. Or likewise, he is not strong enough to articulate the voice of a woman—for him, the Other.

Translation and Transvestism: a Question of Authorship

Dramatic as it may seem, in the midst of historicizing fashion as a strategy to write (about) the subject, Carpentier makes a small change in his column: the "elegant readers" of *Social* will no longer find "De la moda femenina," but rather, beginning with *Social* XI, in January of 1926, readers are treated to a "new" column, "S. M. La Moda." A translation of the title brings to light quite a different matter: "Her (His?) Majesty, Fashion." What is interesting about the inaugural article of "S. M. La Moda" is that it presents for the first time what will become a larger preoccupation for Carpentier/Jacqueline. Here s/he tells us that "[a]nother particularity that continues is the use of somewhat *masculine* lines in *sport* outfits."[43] This initial commentary functions as a prelude to the following month's column:

we notice that the "problem" of the "masculine" within the realm of the "feminine" has become larger, and that Carpentier writes extensively on it. Carpentier begins moving away from the historicizing tendency dramatized in his initial writing of and as woman, and ends moving toward a critique of women's roles *reflected in* women's clothing itself.

> Recently, a subtle Parisian writer wrote in some article a somewhat cruel, yet just, phrase affirming that soon the exegetes of the feminine wardrobe would see themselves obligated to refer simultaneously to the fashions of women and men, since the charming representatives of the weaker sex (*sexo*) tend to *masculinize themselves* more each time.
>
> A moralist would not miss this moment to raise his arms in the air and to denounce from the top of his lungs the evils of our time—O tempora, O mores!—but as for me, I dare offer the opinion that, seen anew, this orientation for woman toward practical things, and toward the liberty that was unknown to our grandmothers, embraces a necessary minimal amount of flirtation. *No one would dare deny that today as never before, perhaps, woman worries about perfecting the minor details that would interfere with her outfit; she has never had so much art to complicate her existence, in creating for herself new obligations, new necessities of self-aesthetics, so as to have the pleasure of triumphing more brilliantly over all of the difficulties and of making herself more suggestive—in a word, more desirable.*[44] (Please refer to figure 2.1 for original text).

These two richly constructed paragraphs hardly make a feminist statement—maybe an early, crude Marxist statement, but not a feminist one.[45] Let me begin with a critique of the first paragraph, which closes with a most memorable line: "the charming representatives of the weaker gender (*sexo*) tend to masculinize themselves more each time." Again Carpentier flagrantly reiterates the binary opposition male/female, strong/weak, etc. where the first term represents itself as a more desirable state of being. I have chosen to translate the Spanish word *sexo* as "gender," but we all know that it explicitly means "sex." This double translation is very fruitful, since the tendency of the weaker *gender* toward the stronger means something entirely different to that movement of the weaker *sex* to the stronger *sex*. In other words, what is the difference between saying "femininity becomes masculinity" and "female becomes male"—or "vagina becomes penis"? The difference is that changing gender might represent a behavioral modification (say, a transformation of a socially-constructed Self) while sex change refers to a more radical bodily transformation (another expression of a social construction). Thus, getting or losing a penis is a sex change, getting or losing a phallus would suggest a gender change.

Ironically, what Carpentier notices in women's fashion could also be called a transvestitic performance of women in masculinizing their clothing, their form. Carpentier reads this transvestism as both practical and liberatory: practical, in the sense that masculine fashions grant women the mobility necessary for different activities; liberatory, because it gives women a degree of "flirtation." Again, women performing the "masculine" enables them to flirt, to seduce; performing the masculine means that women can acquire rhetoric, the art of seduction, that is, the language of the other. The language of the transvestite is the language of seduction. The language of the other as the language of seduction responds negatively to the question of essentialism: Can the Other be seduced in a language other than his or her own?

Carpentier's language about transvestism as a liberatory act for women is unusual because it inadvertently supplies a critique of himself, the writing subject. Carpentier's construction of Jacqueline figures prominently as an act of the deployment of particular and strategic essentialisms. He has taken a system of signs, which he has identified as "feminine," and has put these signs into motion to reconstruct the Self as other. Carpentier has redrawn the limits of gender not through a subversion of the boundaries of the "masculine" and the "feminine," but, instead, through the appropriation of the other and the transvestitic layering of the Self.

More on the question of women's "liberation." While there might be some truth in arguing that some fashions allow more freedom for the body—we need only think about the excruciatingly painful hourglass fashion figure of the late nineteenth century—there remains the question of freedom for the Self. In other words, does "acceptance" (and already this term is problematic) of women's performance of masculinity necessarily imply an act of liberation? To act like a man is to be free? Listen to this reformulation of the Cartesian paradigm: I think (like a man), therefore I am (free). How does the opposite of this paradigm read? I think *like a woman*, therefore I am *not free*; or, perhaps, I think *like a man writing like a woman*, therefore I am *not free to reveal my name*. That is, I think (am) *homosexual*, therefore I am *anonymous*. In other words, the facile equation of masculinity and freedom that informs Carpentier's writing supports a series of masculinist prejudices in and of his cultural space. Moreover, this equation strangely deconstructs his subject position: his insistence on "fully" becoming Jacqueline, which is further accentuated in his desire for anonymity, complicates and problematizes his freedom. If to be free means to speak, then his not revealing his real name, not speaking, shows him failing to perform the "masculine." Carpentier thus perversely becomes woman, the writer of history, woman, the hysterical, the historical woman "Jacqueline."

Painting Gender on the Body

As I mentioned before, this particular column—*Social* XI, 2 (February 1926)—marked a change in how Carpentier writes "woman" and how he writes as a woman. Not only does Carpentier introduce the problem of women and masculinity, but immediately after his opening remarks, examined above, he turns his attention to the matter of cosmetics, "And proof of the amount of femininity hidden by this apparent tendency towards the masculine, can be foreseen in the importance that the arts—for example, the art of putting on cosmetics (*pintarse*) which for a long time was abandoned to the tact and the good taste of anyone interested—have gained."[46] Following this observation, Carpentier adds that, "Recently, the great writer Mme. Lucie Delarue Mardus published in Paris a book, entitled *Séduire*, in which all of the conceits that a woman may put into play to be attractive were detailed with extraordinary knowledge and insight. The author concedes its deserved importance to the art of applying make-up (*pintarse*)—of *maquillage* as the French call it—considering this one of the greatest factors of beautifying that a woman has available to her."[47] The emphasis that the author places on the act of applying make-up (in Spanish *pintarse*, literally "to paint oneself") makes me question the centrality of this particular task. If performing the "masculine" means that women now possess the masculine empire of rhetoric, what is the relationship between maquillage and rhetoric? What logic constructs *maquillage* as a continuation—if not only, a function—of masculinity? Again, the reflexive verb *pintarse* reminds us that the subject is also object of the action. Transvestites become subjects at the moment they objectify the Self. For the transvestite, the penis no longer matters as a signifier of the male subject; it remains passively hidden and ignored, waiting to surprise and to reveal itself unexpectedly. Now the phallus, the signifier of masculinity as an agent for representation, becomes the defining figure that regulates the transvestite's subjectivity; thus, the simulation of castration—that is, by phallic imposition and aggressiveness—is the signifier of the Eternal Masculine. Carpentier is most masculine when he castrates himself to become "feminine" insofar as he regulates the illusion of "femininity," that is, the illusion of a castration. He does not suffer any pain of a disfigured subject because he

S. M. La Moda
por Jacqueline

Un hermoso mantón, cubierto por un verdadero jardín de flores ejecutadas en colores vivos.
(Cortesía de Bonwit Teller Co.)

obligado caudal de coquetería. Nadie se atrevería a negar que nunca como hoy, tal vez, la mujer se ha preocupado mas en perfeccionar los menores detalles que han de intervenir en su atavío; jamás ha tenido tanto arte en complicarse la existencia, en crearse nuevas obligaciones, nuevas necesidades de auto-estética, para tener el placer de triunfar más brillantemente de todas las dificultades y hacerse más sugestiva, en una palabra, más deseable.

Y la prueba de la cantidad de feminidad que encierra esta aparente tendencia hacia lo masculino, se advierte en la importancia que adquieren artes, como el de pintarse, por ejemplo, que durante mucho tiempo se abandonaban al tacto y buen gusto de la interesada. Recientemente se publicó en Paris un libro de la gran escritora Mme. Lucie Delarue Mardrus, titulado *Seducir*, en que todos los sortilegios que puede poner en juego una mujer para gustar eran detallados con un extraordinario conocimiento de causa.

Un grácil mantón de seda ligera, fabricado en Francia, embellecido por nutrida orla de franjas.

RECIENTEMENTE, un sutil escritor parisiense escribió en cierto artículo una frase algo cruel pero bastante justa, afirmando que pronto los exegetas de la indumentaria femenina se verían obligados a referirse simultáneamente a las modas de la mujer y a las de los hombres, pues las encantadoras representantes del sexo débil tienden a masculinizarse cada vez más.

Un moralista no perdería esta ocasión de alzar los brazos en aspa y poner el grito en el cielo denunciando los males de nuestra época—¡o tempora, o mores!—, pero por mi parte, me atrevo a opinar que, bien mirada, esa nueva orientación de la mujer hacia las cosas prácticas, y hacia una libertad que desconocían nuestras abuelas encierra su

Un mantón en crepé de seda, muy ligero, que ostenta el precioso motivo decorativo de unos crisantemos japoneses.

La autora del libro concede una merecida importancia al arte de pintarse —del *maquillage* que dicen los franceses—considerándolo como uno de los máximos factores de embellecimiento que puede tener a su disposición una mujer.

Hablando de los ojos, afirma que, vistos aisladamente, separados del rostro, sin sus párpados, "tal cual se mirara una piedra preciosa", todos los ojos son bellos. Los hay más grandes que otros; los hay de colores más o menos raros; eso es todo. Lo que a su juicio hace la belleza de los ojos, no es el iris en sí, sino el modo con que viene a exteriorizar su fuerza expresiva en el conjunto del rostro, la forma y el color de los párpados, la forma de las cejas, las ojeras. La verdadera belleza

Figure 2.1 (*continued*) *Social* XI (2), February 1926, pp. 63–65.

de los ojos proviene, pues principalmente de lo que los rodea.

Para embellecer entonces esas regiones que circundan el ojo, es menester utilizar el creyón con verdadero virtuosísimo, ya que de ellas depende una mayor o menor fuerza expresiva. A fin de aumentar el brillo del iris, de darle vida a los ojos, es menester proceder del modo siguiente: iniciar el proceso marcando dos puntos fuertemente a ambos extremos del ojo, es decir en la intersección de los párpados. Señalar el borde del párpado inferior con un trazo, grueso en los lados, y cada vez menos importante, hasta no ser más que una mera sombra en el centro. En el párpado superior ha de hacerse justamente lo contrario, colocando el punto de máxima intensidad de pintura en el centro. A continuación se repartirá sobre los párpados, con mucha discreción, un poco de polvos azulados u ocre—según la entonación del cutis—destinados a crear una especie de penumbra alrededor del ojo, y a amortiguar las marcas del creyón... Probad y ve-

Dorothy Mackaill la célebre actriz se ha dispuesto a lanzar la moda excéntrica de rodilleras de piel, análogas a las que aparecen en esta fotografía. ¿Le auguráis algún éxito?

(Foto First National)

réis los maravillosos resultados de estos consejos...

Otra parte del rostro que debe atraer nuestra mayor atención en punto a pintura, son los labios. Según opina la escritora, tampoco es fácil utilizar aquí la pintura. Hay labios en que el *rouge* no prende bien, pues, o tienen tendencias a estar siempre demasiado húmedos o se resquebrajan por excesiva sequedad. En este último caso el empleo de una pequeña cantidad de glicerina por las noches puede ser muy saludable, o sino debe aconsejarse el uso del *rouge* graso, en caja. Para iniciar el acto de pintarse los labios, es menester extender estos sobre la superficie de los dientes, a fin de que reciban equitativamente su cantidad de pintura. Después de haber pasado el creyón horizontalmente sobre ambos labios, debe volverse al superior verticalmente para igualar mejor el color en el centro.

Refiriéndose a la cuestión importantísima del cutis, Lucie Delarue Mardrus, dice: "Este es el momento de referirnos a algo trascendental: la nariz. La juventud auténtica de

Un elegante modelo de abrigo de tarde. Está confeccionado en brocado de oro con bordados en azul y rosa. El cuello y los puños son de piel de zorro.

(Foto Borgdorf-Goodman)

El gran costurero L'ionnet puede jactarse de haber realizado una verdadera creación en el dominio de las "robes de style", con este bellísimo modelo hecho en moiré plateado con ricos adornos de broderies de oro. (Cortesía de Bonwit Teller Co. Foto Maurice Goldberg.)

Figure 2.1 *(continued)* Social XI (2), February 1926, pp. 63–65.

Obsérvese la utilización de plumas de paraíso en este atavío de tarde.

(Foto Bonny)

Jessie Morris, la linda estrella nos muestra aquí una combinación de ropa interior extraordinariamente sugestiva y ligera.

(Foto Metro Goldwyn)

una mujer se debe a muchos detalles de su persona, pero hay uno, muy pequeño, que parece insignificante y dice mucho acerca de la verdadera edad de su propietaria: el borde de la nariz.

"Miradlo en un niño. Liso, intacto, sin grasa, se une a la mejilla sin relucir, sin matizarse de pequeñas venas ni llenarse de oquedades imperceptibles, ni cubrirse de minúsculos puntitos negros. Para el borde de la nariz, aunque solamente se utilice leche de almendras, debe reservarse siempre una cantidad— —aunque sea pequeñísima—de crema, a fin de devolverle la pureza que pierde forzosamente alrededor de los treinta años. Por esto debe insistirse en la ranurita semicircular que determina el punto de intersección con la cara.

"Ahora pueden aplicarse los polvos. La mayoría de las mujeres se aplican el colorete por encima de los polvos, pero creo más práctico

Aquí tenéis una preciosa boquilla cubista, hecha en onix y marfil.

(Foto Bonney)

hacer lo contrario, pues *debajo* de los polvos, el colorete tiene más oportunidades de adquirir un color de acuerdo con la naturaleza.

"Para colocar el colorete en su verdadero lugar, lo cual no se hace al azar, debe sonreirse a fin de que los pómulos se marquen, pues deben ser el punto de máxima intensidad en la repartición del color. Debe tenerse el cuidado de no propagar el colorete ni en el párpado inferior, ni en las sienes, ni muy cerca de la boca. Tampoco debe abusarse del colorete si no se quiere envejecer, en lugar de lo contrario."

Paris, Enero 1926.

Una libra y cuarto es todo lo que debe pesar el atavío femenino, según nos demuestra Kathleen Key, la linda estrella de la Metro-Goldwyn-Mayer, que ha colocado en la balanza todas sus prendas de vestir sin omitir aquello que quizás pudiera ser considerado de superfluo. He aquí lo que nos revela la balanza: Pantalones, dos onzas; un brassiere, una onza; un par de medias de seda, dos onzas; traje, seis onzas; sombrero, cinco onzas; zapatos, una libra.

Una de las más bellas creaciones de Joseph Paquin.

(Foto Manuel Freres)

manages to copy or simulate a woman's voice the way he would want her to do. The possibilities of being a different subject (of claiming other subjectivities) define his privilege as male, his privilege as author. Carpentier writes not only the body *of* feminine fashion, and *of* make-up, cosmetics, or *maquillage*; rather, he writes the body *with* texts of feminine fashion.

After the introduction about women's masculinizing tendencies and its relationship to cosmetics, Jacqueline finally tells us how to make ourselves effectively more beautiful. She begins with the eyes.

> Talking about the eyes, she [Mme. Delarue Mardrus] affirms that, when isolated, separated from the face, without lashes, "as if one were looking at a precious stone," all eyes are beautiful. There are those which are bigger than others; those rarer or less rare colors; that's all. What in her judgment makes the eyes beautiful isn't the iris itself, but the way in which the iris comes to extend its expressive force to the whole face, the form and the color of the lashes, the form of the brows, the bags. The true beauty of the eyes comes primarily from what surrounds them.
>
> Then to make the eyes more beautiful, for those areas that surrounding the eyes, it is necessary to use a crayon with true virtuosity, since from it depends the greater or lesser expressive force. In order to heighten the shine of the iris, to give life to the eyes, it is best to proceed in the following manner: begin the process marking two strong dots . . . [48]

Truly a fascinating dissection of the face. We see yet another strategy that the author uses to articulate himself as woman: translation. Carpentier has borrowed Delarue Mardrus's fashion tips and translated these (into Spanish) for his Cuban readers. Throughout this particular entry he will quote Delarue Mardrus directly, and then proceed to appropriate her voice. This ventriloquism would be in itself a forceful adaptation of Madame's text, *Séduire* (?), if only we knew that the text actually existed.[49] Perhaps, this title is a deliberate mistranslation of Delarue Mardrus's known text *Embellissez-vous!* [Make yourself beautiful!]. Carpentier's mistranslation would point to his imposing the ideology of seduction over that of beauty; after all, seduction is what Jacqueline equates to being "masculine," and not the act of making oneself beautiful like a woman, in other words, transvestism. What Jacqueline promotes as a figure of seduction is precisely a masculine representation of woman; indeed, "Jacqueline" is the figure of otherness for men—but also, for women.

I want to add another queer detail to Carpentier's translation. Lucie Delarue-Mardrus was a lesbian and she was involved in early feminist politics.[50] It is necessary then to consider that the model of femininity that Carpentier was promoting was one held and articulated by a lesbian feminist. While this fact may highlight a certain conservatism, that is, a sexual dissident being the purveyor and promoter of a traditionalist feminine aesthetic and "look"; it ironically highlights a certain distance that Carpentier has with the subject of femininity and beauty. In other words, he is negotiating a very mediated form and articulation of the "feminine," which again represents textual and sexual otherness.

Fashion's Lost Word . . .

"¿Adónde vamos este año?", las mujeres recorren afanosas las colecciones para proveerse de todos aquellos vestidos y trajes apropiados a los lugares de veraneo. Pocas cosas agradan tanto a la mujer como sentirse libre de trabas por algún tiempo, vistiéndose ligeramente con aquellos vestidos de *sport*, de catadura masculina, que más que ningún otro dan a las del sexo débil la justa sensación del terreno ganado en los fueros de los eternos "fuertes" del opuesto.[51]

["Where are we going this year?" Women are thoroughly and carefully running through the collections to get all those dresses and outfits appropriate for summer vacation. Few things please women so much as feeling free from snaps (*trabas*) for some time, dressing lightly with those sport dresses with a masculine cut, which more than any dress give those of the weaker sex the right sensation of having gained territory within the privileges of the eternal "strong ones" of the opposite sex.]

First, we cannot help noticing how Jacqueline uses the third-person "women," as well as the phrase "the weaker sex," as subjects of her statements; she does not position herself within either category. In other words, Jacqueline does not see herself implicated in these categorizations. This, of course, seems in direct contrast with her opening question: "Where are we going this year?" Jacqueline's question seems to encapsulate more than just the question regarding the readers' summer plans, but it also evaluates the masculine direction or orientation of feminine fashions. This preoccupation had already been foreshadowed in earlier articles. And while a signaling of this tendency toward the masculine within feminine fashion can be seen by some as a progressive position by the author, this attitude nonetheless revisits the column with a sense of fear, of resistance.

Muchas mujeres contemplarán estos vestidos [una nueva forma de traje sastre, conjugando caprichosamente las líneas masculinas del austero *smoking*] con justificado temor: en efecto, si añadimos al pelo corto, a la silueta extra sencilla de estos últimos tiempos trajes de catadura masculina, ¿qué quedará de nuestra encantadora feminidad?...[52]

[Many women will contemplate those dresses [a new form of tailored suit, which play whimsically with the masculine lines of an austere tuxedo] with justified fear: in effect, if we add outfits of masculine cut to the short hair and to the ultra simple silhouette [figure] of these recent times, what will remain of our charming femininity?...]

This closing remark exposes a contradiction: on the one hand, the author has celebrated the movement toward the masculine as an act of liberation, of seduction, of closing in on the space of the masculine; on the other hand, however, the movement poses a threat—the loss of a "charming femininity." This contradiction signifies a binary opposition that we have seen over and again to regulate the transvestitic narrative. "What will *remain* of our charming femininity?" suggests that femininity loses its definition and force when filled or covered up with masculine signifiers. Furthermore, the very question seems to suggest that "femininity," for Carpentier, is quantitative; by extension, "femininity" marks the site of negation, of castration. Hence, the author repeats the classical Freudian definition of "femininity," which has occupied the central basis of gender difference up to our own *fin-de-siècle*.

In his essay "Shelley Disfigured,"[53] Paul de Man defines Romanticism as an archaeological project, an interpretive labor that duplicates the questions of Romanticism: "Who am I?," "Where am I?," and especially, "Where do I come from?" These questions prefigure the answer to the origins of Romanticism. Romanticism is thus re-defined as an act of auto-referentiality, of self-consciousness. What stands in opposition to this search for the Self as described by Romanticism as repetition is found by shifting the focus of the question from "being" to "becoming"; from "form" to "process"; from repetition to deconstruction. In other words, de Man displaces the concept of a complete Subject to the process by which that Subject is constituted. Having said this, we can see that Carpentier's "failure" or "defect" as a transvestite lies precisely in his conceptualization of "woman"—in this case, the figuration of Jacqueline—and "man" as integral representations of the Self that lie opposite each other on a gender/sexual spectrum.

Rather than completeness, de Man will focus on fragmentation: "What relationship do we have to such a text that allows us to call it a fragment that we are then entitled to reconstruct, to identify, and implicitly to complete?"[54] His question could be used to re-evaluate the "completed" nature of what Carpentier refers to as the masculinizing tendency of the feminine, thus positioning masculinity as completed state. Masculinity is a fragment that, like the "feminine," requires continual examination and articulation. All masculine Subjects, like the "feminine" texts produced, are fragments; that is, all Subjects become fragments when engaged in the dialectics of reading, of completing them. The Subject is like a "question," the most radical manifestation of a textual fragment because it calls for its completion. Asking "Where do I come from?" erases *self*-knowledge. Questions fundamentally figure criticism, but double and disfigure the "original" text/Subject. Our imperatives become how to shatter this constant repetition of discursive modes as a way to promote "intentionality" as well as how to break with the limiting project of insisting that subjectivity can be reduced to an integral and definable Self.

Carpentier takes a very definite position on that gender spectrum that he has designed. The author's position prizes the masculine *look* as that which confers on "those of the weaker sex the right sensation of having gained territory within the privileges of the ever 'strong ones' of the opposite sex," and his position also signals his resistance to accepting his status as transvestite, but supports the superficially cosmetic behaviors of transvestism. Again, Carpentier does not want to give up "masculinity" as the privileged position within the gender construct; this yielding would represent an act of castration of his phallogocentric discourse. The author's resistance denies the sexual reconciliation of the (masculine) Self and Woman as Other. In other words, Carpentier does not erase the borders of gender and social limitations imposed between men and women. This erasure and deconstruction of gender binarisms will be more successfully written by other authors, Donoso and Puig, for instance. Carpentier's triumph comes in establishing and reifying such binarisms.

. . . *Sadomasochism*

A small detail of impertinent erudition: as an almost desperate turn or return to femininity, Jacqueline recommends the use of flowers to feminize fashion. The art of womanhood suffers according to the author; restoring that art becomes a small obsession for him:

Es indiscutible que vivimos en una de las épocas más pintorescas que puedan imaginarse, en lo que respecta los usos y costumbres impuestos por la Moda. Jamás, como actualmente, la moda ha ejercido tan absoluta dictadura espiritual, a punto de controlar hasta cierto punto los gustos de los hombres de este siglo y de imponer a las mujeres una serie de disciplinas cada vez más rigurosas.

La belleza del rostro femenino, alabada por los hombres desde que aprendieron a exteriorizar sus pensamientos, a pintar o a escribir, se ha vuelto en una preocupación secundaria, al lado de una nueva preocupación de hoy, que ha llegado a imponerse cada vez más en nuestras nociones de lo bello: la elegancia de la silueta . . . Pero resulta que la silueta actual está enteramente creada para doblegarse a la exigencias de la moda.[55]

[It goes without question that we live in one of the most picturesque epochs that anyone can imagine, with respect to the uses and customs imposed by Fashion. Never before as today, has fashion exercised such an absolute spiritual dictatorship, to the point of controlling to some degree the taste of men of this century and of imposing upon women a series of increasingly more rigorous disciplines.

The beauty of the feminine face, praised by men since they learned to exteriorize their thoughts, to paint or to write, has become a secondary preoccupation, next to today's new preoccupation that has come more and more to impose itself on our notions of beauty: the elegance of the silhouette . . . But it results that the silhouette of today is entirely created to bow to the demands of fashion.]

Carpentier makes an important distinction here; fashion is different for men and women: for men, it "controls" to some degree their taste, their desires; for women, it imposes a series of behaviors. Furthermore, what underlies Jacqueline's preoccupation about how fashion affect the sexes differently is a social and historical order that goes back to the Aristotelian notion of male as form and female as substance. Feminine beauty has been replaced by the elegance of the silhouette (form). What does this aesthetic shift (written both as an imposition of the "masculine" and as loss of the "feminine") represent?

I want to suggest a somewhat perverse reading of these demands of the silhouette through a discussion of sadomasochism and fashion, sadomasochism in fashion, and—why not?—sadomasochism as fashion. The preceding passage is loaded with a vocabulary of imposition and control, that is, of sadomasochism.

To engage in a discussion about sadomasochism is a difficult task. Our understanding of sadomasochist practices is usually clouded by a (misguided) preoccupation with the pain involved. The slightest discussion of sadomasochism is often avoided because of a deep-seated, nearly universal Victorian fear. Let me suggest, however, that critical interests in Barthes's structuralism and Bakhtin's formalism are but veiled attempts at coming to terms with sadomasochism. Formalism calls for the description of a system and the examination of how different elements function or contribute to the whole. Artistic unity and balance are essential. In any of Carpentier's descriptions of feminine fashion and women, the reader will find a care for values such as symmetry, balance of shape, and color. Everything is controlled to produce a harmonious and "peaceful" effect. Everything is controlled to reproduce a stereotypical "feminine" space and subject.

The best way of discussing sadomasochism is by stating some explicit definitions and by refining them along the way. To begin, sadomasochism is about sexual pleasure. It is a different kind of pleasure. Don't think of the pain involved; that venue is only the Imaginary at work. Rather, it is necessary to undergo an epistemoerotic shift[56]: pleasure is not a *telos*, the culmination of a sexual game; pleasure happens when controlling or being controlled by the other[57]—it is a process. This shift locates pleasure not in the climax, but in the *process* of the sexual act. Sadomasochistic practices suspend the difference between pleasure and pain. This shift operates on several levels of Carpentier's writing: on the authorial level, through a powerful engagement with *sadomasochistic behavior* (gazing, writing, framing, editing) *that is deeply sexual*, the objectification of the feminine Subject reproduces Carpentier's sadomasochist urges of control; on the narratological level, the use of standardized forms of "feminine" discourse—in this specific case, the fashion column—permits the author to perform a felicitous, narrative transvestism. Furthermore, on a social level, Carpentier's anonymity allows for a re-creation of woman. Fashion permits the characterization of the Other, and such a practice is *jouissance*. Again, Fashion is a practice that enslaves everyone who buys into it. In other words, Fashion signifies the dilemma and the pleasure of wanting most what most hurts the Self.

Transvestism and Différance

One question still remains: if masculinizing of the feminine subject promotes a virtual equality, what does that elimination of difference—or, the articulation of *in*difference—mean for women? There is an extreme and real danger of interpreting the assimilationist impulse in Jacqueline as a pro-feminist trivialization. The indifference of the "masculine" woman requires some explanation. First there is a pretension that the "masculine" woman is somehow equal to the man; but operating with the language and discourse of the other causes the death of the Self. The pretension of the "masculine" woman is demystified easily with the understanding that this woman operates in the discourse of the other. Remember: transvestism is not only about becoming the other, it is also about disfiguring the Self. This double movement can be observed in Carpentier's articulation of difference.

The difference that Carpentier/"Jacqueline" draws manifests itself, first, as a sexual and gender inequality; second, as a difference of the *social* space of context in and from which the author writes; and, third, as a conflict of sentimentality between the man who writes and the woman who is written. Carpentier's marking of gender difference is a blindness that lies in the contradiction with his discourse that resists "masculine" form while it imposes it. This double movement (dis)articulates the figuration of Jacqueline, and deconstructs the displaced, authorial voice. This insight reveals a new aesthetic of the "feminine."

I conclude this final literary critical tendency and staging of Jacqueline's writing, which seems to resist and criticize the "real" masculine silhouette as an imposition, with a short theoretical meditation. In his fashion *oeuvre*, Carpentier seems to say that *Art is a means of seduction*. This insight suggests something about writing: rhetoric as an art is an act of seduction. Rhetoric is a cosmetic act. Rhetoric, seduction, and cosmetics: this discursive triangle is related in complicated ways and implies a particular performance that is central to Carpentier's transvestitic project.

A final question, what does Carpentier's writing on women mean—*for women*? In the Carpenterian world, it means that the transvestite Jacqueline, who has been set up as a man's other, also represents the other for women. Carpentier's "Jacqueline," the transvestite subject, is as much Other to women as she is to men. To our world, it may mean that the transvestitic mask is necessary to function within the systems of domination, that a woman's desire to realize even "masculine" tasks must be read within the realm of the "masculine" or forfeited altogether. Paradoxically, this criterion does not always apply to men. This insight presents important political challenges to gender and feminist studies. In another world, this asymmetrical relationship as a profound commentary on our yet unaccomplished postmodern condition must be socially and culturally faced.

Chapter 3

Gender without Limits: The Erotics of Masculinity in El lugar sin límites

Uno de los hombres trató de mear a la Manuela, que pudo esquivar el arco de la orina. Don Alejo le dio un empujón, y el hombre, maldiciendo, cayó al agua, donde se unió durante un instante a los bailes de la Manuela. Cuando por fin les dieron la mano para que ambos subieran a la orilla todos se asombraron ante la anatomía de la Manuela.

—José Donoso[1]

[*One of the men tried to piss on la Manuela, who was able to avoid the arch of urine. Don Alejo pushed him, and the man cursing fell in the water, where he joined la Manuela's dances for an instant. Finally, when the men gave them a hand so that both get on the river's bank, everyone was amazed by la Manuela's anatomy.*]

Skirting the Penis; or **Que grand tu as!**

Clothes possess an interesting power of class signification; why else do certain private clubs still insist on "coat and tie for gentlemen." By the same token, race, ethnicity, and nationality can be easily marked by certain clothes or accessories. Moreover, clothing as a marker of gender, class, and race, gains its meaning through repetition: By this I mean that within a specific, discrete, semantic field, clothes repeat the structure of a cliché.[2] However, what is at stake in the signifying element of dress are not the social or cultural assumptions that are repeated by any particular item—say a yarmulke, a dashiki, or a Paloma Picasso choker. Clothes not only gain meaning through a continuous socio-historical displacement, but strangely, what matters most is that any meaning that clothes might have becomes manifest most strongly at the moment a particular object is deployed and recontextualized outside its "intended" use and space. I have been discussing cross-dressing as an explanation of this phenomenon. Transvestism evokes and fixes the intentionality of dress beyond exclusively maintaining what might be "traditional" values of clothes (which incidentally permit some slippage). (Sartorial) meaning appears more lucid through the complex of difference.

Inherent in the act of transvestism is this paradox of difference, which reveals the structuring of meaning and echoes the paradigm of displacement and decolonization—to which I alluded in the last chapter. We witness this paradigmatic scene awry in José Donoso's *El lugar sin límites* (*Hell Has No Limits*). *El lugar sin límites* is a bold representation of this chaotic, albeit pleasurable, moment of reading.

Although written at the height of the Latin American "Boom," Donoso's text, *El lugar sin límites* (1966), has been displaced as a minor text; this displacement happens from the very beginning, even as the work's very author claims that it would not be his great *oeuvre*. He would designate his gothic *El obsceno pájaro de la noche* his contribution to the "Boom." But like all that is repressed, *El lugar* returns to haunt the author and us.

El lugar sin límites is a simple story. On a cold Sunday, in the middle of nowhere, the famed madame, la Manuela, learns that Pancho Vega has returned to town. A year earlier he had tried to beat her physically but failed; the rumor was that this time he was "going to get her." The entire Sunday is full of anxiety, but Manuela tries to run her errands as if things were not any different. In the course of the day, she decides to fix her red flamenco dress, in the event that she might need it to entertain Pancho. This shows the reader that, although she fears him, she very much desires— or even loves—him. She thinks of the passion that she unleashes in other men. Their passion is hard to articulate because it is unconventional: la Manuela is, after all, a transvestite. That evening Manuela makes every effort to appear calm. She imagines that, if there is any trouble, the town's patriarch, don Alejo, will come to her rescue. She is unsuccessful at pretending that her safety is assured, and once Pancho inevitably arrives at the whorehouse, she runs and hides in a chicken coop. It is there that she remembers another day—eighteen years earlier—when she was raped, and how she and her partner, la Japonesa, "won" the (whore)house where she has lived since.

An analysis of that rape scene (which serves as the opening epigraph of this chapter) shows the representation and construction of the body and the structure of sexual and gender domination that operate throughout *El lugar sin límites*. I will study the ways in which the transvestite's body becomes an object *through* which other subjects rethink their own subjectivity: examples of this are how la Japonesa Grande forges her masculinity, how don Alejo exercises his (heterosexual) authority, how Pancho Vega erases his homosexuality, and, how literary critics of the novel expand other theoretical preoccupations; all of these impositions come about as a misreading of transvestism as imposture. I would argue that nowhere is this misreading of transvestism as plain "ambiguity" more apparent than in the critical reception of *El lugar sin límites*. To wit, it is baffling that almost every critic has discussed la Manuela's transvestism as a symptom of something else: transvestism as Bakhtinian carnivalesque or ambivalence,[3] transvestism as a distorting of "reality,"[4] and transvestism as homosexuality.[5] Whereas the previous chapters involved the reading of social texts, this chapter will focus more on close reading and literary analysis. Here I would like to show the performative potential that literary analysis has as a form of social critique.

Reading / Rape / Other

While hiding in the chicken coop, la Manuela remembers the fateful night of her rape. After much partying, the men at the whorehouse take la Manuela, exhausted from dancing, to the canal and throw her in the water. When she is pulled out, the men get more than a little surprise; they become amazed by her anatomy. Stripped of her red flamenco dress with white polka dots, la Manuela emerges as Manuel; her coming out as a man is certified to the abusive men by the size of her/his large penis. For them, the penis is undoubtedly the most obvious marker of masculinity; the men's comments bear witness to this tautology: "—Mira que está bien armado . . . " [Look he is well endowed (or armed) . . .]. And, "—Psstt, si éste no parece maricón." [Psstt, this man doesn't look like a faggot]. Another man warns, "—Que no te vean las mujeres, que se te van a enamorar." [Make sure the women don't see you; they are going to fall in love with you].[6] The men's reactions merit some explanation: let's go back. First, the "unveiling" of the penis happens at a moment of torture to la Manuela; she had been thrown in the water after her debut performance at la Japonesa Grande's brothel. At a victory celebration party for don Alejo, the community's patriarch and purveyor of the law, the famous dance scene begins when la Manuela takes center stage, only then to be passed around to the guests. First she dances for and with don Alejo, then the mailman, the station chief. Later, another man,

[e]l viñatero jefe de un fundo vecino le arremangó la falda por encima y al verlo, los que se agrupaban alrededor para arrebatarse a la Manuela, ayudaron a subirle la falda por encima de la cabeza, aprisionando sus brazos como dentro de una camisa de fuerza. Le tocaban las piernas flacas y peludas o el trasero seco, avergonzados, ahogándose de risa.[7]

[the chief of a neighboring vineyard rolled up her skirt and, seeing this, those who were hanging around to grab la Manuela helped pull the skirt over her head, imprisoning her arms like in a straitjacket. They touched her skinny and hairy legs or her dry behind, ashamed, drowning themselves in laughter.]

More than a strip-tease, the assault on la Manuela's body represents a moment of pleasure as well as shame for the men: shame because of the pleasure. La Manuela's body literally becomes the site and sight for homosocial exchange. The men (ab)use la Manuela to carry out their desires of sadism. Of course, this sadistic impulse to tie up la Manuela and laugh at her goes hand-in-hand with masochistic shame. I want to suggest that the homosocial is charged and disguised by the scene of sadomasochism. The homosocial exchange is apparent from the very beginning when the different community leaders (don Alejo, the mailman, and the station chief) fight over la Manuela as if trying to establish their authority. Also, the men's snide remarks are meant not only for la Manuela but for each other. It is quite provocative that the men insist on dancing with her and "discoursing" through her. To begin with, they already knew that "she" was a "he," so what exculpates any trace of homosexual panic is the *communal* aspect of their homosocial desire. In other words, la Manuela is a "woman" because that is what the men want. Moreover, she is a "woman" the way they want her to be—in a "straight" jacket (allow me the pun in English). One man's ambiguous exclamation, "—Está caliente" [She is hot. Or, she is horny],[8] unwittingly blurs any compromising position in which the men might find themselves. Ambiguity in language tropes off the body of the transvestite. As a matter of fact the whole narrative structure of the novel hinges on the ambiguity signified by the transvestite's body. To be more precise, transvestism is seen by the men as merely *ambiguity*, which permits them to do whatever they want. The transvestite's influence is not only a centrifugal force that changes the scene of reading, but it is also a centripetal force that creates and recreates the very subject, constantly calling into question the very notion of referentiality. More than just a man wanting or pretending to be or playing at being a "woman," la Manuela wants to be seen as just that, a woman—without any sense of irony. Scenes in which she insists vehemently that she *is* a woman abound in the text. To drive this point further, we see that her name, "Manuela," is the feminine form of her original "Manuel." The letter *a,* which codifies and renames her, signals a complexity more profound than the commonplace notion that the *a* is a marker for what is grammatically feminine in Spanish. The letter *a* permits the representation of the Other. If we as readers remain within the context of the heterosexual matrix, the binary that situates otherness as the subject polar opposite to a gendered self, we would commit an error of being simplistic; what the letter *a* in Manuela's name represents is a much more radical Other that deconstructs the pretense of locating gender within the heterosexual matrix. La Manuela represents a third gendered subject that reveals, in effect, both the indeterminacy as well as every unique conceptualization of gender.

The Place without Limits?

The novel opens with la Manuela, an aging transvestite and co-owner of the bordello in Estación El Olivo, complaining of a hangover after partying the night before. If there is, indeed, a place without limits it is the scene of the family romance: we learn that la Manuela and her virgin daughter, la Japonesita, are the owners of a bordello that is frequented by the men of the small town.[9] To view the bordello as only a place of economic exchange would be limiting; it is paradoxical, however, that, in the lost and diminishing space of Estación El Olivo, which has been forgotten by the politicians as another barren area in the province of Chile, the bordello is a place of political and sexual—in the broadest sense of the word—production. When the patriarch don Alejo wins the election as the area's deputy, all the men go celebrate at the bordello and "[t]he women of the town [agree] not to protest for having to stay in their homes that night . . . "[10] They knew that don Alejo would appreciate and might even reward their husbands for being there with him in his moment of triumph. The men's visit to the bordello represents more than a rite of passage, more than a boy's fancy to "get it" for the first time; the men go to the bordello to garner political, social, and sexual leverage. I want to argue that the bordello is and has always been of space for re-creation; the fact that it is owned by a transvestite and her "virgin" daughter does not lessen the powerful exchanges and transactions that we witness there—strangely enough, the owners' own sexual predilections and fantasies heighten the degree to which the bordello is privileged as a site of sexual, social, and political commerce. In other words, regardless of the fact that the house is sinking—both literally and figuratively—the men of the town go there to see others and to be seen. It is a space of spectacle and voyeurism.

Looking for Love in All the Wrong Places . . .

As a matter of fact, it was a (per)version of the primal scene, an unbridled moment of voyeurism that transferred proprietorship of the bordello from don Alejo to la Japonesa Grande and la Manuela. Don Alejo mocked la Japonesa Grande's womanliness and femininity and made her an offer that she could not resist:

> —Ya está. Ya que te creís tan macanuda te hago la apuesta. Trata de conseguir que el maricón se caliente contigo. Si consigues calentarlo y *que te haga de macho,* bueno, entonces te regalo lo que quieras, lo que me pidas. *Pero tiene que ser con nosotros mirándote, y nos hacen cuadros plásticos.*[11]
>
> ["That's it. Since you think of yourself so highly, I'll make you a bet. Try to get the faggot horny with you. If you get him horny and *he makes himself a man* (macho) *for you,* well then, I'll give you anything you want, whatever you ask for. *But it has to happen with us watching and you make* tableaux vivants *for us.*"]

It is then, in a bout of rage, that la Japonesa Grande asks for the house. To don Alejo's initial reluctance about such a request, la Japonesa Grande challenges don Alejo: "—Yo la quiero. No se me corra, pues don Alejo. Mire que aquí tengo testigos, y después pueden decir por ahí que usted no cumple sus promesas. Que da mucha esperanza y después, nada . . . " ["I want it. Don't run out on me, don Alejo. Look, I have witnesses here, and later they can go around saying that you do not keep your promises. That you give much hope, and later, nothing . . . "][12] She calls into question his word and, in the context of his election to deputy, his authority. He agrees. What is most important about this exchange—besides the conditions of the bet—is the way in which both la Japonesa Grande and don Alejo radically call into question each other's femininity and masculinity. Don Alejo wanted Japonesa to show her sensuality and sexuality. She wanted him to keep his word and "[n]o se me corra." Here she means both "don't run out on me" and "don't come"—and by extension, "don't get limp." So, not keeping his word would mean that Don Alejo was not being a man. Their struggle to maintain their social stature means questioning the other's sexual prowess.

This obsession with sexual prowess and performance is what the men experienced when they first saw la Manuela naked. What is at stake in the sexual performance of others? What do the men get out of watching others perform sexually? Do they get off? To what degree and in what manner does the sexual performance between a prostitute and a transvestite mitigate—and I am saying that it does—the sexual appetite of heterosexual men? In the final analysis, why do straight men watch "lesbian porn"?

It is following the assault on la Manuela that the bet is made. La Japonesa Grande begins her seduction. After finding la Manuela sitting in the kitchen, la Japonesa joins her and tries to console her. La Manuela explains that

—A mí no me importa. Estoy acostumbrada. No sé por qué siempre me hacen esto o algo parecido cuando bailo, es como si me tuvieran miedo, no sé por qué, siendo que saben que una es loca. Menos mal que ahora me metieron al agua nomás, otras veces es mucho peor, vieras . . .
Y riéndose agregó:
—No te preocupes. Está incluido en el precio de la función.[13]

["It doesn't matter to me. I'm used to it. I don't know why they always do this or something similar to me when I dance, it's as if they were afraid, I don't know why, being that they know that one is queer (*loca*). At least this time they just threw me in the water, other times it's much worse, you see . . . "
And laughing la Manuela added: "Don't worry. This is included in the price of the show."]

It is amazing to see how la Manuela has already become used to (*acostumbrada*) the violence against her, how she has to a greater or lesser degree internalized the pain of rape. There is a hint of self-awareness when she uses the third-person form to refer to her sexuality, "they know that *one* is queer."[14] Manuela seems to be saying that her masquerade is doomed to suffer the violence of strangers. Another thing that strikes us about the transvestite's explanation and exculpation of the men's behavior is the repetition of the phrase, "I don't know why." This repeated ignorance seems quite dramatic, especially because she tells la Japonesa why they beat her: "they (the men) were afraid." She knows that the men are afraid of her, not simply what she is but rather what she represents in their lives. The question here is not what la Manuela's performance means for herself, but what la Manuela's performance means for the men. The beating, the psychological violence, the death wish against the transvestite signals her success as a woman. For the men, however, la Manuela's successful performance represents a sinful erasure of the sexual and gender boundaries that they have neatly drawn. She is right: the men were afraid that she could get them excited, *calentarlos,* thus discounting for them the impossibility of homosexuality. Finally, one cannot escape the symbolism of being thrown in the water as a kind of (en)forced baptism to purify, to remove original sin. It is necessary to remind ourselves that the notion of "original sin," a stain of the body, which the transvestite conveniently embodies for the men, lies within each of them; so, again, la Manuela's words signify on the men and on us as readers of *El lugar:* "they know that one *(una)* is queer."[15]

It is precisely this *locura,* queerness, this strange and untranslatable sexuality that the men want to see in a *tableau vivant* that don Alejo demands as proof of la Japonesa Grande's stimulation of la Manuela. Let us imagine for a second what we would call the sexual scenario between a prostitute and a transvestite. Let us call it a "heterosexual" relationship. Or, perhaps, a "lesbian" relationship? But, as we shall see, the terms "heterosexual" and "lesbian" prove to be inefficient when describing the seduction and the orgasm. Also, what the men want out of witnessing this event needs to be explained. The difficulty of talking about what a transvestite and a prostitute might do in bed lies in the fact that, while we have been successful in discussing sexuality and gender, we have failed to account for what might commonly be called sexual practices or erotic imagination. Accordingly, let us look closely at what happened.

Basic Instinct

It is not hard to believe that la Japonesa Grande's seduction of la Manuela was not easy. From the outset the very idea of sleeping with a woman repulses la Manuela: "—¿Estás mala de la cabeza, Japonesa, por Dios? ¿No ves que soy loca perdida? Yo no sé. ¡Cómo se te ocurre una cochinada así!" [My God, Japonesa, are you sick in the head? Can't you see I'm a hopeless fag? I don't know. How dare you think up such a disgusting thing like that!][16] We see that, after questioning Japonesa's mental health and her vision, Manuela focuses on the sexual act itself as some perversion that la Japonesa Grande devised. This sets up the scene for what follows. Japonesa tries holding Manuela's hand; Manuela then pushes it away. The failure of this back-and-forth touching and pushing away (familiar to anyone who has tried) opens up a textual space where competing narrative voices struggle to arrive an accord:

No, si no quería, que no hiciera nada, ella no iba a obligarlo, no importaba, era sólo cuestión de hacer la comedia. Al fin y al cabo nadie iba a estar vigilándolos de cerca sino que desde la ventana y sería fácil engañarlos. Era cuestión de desnudarse y meterse a la cama, ella le diría qué cara pusiera, todo, y a la luz de la vela no era mucho lo que se vería, no, no, no. Aunque no hicieran nada. No le gusta el cuerpo de las mujeres. Esos pechos blandos, tanta carne de más, carne en que se hunden las cosas y desaparecen para siempre, las caderas, los muslos como dos masas inmensas que se fundieron al medio, no. Sí, Manuela, cállate, te pago lo que quieras.[17]

[No, not if Manuela did not want to, let him do nothing, she was not going to force him, it didn't matter, it was a question of putting on a comedy. In any event, no one was going to watch them closely but from the window and it would be easy to fool them. It was about taking off their clothes and getting into bed, she would tell him what faces to make, everything, and by candlelight there wasn't much that could be seen, no, no, no. Even if they didn't do anything. Manuela doesn't like the body of women. Those soft breasts, so much extra flesh, flesh where things sink and disappear forever, the hips, the thighs like two immense masses that melt in the middle, no. Yes, Manuela, shut up, I'll pay you whatever.]

Denial, comedy, fear, the narrative voices battle to set the terms of a new pact. Of the distinct voices that we can discern, nothing is more surprising than the reversal of roles that we hear: On the one hand, la Japonesa Grande's persuasive strategy to bring the whole event to the level of a comedy, of performance. While, on the other hand, Manuela resists this performance, most strikingly, for misogynistic reasons. Japonesa's view of the scene is reduced to nothing (" . . . no, no, no."); I suspect that this attitude responds to her professional regard of sexuality as a performance for men. She seems to realize that sexuality—especially, in this case—is constructed and located to please men, that women's role in the sexual act is liminal, almost subliminal. If we anchor the sexual comedy in this rigid framework of what sexuality might mean for a prostitute, we can then begin to understand la Manuela's aversion to women's bodies. The misogynistic voice we hear, then, is really Manuel's, here and now a "militant" homosexual so involved within the matrix of the homosocial that women's bodies—what the compulsory heterosexual mind attributes and assigns as his ultimate desire, reemergence, and appropriation—bother him.

Manuel's distaste for and representation of women's bodies as a threat to the masculine phallus reminds me of Freud's description of the primal scene in the famous case of the Wolf Man: "When he [the patient, at the age of four] woke up, he witnessed a coitus *a tergo*, three times repeated; he was able to see his mother's genitals as well as his father's member; and he understood the process as well as its significance."[18] And later, the complex significance of the primal scene is presented: "When the patient entered more deeply into the situation of the primal scene, he brought to light the following pieces of self-observation. He seems to have assumed to begin with that the event of which he was a witness was an act of violence, but the expression of enjoyment which he saw upon his mother's face did not fit in with this; he was obliged to recognize that what he was faced by was a process of gratification."[19] Without going too deeply into the manifolds of the case history,[20] let me jump ahead and give some conclusions. That is, the patient's witnessing—really, fantasizing—of his parents during sexual intercourse is an act that he interprets, on the one hand, as an act of violence by his father against his mother. On the other hand, the "process of gratification" is misread as the mother castrating the father: every time the father penetrates the mother, the penis disappears; the mother's laughter is interpreted as an act of vengeance. Now, if I have juxtaposed this scene with la Manuela's fear of women's bodies, it is evident. La Manuela, like the child, envisions women's bodies as a threat to his "masculinity." Of course, this does not solve his dressing up as a woman; in fact, on the surface, it complicates the whole scene of transvestism. How do we explain this conflict, la Manuela dresses up as a woman, insists on being called a woman, yet finds women's bodies a threat. I would find the explanation that a transvestite is not a "real" woman, hence not a "real" threat for Manuela, banal—to say the least. Or, that the masquerade of transvestism is an act of appropriation as a means for Manuel to control his biggest fear, also rings too simplistic. Transvestism is not only about appropriating "woman," but rather about reinscribing the excess of "woman." Again, linearity presents an obstacle to finding a solution. I suggest that la Manuela, like the Wolf Man, lacks a language to describe her/his sexual subjectivity. She conceives her *liaison* with la Japonesa as the primal scene, as an original moment and screen upon which to mount the dynamics of her sexual persona and to re-present her sexual identity. Her paradoxical difficulty with gender could be explained more fully by arguing that la Manuela is a homosexual male, yet given the specific and narrow cultural definition of what it means to be a homosexual—that is, a man who acts *like a woman*—in the context of Latin America, the subtleties of gender are lost. National language (Spanish, in this case) both opens up and exacerbates the notion of gender almost literally to a *letter,* thus setting certain the limits or possibilities of subject formation. As a side note, through and with the power of language, the "national" constructs the closet. Consequently, la Manuela (ad)dresses and disguises her sexual orientation with clothing, the very codes of gender. In other words, la Manuela's only way of being a homosexual is being *like a woman.* Once more, la Manuela lacks the language of gender, so she assigns culturally-defined gender signs to mark the parameters of the sexual. Certainly, there is a relationship between sexuality and gender; however, given the instability of that relationship, it behooves us to suspend the different conceptualizations of each axiom to see the texture and complexity of a transvestite-homosexual matrix that la Manuela designs. Her basic instinct is to (con)fuse the two practices into one. Perhaps it is this insight that makes la Japonesa Grande realize that, in the end, la Manuela is a man like the others, another version of masculinity, and she warns him: "—Oye, Manuela, no te vayas a enamorar de mí . . . " ["Listen Manuela, don't go falling in love with me . . . "][21]

Orgasms in Unison

The sex scene between la Japonesa Grande and la Manuela can be recorded as one of the most erotic and explicit in Latin American literature. I shall quote it at length because it frames the complexity and obsession with gender and sexual roles more than any other text. The absence of this scene of sheer pleasure and erotica would be glaringly obvious in any discussion of *El lugar sin límites.*[22] La Japonesa Grande tries to make la Manuela feel at ease. La Manuela is anxious and not easily put at ease, as she cannot perform as is demanded of her. The only things that la Manuela senses are the smells of the cheap wine, of Japonesa's breath, of her sweat, "[de] ese olor, como si un caldo brujo se estuviera preparando en el fuego que ardía bajo la vegetación del vértice de sus piernas [de Japonesa], y ese olor se prendía en mi cuerpo y se pegaba a mí . . . " [(of) that odor, as if a witch's brew were being prepared on the fire that burned under the vegetation on the vertex of Japonesa's legs, and that odor clung to my body and was stuck to me . . .]; she also feels nothing: " . . . y yo allí, muerto en sus brazos, en su mano que está urgiéndome para que viva, que sí, que puedes, y yo nada . . . " [. . . and I am there, dead in her arms, in her hand she is urging me to come alive, that yes, that you can do it, and I nothing . . .]; and, la Manuela also hears with paranoia "en el cajón al lado de la cama el chonchón silbando apenas casi junto a mi oído como en un largo secreteo sin significado." [in the armoire next to the bed the kerosene lamp barely whistling almost next to my ear as if revealing a long secret without meaning.]²³ And, finally, she also sees don Alejo watching: "don Alejo mirándome, mirándonos, nosotros retorciéndonos, anudados y sudorosos para complacerlo porque él nos mandó hacerlo para que lo divirtiéramos y sólo así nos daría esta casa . . . " [don Alejo watching me, watching us, we are twisted, tied up and sweaty to please him because he ordered us to do it to entertain him and only so he would give us this house . . .]²⁴ It is important to understand don Alejo's position in the erotic scene, in the erotic triangle. He, too, is a participant insofar as he choreographs this revisiting of such a primal scene. By regulating the roles, conditions, and stakes, he stands in the place of the Symbolic.

In these same terms we can explain la Manuela's anxiety. A Freudian reading would necessarily explain the transvestite's participation in this "comedy" as anxiety of castration, represented here by the loss of authority and willful performativity. Freudian discourse may appear to fail us because the metaphorics of castration are too rough a lens through which to analyze the figure of transvestism. Rather than focusing on la Manuela's anxiety of castration, it is best to understand it as a shifting between the Symbolic to the Imaginary.²⁵ The transvestite, who erases the boundaries of the binarism male/female by becoming the Other, occupies the role of the Symbolic.²⁶ And, in such a capacity, she structures and regulates subjectivity: we know that her celebrated presence as a flamenco dancer always, already causes the kind of commotion and violence in men that, ironically, guarantees her Symbolic presence. The Lacanian Imaginary relates to the act of projection and mirroring, that is, entrapment within the binarism. La Manuela's own description of the event, her attention to detail as she lies in bed, shows her new situation within the Imaginary and her exit from the Symbolic that she so much enjoys. She is literally trapped in bed, being forced to put on a role that she does not want or enjoy, performing as the "heterosexual man" that don Alejo would like her to be. Don Alejo usurps the role of the Symbolic and displaces la Manuela. This displacement accounts for her anxiety, for her non-performance. But what is absolutely marvelous about *El lugar sin límites,* and this scene in particular, is seeing how la Japonesa manages to seduce la Manuela to deliver a performance that neither would ever forget. To accomplish this, la Japonesa conjures up an important character in Spanish literature, la Celestina. La Japonesa uses Celestina's incredible skills of rhetoric—of seduction—to make la Manuela come (out as a man).

At every turn, la Manuela resists la Japonesa's advances. Japonesa begins with tenderness. She tells Manuela:

muy despacito al oído, mijito, es rico, no tenga miedo, si no vamos a hacer nada, si es la pura comedia para que ellos crean y no se preocupe mijito y su voz es caliente como un abrazo y su aliento manchado de vino, rodeándome, pero ahora importa menos porque por mucho que su mano me toque no necesito hacer nada, nada, es todo una comedia, no va a pasar nada, es para la casa, nada más, para la casa.[27]

[quietly, in a whisper, baby, it's good, don't be afraid, we are not going to do anything, it's all pure comedy so that they think it's real and don't worry baby and her voice is hot like an embrace and her breath stained of wine, enrapturing me, but now it matters less because as much as her hand touches me, I don't need to do anything, nothing, it's all a comedy, nothing is going to happen, it's for the house, nothing more, for the house.]

What we see here is la Japonesa's attempt to remove or pacify the fear that la Manuela has by stating that "we are not going to do anything." This phrase is then repeated over and over by la Manuela trying to literalize it. This process of literalization through repetition subverts and momentarily disarms la Japonesa Grande. The delirious repetition of "nothing is going to happen, it's for the house, nothing more, for the house" shows an economic structure of production that is a central trademark of transvestism.[28] To be sure, the process of recycling the excesses of language permits the transvestite to have a unique talent that often confuses play with reification, fantasy with materiality. I have been careful to notice that the expression "it's a comedy" is repeated by Japonesa and Manuela incessantly, because I want to show that the expression is an empty signifier; it also functions like saying "nothing is going to happen." It would be too formulaic and reductive to assume by this turn of phrase that the narrator seeks to explain away the whole event as some carnivalesque moment. Indeed, in spite of the fact that la Manuela says it to herself, this sexual encounter with la Japonesa is rather tragic—and not comedic at all. Furthermore, to suppose that this sexual encounter is representative of a "comedy," of the world upside down, is wrong considering the fact that the operative heterosexual structure has been stated or reinstated as the norm. Interestingly, la Manuela, who because of her positionality as a transvestite, a marginal figure within the broader social context of what represents the "normal," cannot subvert this turn of phrase, "it is a comedy." Subversion of the signifier "comedy" would represent for la Manuela a deconstruction of her very own subjectivity; she must maintain the illusion of "realness," or proprietorship and authority, within the confines of her own discourse, otherwise she is figuratively dead. Her resistance to the semantics of compulsory heterosexuality is an act of psychic survival that must continue throughout the seduction. She imagines that

> A ella [la Japonesa] le gusta hacer lo que está haciendo aquí en las sábanas conmigo. Le gusta que yo no pueda: con nadie, dime que sí, Manuelita linda, dime que nunca con ninguna mujer antes que yo, que soy la primera, la única, y así voy a poder gozar mi linda, mi alma, Manuelita, voy a gozar, me gusta tu cuerpo aterrado y todos tus miedos y quisiera romper tu miedo, no, no tengas miedo Manuela, no romperlo sino que suavemente quitarlo de donde está para llegar a una parte de mí que ella, la pobre Japonesa Grande, creía que existía pero, que no existe y no ha existido nunca, y no ha existido nunca a pesar de que me toca y me acaricia y me murmura . . . no existe, Japonesa bruta, entiende, no existe.[29]

> [Japonesa likes what she is doing between the sheets with me. She likes the fact that I can't: with no one else, tell me so, pretty Manuelita, tell me that never with any woman before me, that I am the first, the only one, and that way I can enjoy myself my pretty, my soulful Manuelita, I'm going to enjoy this, I like your body afraid and all your fears and I would like to break that fear, no, don't be afraid Manuela, not break it but softly remove it from where it lies to get to that part of me that she, poor Japonesa Grande, thought existed but, that no longer exists and never has existed, and never has existed even though she touches me and strokes me and says quietly to me . . . it doesn't exist, you stupid Japonesa, don't you understand, it doesn't exist.]

La Japonesa Grande's sexual appetite makes la Manuela suspect that the woman enjoys the man's impotence; Manuela's paranoia goes so far as to portray Japonesa as a sadist. Manuela is confused; in effect, it is not that Japonesa cares whether or not Manuela can perform, but whether she is a virgin. The whole line of thinking that Japonesa insists upon, "with no one else, tell me so, pretty Manuelita, tell me that never with any woman before me, that I am the first, the only one, etc." inaugurates the framing of a different mode of seduction; it is no longer a perfunctory act (a comedy that means nothing), but more directly, it acquires a literally comic turn, that is, Japonesa actively takes on the traditional role of a man trying by all means to woo a woman.[30] By reinscribing a heterosexual, repronarrative[31] of a conventional first or wedding night, la Japonesa Grande hopes to give back to (or rewrite) la Manuela to her role as a woman, specifically as a virgin. How the repronarrative laces this scene of seduction is quite obvious; for example, when la Japonesa talks about breaking la Manuela's fear, it sounds as if she were breaking her hymen and, later, she corrects herself, she says she will "softly remove it." It does not cease to amaze me how flagrantly repronarrativity dominates any discourse of seduction; I would insist that this accounts for the seductive failure again. La Manuela's abrupt response that *that* passion which Japonesa seeks does not exist accosts any pretension about the centrality of repronarrativity. How la Japonesa ultimately seduces la Manuela satisfies the risky essentialist question that I have posed before: Can one seduce the Other in a language other that his/her own? Does the Other have authority?

Perhaps, as a desperate measure to all of the resistance that she encounters, Japonesa ventures to suggest

> No mijita, Manuela, como si fuéramos dos mujeres, mira, así, ves, las piernas entretejidas, el sexo en el sexo dos sexos iguales, Manuela, no tengas miedo el movimiento de las caderas, la boca en la boca, como dos mujeres cuando los caballeros en la casa de la Pecho de Palo les pagan a las putas para que hagan cuadros plásticos . . . no, no, tú eres la mujer, Manuela, yo soy la macha, ves cómo te estoy bajando los calzones y cómo te quito el sostén para que tus pechos queden desnudos, y yo gozártelos, sí tienes Manuela, no llores, sí tienes pechos, chiquitos como los de una niña, pero tienes y por eso te quiero.[32]

> [No baby, Manuela, it's as if we were two women, look, like so, you see, the legs intertwined, the sex member in the other two members the same, Manuela, don't be afraid the movement of the hips, the mouth in the mouth, like two women when the gentlemen at the Ice Princess' house [another bordello] pay the whores to put on a show . . . no, no, you're the woman, Manuela, I'm the butch (*macha*), you see how I am pulling your panties and how I take off your bra so that your breasts become naked, and I can enjoy them, indeed you have breasts Manuela, don't cry, you have breasts, small ones like a girl, but you have them and that is why I love you.]

Substituting a new lesbian erotics and discourse for repronarrativity frees the tired, unproductive *mise-en-scène*, while it presents and maintains the illusion of "normal" heterosexuality for the men who are watching all of this. I play with the very notion and call into question the "normal" state of the heterosexual *tableau* because something else is going on. To wit, I am talking not only about the "secret" lesbian relation that has developed, but provocatively that there are men watching and talking. Their voyeurism constitutes a (per)version of heterosexuality—and here I refer to the casting of a prostitute and a transvestite in the heterosexual matrix as well as the erotics involved in the process itself of framing. Let us look in more detail at the newly articulated version of a *homosexual* matrix, then move on to the question of the erotics of revising the heterosexual matrix.

I should start by saying that la Japonesa has had sex with other women before. Her words unwittingly leak that secret: "look, like so, you see, the legs intertwined" and also "I'm the butch (*macha*)." Furthermore, she chooses la Pecho de Palo's [whom I refer to as the Ice Princess's][33] house, a bordello where la Manuela has been working, as a point of reference; this shows that lesbian sex *tableaux* are commonplace, and that they are part of male sexuality and erotic imagination. As an aside, one can see that at this specific discursive sexual moment, questions about the gender, sexuality and sexual orientation of la Manuela are difficult to fasten: is Manuela imagining herself as female, as a lesbian, as a passive man? These questions of subjectivity that are customarily well secured by the signifiers, "heterosexual," "woman," "sadomasochist," and the like, become irrelevant unless there is a clear understanding of how and under what conditions these signifiers are constructed, and what impact the performance of these signifiers effects. In other words, gender, sexuality and sexual orientation are axioms that define identity; they are historically and culturally produced, cannot be grounded, only effected. Moreover, I speculate that these axioms are structured generally as a speech act, specifically as a de Manian insight.

The seduction is subtle, to the extent that Japonesa knows that she must define her role as "butch," *macha*, while convincing la Manuela that she is a girl. When she says to Manuela "you see how I am pulling your panties and how I take off your bra so that your breasts become naked," she pronounces a speech act; she "reads" for Manuela a lesbian erotica.

> Hablas y me acaricias y de repente me dices, ahora sí Manuelita de mi corazón, ves que puedes . . . Yo soñaba mis senos acariciados, y algo sucedía mientras ella me decía si, mijita, yo te estoy haciendo gozar porque yo soy la macha y tú la hembra, te quiero porque eres todo, y siento el calor de ella que me engulle, a mí, a un yo que no existe . . . [34]

> [You speak and stroke me and suddenly you tell me, now that's it Manuelita, my sweetheart, you see you can do it . . . I dreamed of my breasts being stroked, and something was happening while she was saying to me, yes baby, I am making you happy because I am the butch one (*macha*) and you are the

femme (*hembra*), I love you because you are everything, and I feel her warmth that engulfs me, me, an "I" that does not exist . . .]

Here we can see how the seduction continues and builds up. La Manuela sees herself as part of the lesbian act that la Japonesa Grande has designed. That line "I am the butch one (or the manly woman) and you are the female" conveys the complexity of the roles with which each woman identifies. First, la Japonesa would embody the virility and masculinity that will attract la Manuela later. The sexual figure and imagination of la Japonesa will appear later in the plot of the novel not as a *macha*, but as the *macho* Pancho Vega, very butch, very masculine and very repressed, with whom la Manuela will fall in love. Second, la Manuela gets an erection (becomes a man) as la Japonesa talks: in an oppositional movement, la Manuela identifies at that specific moment with the role of the woman (*hembra*). The temporality of subjectivity hinges on an awareness of difference that is lucidly articulated by la Manuela, "me, an 'I' that does not exist . . . "; these fleeting moments where identity is registered climax at la Manuela's almost existential realization. These insights into the making of the Self explode and leak like a (male) orgasm, always uncertain, sometimes premature, tiring and messy. It would only make sense then for la Manuela, who denies her subjectivity, to deny or reinterpret her ecstasy:

> y ella me guía riéndose, conmigo porque yo me río también, muertos de la risa los dos para cubrir la vergüenza de las agitaciones, y mi lengua en su boca y qué importa que estén mirándonos desde la ventana, mejor así, más rico, hasta estremecerme y quedar mutilado, desangrándome dentro de ella mientras ella grita y me aprieta y luego cae, mijito lindo, qué cosa más rica, hacía tanto tiempo, tanto, y las palabras se disuelven . . . [35]

> [and she guides me laughing, together because I am also laughing, dying of laughter to veil the shame of the agitation, and my tongue in her mouth and what does it matter that they are watching us from the window, better yet, it's hotter, until I shudder and become mutilated, bleeding inside her while she screams and squeezes me and then falls, my beautiful baby, what a wonderful thing, it's been so long, so long, and the words melt . . .]

One thing strikes me here: shame. It is not the shame of being watched for, as we might imagine, the transvestite's obsession with spectacularity, with being seen and praised, is known. La Manuela specifies that it is the "shame of the agitation," of the commotion that she is causing. This is a major and perspicacious recognition of the transvestite's power to transform herself and the subjectivity of others. Shame replies to an epistemological disjunction, a crisis in the categorization of gender—to use a wording introduced by Garber to describe a transvestite effect.

It is this shame that affects how la Manuela expresses her orgasm; she is castrated, she bleeds. It is also la Manuela's first and last period. She has lost her penis, her "period," as well as her phallus, her "words melt." This loss of authority can be seen in the very narrative structure of the event. Her phrases are joined by a series of conjunctions; language has lost its grammar; genders have lost their grammar. La Manuela's delirious grammar creates a palimpsest of this and that and something else. This layered discourse repeats and structures the very trials of subject formation and the writing of the text. Meaning is not only found within each part or episteme but, importantly, between the relationship and deployment of each. Transvestism continuously (dis)embodies that conjunction and rearrangement.

Returning to the scene of the crime: I think it is a bit too much that the prostitute and the transvestite "came" together. If I may be so bold as to claim that reaching orgasm in unison, most unusually having la Japonesa coming through penile penetration, is much too much a heterosexual male's fantasy of the perfect orgasm. It is an event of fictive dimensions, which makes us wonder whether La Japonesa is not playing it up for the men, in other words, she is giving them the performance they want. La Manuela is quick to deny that what happened happened. And la Japonesa tells her not to worry that they won the house, really that Manuela won the house for her. Also, Manuela inadvertently got la Japonesa pregnant with la Japonesita.

Nevertheless la Manuela is fixated on one and only one issue, "júrame, que nunca más, Japonesa por Dios qué asco, júrame, socias, claro, pero esto no, nunca más porque ahora ya no existe ese tú, ese yo que ahora [dieciocho años más tarde] estoy necesitando tanto . . . " [swear it, that never again, in God's name, Japonesa, how disgusting, swear it, partners, okay, but not this, never again because that "you" doesn't exist, that "I" that I need so much now (eighteen years later) doesn't exist . . .][36] The end of the bet is important for two reasons. First, we are taken forward to the chicken coop where la Manuela is hiding from Pancho Vega who has threatened to rape her. The winning bet contextualizes (gives texture to) the present. There she is shaking and fearing for her life, holding on to her famous red flamenco dress; she remembers that occasion when she was that virile "man" who impregnated la Japonesa—or, as she sighs nostalgically, "that 'I' that I need so much now [and who] doesn't exist." Second, la Manuela conjures up this performance of masculinity, which won her the house, so that she may face this brute Pancho Vega, just another of "[t]hose big men with thick eyebrows and harsh voices [who] are all the same: as soon as dusk comes, they begin manhandling you."[37] In other words, if la Manuela is going to meet this man face to face, she must do so on *his* terms.

Heterosexuality as a Symptom of Pornography

Who are those big men? What do they want? Earlier I suggested that the same *tableau vivant* represented a double perversion of the idea of heterosexuality: on one level, heterosexuality sets itself up as a polar opposite of lesbian sexuality; on another level, male heterosexuality eroticizes the process itself of framing this binarism. In other words, the direction and choreography of lesbian sexuality by heterosexual men spotlight a special relationship between the men themselves—call it homoeroticism. The pleasure for the men may not be so much in watching two "women" having sex, but rather in having the power to force them into this situation. Likewise, pornography is not necessarily the representation of sexualities, but a structural relation of power. Furthermore, with respect to the *tableau,* the men's relationship is not one of inclusion, but of exclusion and exclusivity. Homosocial bonding happens as the first step of defining heterosexuality; the homosocial is a discursive space created by repression along the lines of gender within the heterosexual matrix. The next step, of course, which insures the enterprise of the "heterosexual," is homophobia, another repressive measure that hinges on and delimits the sex coordinate. The archaeology of heterosexuality, then, is a palimpsest of repressions, which make for a difficult articulation of referentiality. Cutting through this complex called "normal" heterosexuality is messy, always uncovering unsuspected gender and erotic fantasies.

Masculinity as Parody

> The repetition of heterosexual constructs within sexual cultures both gay and straight may well be the inevitable site of the denaturalization and mobilization of gender categories. The replication of heterosexual constructs in non-heterosexual frames brings into relief the utterly constructed status of the so-called heterosexual original. Thus, gay is to straight *not* as copy is to

original, but, rather, as copy is to copy. The parodic repetition of "the original" reveals the original to be nothing other than a parody of the *idea* of the natural and the original.[38]

Thus Judith Butler disarms the notion of originality of heterosexuality and decenters its powerful, regulating positionality. While homo- and heterosexualities operate in this non-hierarchical plane, an imposition of compulsory heterosexuality prevails and locates itself centrally as the regulating metaphor for the natural and normal, for the law. All the seams of sexual and gender difference are erased, ignored, or conveniently overlooked. An occasional awareness of the effects of this differentiation creates an anxiety that threatens "normal" subjectivity and leads often to a violent response.

In the previous sections I have chosen almost deliberately, sometimes unknowingly, to confuse masculinity and heterosexuality. I would argue that this blurring is the result of a tautology so prevalent in Latin American culture: "men" are always masculine and heterosexual. The signifiers "men," "masculine," and "heterosexual" point to the exact same signified or idea, and referent or body. In other words, to call Pancho Vega "el macho Pancho Vega" is redundant because, in the minds of la Manuela and la Japonesita, he reeks of machismo. I insist that this excessive and brutal masculinity clothes and hides a "fault"; in other words, the figuration of "masculinity" doubles the act of transvestism. A critic once criticized this particular theoretical point as "silly": it *is* a silly masculinity that is a form of transvestism. The whole idea of silliness—in opposition to queerness—replicates the fierce homophobia inherent in the "masculine." The queer readings of this book delight in the instability that "transvestism" and "machismo" put forth; this instability ironizes how infertile "straight" readings can be.

La Manuela insists that "[m]aricón seré pero degenerado no. Soy profesional." [I may be a faggot but not a degenerate. I'm a professional.][39] What makes Pancho Vega such an attractive man is not that he doubles transvestism as a "professional," but that he does so amateurishly—there are too many slips in his performance—trying to hide his homosexual desire and love for la Manuela. Pancho Vega would never think about his "masculinity," much less that it is a performance; he reveals this masculine strength through threats.

It is precisely this circulation of threats that opens the novel and creates the sense of fear that invades la Manuela. She has been told that Pancho Vega is in town and that he has promised to hurt her. A year earlier, Pancho had come with some men to the bordello and had tried to force la Manuela to put on her red flamenco dress with white polka dots. After refusing, Pancho got angry and began destroying the place and coercing Manuela into the dress, which got ripped. Had it not been for don Alejo's arrival, the virginal Japonesita, too, would have been hurt. What is extraordinary is the reason la Manuela gave for not dancing:

> ¡Cómo no! ¡Macho bruto! ¡A él van a estar bailándole, mírenlo nomás! Eso lo hago yo para los caballeros, para los amigos, no para los rotos hediondos a patas como ustedes ni para peones alzados que se creen una gran cosa porque andan con la paga de la semana en el bolsillo . . . y sus pobres mujeres deslomándose con el lavado en el rancho para que los chiquillos no se mueran de hambre mientras los lindos piden vino y ponche y hasta fuerte . . . no.[40]

> [Oh sure! Macho brute! He wants someone to dance for him, just listen! I only do that for gentlemen, for friends, not for such stinking small-town folks, nor for bankrupt peons who think so highly of themselves because they are carrying their weekly earning in their pockets . . . and your poor wives are breaking their backs washing clothes so that the children don't starve to death while these pretty boys ask for wine and punch and even refuge . . . no.]

The transvestite's protest defines her audience. She will only perform for those who can afford her. She seems to suggest that transvestism is born out of a particular social class, that somehow others will not understand her. Interestingly, la Manuela is once described as someone who was well-known around town and that she had "muy buen trato con la policía." [a very good relation with the police.][41] The transvestite is socially and politically protected.[42] This unholy alliance between the police and the sexual outcast seems important; however, I can only speculate into its significance because it is so veiled. Perhaps the fact that the police (law) define the space and monitor the limits of the "underground" where the drag queens and homosexuals live, brings them together; the drag queens are figures that crossover and inhabit both the interior and exterior of society, and, in the mind of mainstream, heteronormative society, homosexuals personify the perfect stereotype of an informant, easily blackmailed by international spies. This paranoia about the instability of sexual minorities regulates, legislates, and disciplines their uneasy presence within the social and political structures of power. The fact that Manuela can be so haughty means that she has the comfort provided by the support of don Alejo and the police. At an earlier time, we note likewise that la Japonesa had a similar philosophy about her business:

> La Japonesa no abría las puertas de su casa a cualquiera. Siempre gente fina. Siempre gente con los bolsillos llenos. Por eso ella pertenecía al partido político de don Alejo, el partido histórico, tradicional, de orden, el partido de la gente decente que paga las deudas y no se mete en líos . . . [43]

[La Japonesa would not open her doors just to anyone. Always refined people. Always people with their pockets full. That is why she belonged to don Alejo's political party, the party of history, tradition, and of order, the party of decent people who pay their debts and don't get into trouble . . .]

We have another example of the relationship between the authorities and the underground. Obviously, la Manuela is not as strict about who comes into her business as Japonesa. There is a difference between both women as to what deserves respectability: la Japonesa sees that her business, the institution, is respected by only inviting those who deserve being there; la Manuela, otherwise, demands the respect for her own person, for her reputation, not for the bordello. The idea that those who cannot pay should not see her performance echoes Darío's pretension that *celui-qui-ne-comprends-pas* is excluded from reading and understanding.

In this highly stratified social context, la Manuela's upper class pretensions are troubling to Pancho because they remind him that he is in debt to don Alejo. To be sure, in the economy of this remote and rural town, to be without money means to be less of a "man." It will be only after clearing this debt that Pancho will feel secure enough—or "man" enough—to return to the bordello a year later to get what he wants. Masculinity is presented not only as a qualitative, but also as a quantitative characteristic. Masculinity can be bought. The accessories that fashion the "masculine" are many: those which are inherited like a deep voice, hairy chest, big biceps, and the like as well as those that are performed or purchased like a deeper voice, bigger biceps, a stiffer walk, and the like. That such an economy exists to support masculinity only means that the "masculine" designs itself from the outside of culture and society, and doubles an idea of itself as the very interior of that culture and society—thus, I am reminded of Butler's whole argument of the "original" as a parody of the *idea* of an "original."

What makes it more difficult for Pancho to keep this delicate structure from breaking is his inability to conceal his homosexual desire. Here we can see the importance of the "closet" as a discursive space that protects the conceit of masculinity. Were it not for Pancho Vega's closet door flinging open so often, revealing his desire for another man, he might be more successful in keeping up the show of the "masculine." There are moments in the text when Pancho most flagrantly reveals his queer desire. On those occasions, Pancho will require more than a veneer of solemnity and straight-acting calmness to hide his true desires and impulses convincingly from other "men" like his brother-in-law Octavio. As I suggested before, masculinity and male heterosexuality are often one and the same; for that reason, only the destruction of la Manuela, the strongest or most radical reminder of what Pancho does want, will "save" him from having his masculinity questioned.

Diva's Time; or, The Transvestite Must Die

I have been intrigued throughout this chapter with the junctions and disjunctions of gender, sexuality, and eroticism, and how these different perspectives and conceptualizations of the Self knit together a maddening web from which it is difficult to escape. Listening to Mozart's *Die Zauberflöte*, the Queen of the Night's *staccato* reminds me of the defenses that we as subjects put forth to save ourselves. The accentuation reveals and blurs the linguistic details of the aria. La Manuela sings a similar aria; when she confronts Pancho she sets the scene: "avanza hasta la luz y antes de entrar escucha oculta detrás de la puerta, mientras se persigna como las grandes artistas antes de salir a la luz." [she advances to the light, and before making her entrance she listens hidden behind the door, while she makes the sign of the cross as great artists do before coming to the light].[44] I could have opened this chapter with this self-conscious moment, but I opted for straightening out the narrative; first, la Manuela dances and gets molested by the men, then, she takes part in the "comedy." Years later, she is molested again, but this time by Pancho and his friends; now, he returns to settle what are in his mind some pending debts. In the text, this linearity does not appear to the reader until the very end; the actual narration of the text oscillates between the present and the past, and the narrator is constantly changing. This breaking of time and space belongs to transvestism as a means of recapturing the past glories and making them present, as a way of forgetting the present and replacing it with happier or, at least, more encouraging times. La Manuela's self-figuration, presence, and voice, thus, correspond to what could be called, Diva's time. The Diva is the boldest manifestation of the Eternal Feminine in *El lugar sin límites*. The Diva is always concerned with the "here and now." She disrupts time and space, and remains the same. Listen to the way in which la Manuela remembers and writes herself:

> ella, una artista, recibe aplausos, y la luz estalla en un sinfín de estrellas. No tenía para qué pensar en el desprecio y en las risas que tan bien conoce porque son parte de la diversión de los hombres, a eso vienen a despreciarla a una, pero en la pista, con una flor detrás de la oreja, vieja y patuleca como estaba, ella era más mujer que todas las Lucys y las Clotys y las Japonesitas de la tierra . . . curvando hacia atrás el dorso y frunciendo los labios y zapateando con más furia, reían más y la ola de risa la llevaba hacia arriba, hacia las luces.[45]

[she, an artist, receives the applause, and the light explodes in a countless number of stars. She didn't have to think of the hatred and the laughter that she knew so well because they are part of men's entertainment, that's why they come: to hate her, but on the runway, with a flower behind her ear, even as old as she was, she was more of a woman that all of the Lucys and Clotys [the other prostitutes in the bordello] and Japonesitas on this Earth . . . curving her back and puckering her lips and marking her step with more fury, they laughed more and the wave of laughter carried her up, toward the lights.]

This and the previous quote remark on the lighting of the Diva. She is always on center stage, where she alone can be seen and no one else. This need to be the one who gets all of the attention verges on and, at times, culminates in the delirium of la Manuela's imagining herself climbing into the light, propelled by the laughter of the men. The men's hatred, which she excuses as part of their nature, becomes a lift into the glory of the spotlight. La Manuela also shows a kind of self-apotheosis when she mentions that "she was more of a woman than all" of the others. This powerful declaration really shows her blindness; she is blinded by the lights and the fantasy. Her femininity is greater and more excessive than that of the others. Elsewhere and to this effect, she had reprimanded la Japonesita, "[Q]ué sacas con ser mujer, si no eres coqueta." [What good is it that you're a woman, if you are not a flirt.][46] And, "[e]sas no son mujeres. Ella va a demostrarles quién es mujer y cómo se es mujer." [(t)hose are not women. She is going to show them who is a woman and how to be one.][47] Here la Manuela adds and details the practices that make her (or anyone) more of a woman, indeed, a Diva: the curved back, the puckered lips, and the like. In other words, the transvestite becomes the ideal of womanliness (the ever-beautiful and ever-young Diva) that all women strive to imitate. La Manuela animates what have become the empty signs of femininity; again, she recycles those signs. Also, the converse is true:

> Se pone el vestido por encima de la cabeza y los faldones caen a su alrededor como un baño de tibieza porque nada puede abrigarla como estos metros y metros de fatigada percala colorada. Se entalla el vestido. Se arregla los pliegues alrededor del escote . . . un poco de relleno aquí donde no tengo nada. Claro, es que una es tan chiquilla, la gitanilla, un primor, apenas una niñita que va a bailar y por eso no tiene senos, así, casi como un muchachito, pero no ella, porque es tan femenina, el talle quebrado y todo . . . [48]

> [She puts the dress on over her head and the pleats fall around her like a warm bath because nothing can protect her like the yards and yards of the red, tired percale. She adjusts her dress. She fixes the fold around the neckline . . . a bit of stuffing here where I don't have anything. Of course, you know, since one is so young, a little gypsy, so precious, barely a little girl who is going to dance and that's why she doesn't have breasts, so, almost like a little boy, but not her, because she is so feminine, the broken silhouette and all . . .]

The attention to detail that Manuela gives, always highlighting her positive feminine attributes and attitude as well as explaining away her absences, this attention shows how much transvestism is a performative gesture—both in the sense of theatrics and the rhetoric (or discursiveness) of engendering the subject. That marvelous scene when she puts on the dress and how this "red, tired percale" warms her up reminds me of a lyric from *La Cage aux Folles*: "When life is a real bitch again, I put a little more mascara on . . . " Dress and cosmetics become a *pharmakon,* that addictive drug that alleviates the sense of ugliness and pain. Beauty is never easy; it is only addictive. The paradox is that, despite the fact that la Manuela will use every effort and talent to survive, she is growing old; she cannot stop her body from decaying. She imagines herself being raped by thirty men but knows that "[o]jalá tuviera una *otra edad* para aguantar. Pero no. Duelen las encías. Y las coyunturas . . . " [I wish I were younger to hold on. But no. The gums hurt. And the joints.][49] "I wish I were younger," or another translation, "I wish I were of another age," or better yet, "I wish I had an Otherness . . . " I am playing here with the homophone, "otra edad" (another age) and "otredad" (otherness). Manuela seems to realize that she may not be able to maintain her performance, that she is no longer convincing. Consequently, the excess and failure of the *pharmakon*, "the broken silhouette and all," of course, will eventually be what kills the transvestite.

Unfortunately, the transvestite must die because the screen onto which she projects herself, call it "culture" or "men," changes slowly and it cannot support her. She cannot be fixed in the imagination of "normal" people. We, the "normal" ones, often lack the language to understand, to let ourselves go. Letting go of the limiting archetypes of gender and sexuality is moreover the problem for Pancho—and for all the Panchos in the world.

Transvestites, Homosexuals and Other Versions of Masculinity

La Manuela, who had been shaking in the chicken coop, conjuring up the strength to face Pancho as that "man that no longer exists," chooses to face Pancho as the woman he had beaten the year before. She becomes the martyr, the woman who returns to the scene of the crime to face the criminal again. This painful moment has been foreshadowed and internalized already by the transvestite as just "part of men's entertainment" and yet it does not stop surprising us. This threat of violence is disregarded by almost everyone: Any physical or verbal abuse that la Manuela gets is taken for granted. Even la Japonesita at the end of the novel has stopped worrying about Manuela, just saying that her father will return after a couple of days, that she is used to her father's behavior. It could be argued that repetition compulsion obeys a desire to return to the original moment or event, where the subject "failed," and now tries to repair or resolve the "event." However, I would argue that the fact that the scene of violence repeats itself has to do with the transvestite's entrance into the pleasures of sadomasochism. La Manuela's return as la Manuela re-configures a structure, upon which her subjectivity depends. I am not arguing that she is solely asking to being beaten and brutalized for its own sake, but rather that she seeks within this violence the pleasure that the scene of sadomasochism gives her. Pleasure or *jouissance* is dislocated from the climax of compulsory heterosexuality and woven into the process of framing narratives in the text of sadomasochism.

What is difficult to conceive is that when la Manuela enters the bordello as a woman, she is not really what Pancho desires: he wants a man. La Manuela dances for Pancho, and he reveals his passion:

... eso que baila allí en el centro, ajado, enloquecido, con la respiración arrítmica, [...] eso que se va a morir a pesar de las exclamaciones que lanza, [...] eso está bailando para él, él sabe que quiere tocarlo y acariciarlo, desea que ese retorcer no sea sólo allá en el centro sino contra su piel, y Pancho se deja mirar y acariciar desde allá... el viejo maricón que baila para él y él se deja bailar y que ya no da risa porque es como si él, también, estuviera anhelando.[50]

[... that thing that dances there in the center, aged, crazed, with arrhythmic breathing, [...] that thing that is going to die despite of the bursting exclamations, [...] that thing that is dancing for him, he knows that he wants to touch and caress him, he desires that that writhing not only be in the center but against his skin, and Pancho allows himself to be seen and caressed from over there... the old faggot who dances for him and he allows himself to be danced and it is no longer a cause for laughter because it is as if he, too, were coveting.]

"That thing," as Pancho refers to Manuela, becomes "the old faggot." The inchoate and unrecognizable body of the transvestite becomes engendered at the very moment at which Pancho begins to desire. Pancho wants Manuela's dancing to touch him; he wants to feel the transvestite's body against his own. The writhing of the body or—as the silent Spanish *h* would have me saying—the writing of the body, which la Manuela displays for her man, is "that thing" that Pancho wants, indeed. Pancho wants to redress himself. In other words, he wants to be like her. He wants to be her. The gender ambiguity of the language that he uses blurs the identity of the subject "he" in the last line, "it is no longer a cause of laughter because it is as if he, too, were coveting." He is Pancho. He is la Manuela. He is Pancho and la Manuela. Desiring the Other is not a cause for laughter. To laugh is to construct the Other as a parody, a vampire version of the Self. Laughter destabilizes and deconstructs the very idea of the Self. Pancho's silence, thus, becomes a paranoia not to laugh (a moment of identification); however, then, this paranoia shifts to a *méconaissance*. The possibility for recuperation in the act of "misrecognition" is, however, lost because Pancho fears being identified with la Manuela. In the following scene we can see how his initial desire and now paranoia clearly become homosexual panic,

Qué Octavio no sepa. No se dé cuenta. Que nadie se dé cuenta. Que no lo vean dejándose tocar y sobar por las contorsiones y las manos histéricas de la

Manuela que no lo tocan, dejándose sí, pero desde aquí desde la silla donde está sentado nadie ve lo que le sucede debajo de la mesa, pero que no puede ser no puede ser y toma una mano dormida de la Lucy y la pone allí, donde arde.[51]

[Let Octavio not know. Let him not realize what is happening. May no one realize it. Let no one see him letting himself being touched and stroked by the contortions and hysterical hands of la Manuela who doesn't touch him, allowing himself to be touched yes, but from here from the chair where he is sitting no one sees what happens under the table, but that can't be it can't be and he takes Lucy's sleepy hand and puts it there, where it is fiery.]

Despite all of the excitement that has caused Pancho to get an erection, he is paranoid, afraid even, that Octavio will learn or discover that la Manuela's "hysteria" is doing something to him. The desire *and* denial that Pancho has for the drag queen is such that he almost seems to resist that it is happening in a peculiar way; he says that "allowing himself to be touched yes, but from here from the chair where he is sitting no one sees what happens under the table." Pancho talks about himself in the third person, passively—and literally "under the table"—negotiating the eroticism between himself and the old flamenco dancer. I would argue that Pancho's twisted re-construction of the event—which, incidentally, reminds us of the closing scene of *Cien años de soledad* [*One Hundred Years of Solitude*] when Aureliano Babilonia deciphers the manuscripts and begins reading that very moment in which he is living—this desperate effort to create a closed scene of writing and reading, of desire and denial, all these moments of anguish provide the necessary space for the "literary."

I would reevaluate Pancho's "readerly" moment of panic, a classic example of homosexual panic, in other terms. What is at stake in this scene is that Pancho wants not to explain away his desire, but simply to desire within himself. Pancho's reasoning of not wanting to be seen is, in effect, another way of coming to terms with his homosexuality. No matter how perverse the explanation that he comes up with is, Pancho is playing with a new identity. The *macho* is trying to recapture a loss of his subjectivity; the panic that he shows is a symptom of male hysteria. I define the term "hysteria" as a moment of loss, as a crisis of agency, where the "I" cannot comfortably locate itself; in other words, the hysteric results from the act of denial of a "traditionless Self."[52] Pancho suffers from male hysteria when he begins referring to himself in the third person, "he"; this shift to the third person pronoun should not be confused with the "third term" as the signifier of the Symbolic because Pancho's renaming occurs as an act of denial, rather than one of affirmation. Let us revisit the important "third term": it is important to underline its condition of affirmation of agency and subjectivity. Here the "third" is more than just another category, it is an epistemological challenge. Male hysteria is, then, that moment of psychic death, which comes about through the failure to recognize and affirm a subjectivity that is new and changing.

A poignant moment that illustrates Pancho's denial of his homosexuality is when he takes the prostitute's hand and places it on his erection. It is important to see here that his heterosexuality is performed through the use of a real woman's body. In other words, Pancho normalizes his homosexual desire by placing a woman's hand on his penis. This turning of the screw shows, as Juliet Mitchell argues, that "hysteria sometimes presents not the negative of the sexual perversion but the negative of a perverse knowledge."[53] In other words, Pancho's erection signifies a perverse knowledge of his homosexual desire for Manuela; taking the woman's hand to cover up this knowledge represents a moment of male hysteria. Pancho's action negates not just the transvestite as provocateur, but it also hides his homosexuality, a perverse knowledge. "These syptoms of hysteria," concludes Mitchell, "acts of regression to an original situation of the safety and terror of wombs and mother, goddesses of Life and Death, have some historical specificity. Instead of a knowledge of sexuality we have a sexualizing of knowledge, a sort of 'no' or minus sign to a verbal meaning, a 'no' that acknowledges even as it denies."[54]

Upon leaving the bordello, la Manuela

> se inclinó hacia Pancho y trató de besarlo en la boca mientras reía. Octavio lo vio y soltó a la Manuela.
> —Ya pues compadre, no sea maricón usted también . . .
> Pancho también soltó a la Manuela.
> —Si no hice nada . . .
> —No me vengas con cuestiones, yo vi . . .
> Pancho tuvo miedo.
> —Qué me voy a dejar besar por este maricón asqueroso, está loco, compadre, qué me voy a dejar hacer una cosa así. A ver Manuela, ¿me besaste?[55]

> [(la Manuela) reached down to Pancho and tried kissing him on the lips while he was laughing. Octavio saw him and let go of Manuela.
> "Now, compadre, don't you be a faggot too . . . "
> Pancho also let go of Manuela.

"But I didn't do anything . . . "
"Don't give me that, I saw . . . "
Pancho was afraid.
"I'm not going to let myself be kissed by this dirty faggot, are you crazy, compadre, why would I allow myself such a thing. Come on Manuela, did you kiss me?"]

This scene summarizes the points that I have been arguing. First, when la Manuela tries to kiss Pancho, that is, when she takes action, she becomes a threat; as long as she behaved as the men want her to be, everything is fine. Second, being caught or seen with the drag queen is all right; however, when she implicates and threatens the players with the possibility of homosexuality, she must be released. Third, Pancho has homosexual desires and is afraid. Fourth, faced with the name-calling—and, certainly, in the place without limits naming signifies affiliation—Pancho will begin questioning la Manuela in every single respect. That questioning becomes a major issue for Octavio: "¿Lo besaste o no lo besaste?" [Did you or didn't you kiss him?][56] Fifth, in this particular line or question, Octavio locates "being" as a performance. Sixth, a beating follows la Manuela's answer that it was "just a joke"; this suggests that transvestites cannot put into motion or articulate a parody because their very positionality invalidates whatever they might say. And so, seventh, the transvestite must die. The death of the transvestite comes as a brutal awakening: "Octavio la paralizaba retorciéndole el brazo, la Manuela despertó. No era la Manuela. Era él Manuel González Astica. Él. Y porque era él iban a hacerle daño y Manuel González Astica sintió terror." [Octavio paralyzed her by twisting her arm, la Manuela woke up. She wasn't la Manuela. She was he, Manuel González Astica. He. And because it was him they going to hurt him and Manuel González Astica felt terror.][57] At this painful moment Manuela discovers that her body is not that of a woman but of a man. She realizes that her body is deployed, developed, and disposed however others want: Pancho draws upon the different uses that the transvestite has for him when he tells her, "Una cosa es andar de farra y revolverla, pero otra cosa es que me vengái a besar la cara . . . " [It's one thing to go partying and turning things upside-down, but another thing that you come and kiss my face . . .][58] La Manuela's body is used to define the subjectivity of the men, not her own. She is fully baptized Manuel González Astica; the face of a terrified man emerges from the mask of La Manuela. Her "masculinity," like that of all the men, is relayed as an experience with the *uncanny*, a strange familiarity. Manuel manages to escape and runs to don Alejo's vast vineyards, hoping to find some protection. However, going to don Alejo's refuge is the greatest of ironies because we know how futile it is to seek protection from the very institution that oppresses us. He runs in the sure belief that don Alejo awaits him. But he will not get there. The men catch up with Manuel and beat her ruthlessly. The men weigh heavily on la Manuela; they are

> los tres una sola masa viscosa retorciéndose como un animal fantástico de tres cabezas y múltiples extremidades heridas e hirientes, unidos los tres por el vómito y el calor y el dolor allí en el pasto, buscando quién es el culpable, castigándolo, castigándola, castigándose deleitados hasta en el fondo de la confusión dolorosa, el cuerpo endeble de la Manuela que ya no resiste quiebra bajo el peso, ya no puede ni aullar de dolor, bocas calientes, manos calientes, cuerpos babientos y duros hiriendo el suyo y que ríen y que insultan y que buscan romper y quebrar y destrozar y reconocer ese monstruo de tres cuerpos retorciéndose, hasta que ya no queda nada y la Manuela apenas ve, apenas oye, apenas siente, ve, no, no ve, y ellos se escabullen a través de la mora y queda ella sola junto al río que la separa de las viñas donde don Alejo espera benevolente.[59]

[the three men are one viscous mass writhing like a fantastic three-headed animal with multiple wounded and burning extremities, the three united there on the grass by the vomit and the heat and the pain, looking for the one who is guilty, punishing him, punishing her, self-punishing and delighting deeply in the painful confusion, the weak body of la Manuela that no longer resists breaks under the weight, she can no longer moan from the pain, hot mouths, hot hands, spitting and hard bodies hurting her own and they laugh and insult and seek to rip and break and destroy and recognize that three-bodied monster writhing until there is no more and la Manuela can barely see, barely hear, barely feel, she sees, no, she can't see, and they sneak out through the boysenberry tree and she remains alone next to the river that divides the vineyards where don Alejo waits benevolently.]

Back in the bordello, la Japonesita holds down the fort. Unaware of la Manuela's fortune, la Japonesita imagines that her father will return as he always does. La Manuela's escapades are nothing new. She will return, according to Japonesita, after a couple of days of "triumphs." The still virgin prostitute will go to bed in the dark, ignorant that la Manuela has been raped again.

The metaphorics of rape to which I have alluded throughout this chapter as acts of a misreading of transvestism take a literal turn in this scene. The danger of the metaphor is that it suspends the possibility and actualizing of the event. If the men could no longer figuratively rape la Manuela, using their pen(ises) to write on the transvestite, their ultimate alternative—and it is not really an "alternative" *per se* but their unequivocal desire—is to rape, "seek to rip and break and destroy and recognize" and to rename by force. But, transvestism is not a voluntary or involuntary imposition, it is also a desire that seeks recognition.

The men beat la Manuela for the perverse pleasure of affirming their sense of "integrity." They want a single story to be told about them; ambiguity is out of the question. Nonetheless, what is absolutely fascinating about *El lugar sin límites* is the trial and error, the attempting to tell the story right. I mentioned the shifting narrative voice in the text; this voice meanders desperately through the passions of the mind and the body trying to capture who we all are. The event in and of itself, like the fantasy of the Real, is always uncanny and inaccessible. But language allows us to survey the different voices that construct that "event." Transvestism prefigures the assurance that subjectivity is unique through the echoes of many voices. And trying to be univocal, that is, imposing a single voice, chokes and inevitably kills the self-sufficient transvestite.

Chapter 4

Transvestite and Homobaroque Twirls: Sarduy on the Verge of Reading Structuralism / Psychoanalysis / Deconstruction

> [S]etting down and composing by himself his soliloquy, tracing it upon the white page he himself is, the Mime does not allow his text to be dictated to him from any other place. He represents nothing, does not have to conform to any prior referent with the aim of achieving adequation or verisimilitude. One can here foresee an objection: since the mime imitates nothing, reproduces nothing, opens up in its origin the very thing he is tracing out, presenting, or producing, he must be the very movement of truth.
>
> —Jacques Derrida[1]

Sarduy's Critical Essays

When talking about transvestism in Latin American literature, the name of Severo Sarduy is almost synonymous with such a topic. His novels, for example *De donde son los cantantes* [translated as *From Cuba with a Song*] and *Cobra*, feature transvestites as central characters. Furthermore, it is cliché to hear that Sarduy proposes that "transvestism is a metaphor for writing." From his earliest works, one can find traces of Sarduy's obsession with the question of writing and representation.

In this chapter, I shall take issue with Sarduy's critical writings in which he deals directly with transvestism. I am talking primarily about two texts: "Escritura/travestismo" [Writing/Transvestism], an excerpt from *Escrito sobre un cuerpo*, and *La simulación*.[2] Here I would like to examine how Sarduy theorizes the act of reading and, in so doing, how he proceeds to write his own texts. I am also interested in different theories of reading and writing, namely Jacques Derrida's and Paul de Man's, to see what points of contact they make with Sarduy's. Further, I am mindful of how the notion of transvestism is related to Lacan's idea of the Symbolic; I consider the Symbolic to be a turning back to privilege or a return of the language of the Father, hence a trope of prohibition and authority. This particular analysis will enable us to understand and fine tune what Sarduy means when he says that transvestism points to the very structure of inversion. De Man's theories of autobiography and disfiguration in his important work *The Rhetoric of Romanticism* will be useful to contextualize that Sarduyan truism about the relationship between writing and transvestism. Furthermore, I hope to explain how writing contains the "autobiographical" to evaluate Sarduy's interest in the Baroque as a queer imperative, a sensibility that I call the "homobaroque." In the final part of the chapter, I will look at how Sarduy puts into action some of his theories in one of his most important literary works, *De donde son los cantantes*.

On the Verge of a Sexual Breakdown: Structuralism/Deconstruction

Recapitulations.[3] Readers familiar with the work of Sarduy will have noticed a flagrant absence in the third chapter of this collection: I am talking about my not mentioning there Sarduy's influential reading of *El lugar sin límites*, which, under the title "Escritura/travestismo," is nested in the middle of *Escrito*. I have deferred this discussion until now—rather than incorporating it in the previous chapter—because it is one of the few instances where a Latin American author writes critically about crossdressing and transvestite subjectivity. I am interested in deciphering Sarduy's way of reading transvestism and the figure of the transvestite in different literary and theoretical texts, so that he may then proceed to write his own literary texts based on his theorization. In other words, how does Sarduy catalog and distinguish the "excess" of other texts to deploy it in his own work? To wit, I am fascinated by Sarduy's reading of *El lugar sin límites* as the narrative figuration and structured deployment of the term "inversion." Sarduy notes that

> La inversión central, la de Manuel, desencadena una serie de inversiones: la sucesión de éstas estructura la novela. En ese sentido *Un* (sic) *lugar sin límites* continúa la tradición mítica del "mundo al revés," que practicaron con asiduidad los surrealistas. El significado de la novela, más que el travestismo, es

decir, la apariencia de inversión sexual, es la inversión en sí: una cadena metonímica de "vuelcos," de desenlaces traspuestos, domina la progresión narrativa.[4]

[The central inversion, that of Manuel's, unleashes a series of inversions: their very sequence structures the novel. In this sense, *Un* [sic] *lugar sin límites* continues the mythic tradition of the "world upside down," that the Surrealists practiced assiduously. The meaning (indeed, the "signified") of the novel— more than just tranvestism, that is, the illusion of sexual inversion—is inversion in and of itself: a metonymic chain of "turns," of transposed endings, dominates the narrative progression.]

This is a tightly knit passage that, like many of Sarduy's insights, merits some fleshing out. First, Sarduy is clearly aware that Manuel's transvestism, which he locates as the "central inversion," signifies outwardly to every single aspect of the text. This is a crucial point to understand in Sarduy's reconstruction of la Manuela's transvestism—it all begins with a male body. He does not talk about la Manuela as transvestite subject; rather, he positions a "masculine" Manuel at the center of his analysis. Furthermore, it is imperative to recognize that a body is set up beforehand in his analysis: gender is not performative here; it is a bodily presence that then undergoes changes. I have proposed that this particular pattern that presupposes and gives priority to the body is quite powerful in Latin American writing. Second, Sarduy perspicaciously situates the novel on a similar plane with Surrealism in a literary historical tradition, yet he does not keep it there. Both of these acts of reading that privilege "inversion" and Surrealism, if anything, can be read as a continuum of the significant influence that Freud's work has on Sarduy. We remember that the term "inversion" has many connotations in Freud—from homosexuality as "sexual inversion" to jokes as "linguistic inversions." Of course, Surrealism has direct links to psychoanalysis. González Echevarría assures us that "Sarduy's Freud, given his Lacanian veneer, is a very literary one. Yet, because of Freud, Sarduy is able to dismantle Latin America's cultural fictions. This is his master story: the other Latin American novel."[5] This evaluation reminds me of Michel de Certeau's discussion of the "Freudian novel" as an object of affect and theory[6]; he argues specifically that "For Freud, the nation and the individual are equal disguises for a struggle, a dismemberment (*Zerfall*), which always returns to the scene from which it is erased; and the novel is the theoretic instrument of this analysis."[7] In this context, then, Sarduy's conceptualization of "inversion" lies as the unconscious since it is a principle that "dominates" or regulates the narrative progression; in other words, "inversion," according to Sarduy, represents the signified of the text and of its structure. Language in *El lugar sin límites*—as in all of Sarduy's own work—is continually subversive, always already self-subverting. Sarduy gives another turn of the screw to interpret Lacan's patent insight that language is structured like the unconscious: language is structured as a paradox, a "turn" or trope inside another one—in fact, Sarduy conceptualizes Baroque language as "metaphor to the second power" or metaphor squared.[8] Language contains for Sarduy oppositional tensions by which the act of reading will highlight one and undermine others; that is to say, language for Sarduy performs the mechanics of *Verdrängung,* repression. Language shoves aside *(drängen)* and overturns certain meanings, while highlighting them. Importantly, what gets casts aside or repressed becomes isolated, and ironically, rendered highly visible. Certainly, I find in this redoubling or inscribed "turning" a truly neo-Baroque pulsion that is a signature of Sarduy's work.[9]

Nevertheless, what remains unexplained in Sarduy's opening reading of the narratological structure of *El lugar sin límites* is what he means by "inversion in and of itself." Given his Freudian predilection, an "inversion" is not just machinery that operates to twist everything; that interpretation would be banal. In Freud's *oeuvre,* "inversion" has at least two general applications *per se.* On the one hand, inversion is part of Freud's discussion of homosexuality.[10] It seems that Sarduy is aware of this when he defines transvestism as "the illusion of sexual inversion." On the other hand, Freud uses the notion of "inversion" to describe a type of joke, of linguistic play.[11] In his *Jokes and Their Relation to the Unconscious,* Freud gives an example of "inversion" as the "flipping" or displacing of semantic structure to create a *double entendre.* This notion of the *double entendre* relates directly to the double tension found in language, where one part represents a socially and culturally acceptable meaning, and the other subverts the propriety of the first through the devices of the "return of the repressed." Both of these categorizations are applicable to understanding Sarduy's notion of "inversion." As I have shown in analyzing Donoso's text, sexual signifiers (e.g., heterosexual, *macho,* woman, etc.) are often times insufficient to describe the desires or signifieds that motivate and define sexual personae. The language of sexuality fails to comprehend the erotic imagination. To boot, "inversion" symbolizes the utter and complete inability of language to grasp meaning, to describe the "event." Also, "inversion" as a literal figure for the turning and slippage inherent in language seems to suggest indirectly the attempt and inevitable failure for linguistic closure; again, "inversion" represents the "return of the repressed." What Sarduy does so far is provide a provocative introduction to Donoso's complex narrative by subtly unfolding the possibilities of reading the mechanics of "inversion" in the novel. From a more directly Foucauldian or gender-based analysis, I have arrived at similar conclusions about the difficult relationship between language, narrative, and transvestism in *El lugar sin límites*. From this delicate structure that the transvestite's presence seems to embody, there springs a complex of signification that describes and carries away time, space, and identities in *El lugar sin límites*.

Up to this point, I generally agree with Sarduy's reading of *El lugar sin límites*. As a matter of fact, I appreciate his definition of transvestism as an illusion or appearance, an image or imagining of Otherness. Although he does not say it directly, he almost wants to say something about the theatrics of transvestism, that is, about performance. And it is here that our respective readings of the novel begin to differ. Plainly stated, Sarduy focuses on transvestism as a series of inversions; I insist on reading transvestism as the exposure of gender performativity. Reading further, Sarduy will analyze the *tableau vivant* that marks an originary event in the text; he will designate the figure of la Manuela as a series of inversions, a "take-off," an inversion after another:

> La Manuela, que novelística (gramaticalmente) se *significa* como mujer—primera inversión—, *funciona* como hombre puesto que es en tanto que hombre que atrae a la Japonesa. Es una atracción lo que induce a la curiosa matrona a ejecutar el "cuadro plástico"; su ambición [. . .] no es más que un pretexto, ese con que el dinero justifica todas las transgresiones.
>
> En el interior de esta inversión surge otra: en el acto sexual el papel de la Manuela, hombre por atribución narrativa, es pasivo. No femenino—por eso se trata de una inversión dentro de otra y no de un simple regreso al travestismo inicial—, sino de hombre pasivo, que engendra a su pesar. La Japonesa lo posee haciéndose poseer por él. Ella es el elemento activo del *acto* (también en su aceptación teatral: una sola mirada basta para crear el espacio de la representación, para instituir el Otro, la escena).[12]

> [La Manuela, who novelistically (grammatically) *signifies* (on) herself as a woman—first inversion—*functions* as a man, since it is as a man that he attracts la Japonesa. It is an attraction that makes the curious prostitute stage the *tableau vivant;* her ambition [the money that don Alejo offers her] is nothing more than a pretext, one for which money justifies all transgressions.
>
> In the interior of this inversion we see another one emerge: in the sexual

act the role of Manuela, narratively designated a man, is a passive one. He is not at all feminine—this is why the issue is about an inversion inside another inversion, and not about a return to an initial transvestism—but a passive man, who engenders (or becomes a father to) his sorrow. La Japonesa possesses him by allowing herself to be possessed by him. She is the active element of the *act* (furthermore in her theatrical activity: a single gaze is enough to create the space of representation, to institute the Other, the scene).]

First, I would like to indulge in a critique of translation. As I mentioned above, there are two translations of this text—one by Alfred MacAdam, another by Carol Maier. Let us look at Maier's translation of the first sentence: "Manuela, who novelistically (grammatically) *signifies* that he is a woman—the first inversion—*performs* as a man since as a man he attracts Japonesa."[13] Another translation of the same line by MacAdam reads thus: "Manuela, who novelistically (grammatically) is defined as a woman—first inversion—*functions* as a man, since it is as a man that he attract La Japonesa."[14] Both translations make some useful, critical errors. First Maier forgets the reflexive verb, *significarse;* I have exaggerated the importance of the reflexive act because the transvestite signifies *on herself:* She is subject and *object* of the process of assigning value to her acts. MacAdam does not deal with the reflexive verb at all; instead, he opts for a correct, though simplistic, translation in the passive voice. Second Maier translates *"funciona"* as "performs"; this misreading, while very attractive to me as a critic who uses speech act theory, greatly ignores the complex history and connotations of the term "performance." MacAdam gives here a more literal translation. These problems in translation expose the difficulty of reading Sarduy's conceptualizations about gender and transvestism. Translation is an approximation; it is always incomplete, although this simple insight is a crucial fact of transvestism.[15]

Sarduy's reading of the event of seduction between la Japonesa and la Manuela is problematic. Certainly, there is a way in which la Japonesa manages to seduce la Manuela, constantly naming and renaming her, convincing la Manuela that she is a virginal, prepubescent girl. Rhetorically, la Japonesa is the "active" one in this relation. Her self-figuration is complex, and it appears that she is an active sadist. Additionally, in Sarduy's portrayal of la Japonesa, she "possesses him by allowing herself to being possessed by him"; she is, in effect, what we might call a "greedy bottom," in other words, a true masochist. What we see here is a double representation of la Japonesa as sadist and as masochist. In any event, I would argue that what attracts la Japonesa is not la Manuela's "anatomy," her manhood, as the men who threw her in the canal would imagine; it is indeed getting the house from don Alejo that moves la Japonesa. If we remember, throughout the scene she insists to la Manuela that they are putting on such a show or production to get the house. La Japonesa wants the house so that she does not have to depend on don Alejo or any other man. A problem with Sarduy's reading is his evaluation that la Manuela functions as a "man" in this scene, *and* that this masculinity attracts la Japonesa. La Japonesa likes Manuela because she is a good housekeeper and party organizer (the traditional, heteronormative duties of "being a woman"), not because Manuela is any "man." The only moment in the whole scene where we are reminded that the transvestite is really a "man" happens as an afterthought (eighteen years later): In the chicken coop, a frightened Manuela explicitly seeks "that 'I' that I need so much now that doesn't exist." That "I" to which la Manuela alludes is the "man" who impregnated la Japonesa. In the coop, la Manuela wants to conjure up that idea of a man, a virile man who can get a woman pregnant, so that (s)he may then face Pancho Vega. It is in this very specific context and manner that la Manuela defines being a "man," not any manly behavior or attribute.

I do not totally disagree with Sarduy's assessment; he makes important observations about the role that the transvestite plays in the structure of the text. For example, his idea that the transvestite *signifies herself* as ("se significa como") "woman" is a significant insight: to define transvestism as a process of self-signification allows the possibility of autonomy and self-sufficiency to be discussed with respect to the design of subjectivity, and in some ways dislodges the figuration of transvestism from the heterosexual matrix, which is what the notion of "inversion" maintains. I understand here that Sarduy's vision of "woman" as a mask, décor, or cosmetic still needs revision, but I want to capture the importance of agency that the process of self-signification gives the transvestite.

It is surprising that, despite this acute critical definition, Sarduy would fall into the trap of essentialism, blindly insisting on such categories of "man," "woman," that is, "not feminine, but passive man," and the like. But why is it that Sarduy fails to show the complexity of performance and lands in a game of a back-and-forth categorizations? Let me suggest that the problematics of reading are the product of the structuralist approach that he uses. Continuing his discussion, he remarks that

> La sucesión de *ajustes,* la metáfora de la muñeca rusa, podría esquematizarse en un cuadro.

Inversiones:
1° un hombre se traviste en mujer
⇓
2° que atrae por lo que de hombre hay en ella
⇓
3° que es *pasivo* en el acto sexual[16]

[The sequences of *adjustments,* the metaphor of the Russian doll, could be schematized in a diagram.

Inversions:
1st a man crossdresses as a woman
⇓
2nd who attracts because of the man in her
⇓
3rd who is passive in the sexual act]

First, in order to understand Sarduy's structuration of the novel as a chain of inversions, it is imperative to see that this diagram is framed by a tacit or forgotten context, which is the heterosexual matrix. That is, Sarduy organizes his concept of transvestism through a heteronormative discourse. Sarduy could never have made such a chain of relations were it not for the underlying and necessarily tacit understanding of this matrix. His blindness allows him such a reading of *El lugar sin límites,* for without the cultural scaffold provided by the heterosexual matrix, the critic would have been unable to construct such a chain discourse. An awareness of how the heterosexual matrix supports the enterprise of structuralism deconstructs that enterprise. While we can dismiss this "error" as a lack of rigor in his reading, Sarduy never stops amazing us with other insights that would strangely deconstruct the constructions or "orders" upon which he has meditated. In the following passage, we can hear, in Sarduy, a keen yet subtle reader:

> Este juego de "vuelcos," que he esbozado, se podría extenderse a toda la mecánica narrativa: al esquema novelesco del relato en el relato, Donoso substituye el de la inversión en la inversión. Si esta serie de virajes, contenidos unos en otros, no dan jamás una imagen análoga a la del "mundo al derecho," sino que van cada vez más lejos en su revolución, es porque lo que se invierte en cada caso no es la totalidad de la superficie—lo económico, lo político, las tensiones de clase no se modifican en los vuelcos y corresponden siempre a

la "realidad"—, sino únicamente sus significantes éroticos cada vez diferentes, ciertos planos verbales, la topología que definen ciertas palabras.[17]

[This game of "turnings" that I have described could be extended to the whole narrative mechanism: Donoso substitutes the "inversion within an inversion" scheme for the "story within a story" (or "play within a play"). If this series of twirls, contained one within another, never gives the analogous "world right-side up" image, but instead goes further away in its revolution, this is because what becomes inverted in each case is not the totality of the surface—economics, politics, class tensions are not included in the twists of the plot, and they always correspond to "reality"—but inverted are only the ever different erotic signifiers, certain verbal planes and the topology, all of which certain words define.]

Although I have argued that the Sarduyan idea of the "inversion within an inversion" needs a few "adjustments"—to use the critic's own words—in order to be applied so neatly to la Japonesa and la Manuela's erotic encounter, I would like to be more playful and suggest another reading of *inversión:* another translation is "investment." It would be worthwhile to rethink the seduction of la Manuela as a series of "investments." Rereading *El lugar sin límites* as a series of investments—language, gender, and economy—that are doomed to fail affords us an opening to interpret the economy of text, desire, and prostitution. "Investment" introduces the problem of profit and loss, of supplement. Transvestism, not as a gender inversion, but rather as a gender investment, allows us to break away from a binary thinking, where "femininity" is the inverse of "masculinity"; transvestism as investment suggests the possibility of entering and inhabiting genders, which can also mean that transvestism is about existing and thinking through gender, with all the possibilities of profit or loss that such enterprise might entail.

Going back to Sarduy's theoretical extrapolation, I would like to underline two issues. First, the issue that with each inversion what gets changed is the signifier, and not the totality represented by the surface, the sign. This can be seen as an critique of the carnivalesque, for therein, even though we find a cosmetic difference, that "inversion" points to the *desire* of difference and not to difference itself. Second, when Sarduy observes that the shifting of erotic signifiers, verbal planes, and topology defines certain words, he is talking about shifting epistemologies. That he is unable to apply this observation to his previous analysis dramatizes his "structuralist" blindness even further.

It is out of (or because of) these two conclusions that I define transvestism as a performance. To elaborate his theory of transvestism and literature, Sarduy articulates a critique of the Saussurean sign in his conceptualization of "simulation." Sarduy's transvestites bridge the elementary parts that constitute the sign through the act of "simulation," a kind of simulacrum effect, thereby producing an "excess" with which the transvestite (de)constructs subjectivity. I read transvestism otherwise by defining language as a function of speech acts. "Semiology, as opposed to semantics," states de Man, "is the science or study of signs as signifiers; it does not ask what words mean but how they mean."[18] De Man argues, then, that language takes part of a performative activity that can be largely disengaged from and goes beyond reference and referentiality[19]:

> By an awareness of the arbitrariness of the sign (Saussure) and of literature as an autotelic statement "focused on the way it is expressed" (Jakobson) the entire question of meaning can be bracketed, thus freeing the critical discourse from the debilitating burden of paraphrase. The mystifying power of semiology [. . .] demonstrated that the perception of the literary dimensions of language is largely obscured if one submits uncritically to the authority of reference. It also revealed how tenaciously this authority continues to assert itself in a variety of disguises, ranging from the crudest ideology to the most refined forms of aesthetic and ethical judgment.[20]

With this Demanian perspective that circumvents the mechanics and acrobatics to ascertain reference, it is possible to focus on the ways in which the transvestite creates meaning as her performance. Performativity, like semiology, focuses on the ways in which language means, not on what it means. The meanings of a man putting on a dress range from a joke to a carnival to erotic "deviance." But *how* (or under what conditions) a man puts on a dress or what desires and instincts motivate a man to put on a dress is a much more tantalizing question. This reading that privileges the style and performance over the mechanics and semantics of language participates in similar pleasures of performativity as the transvestite.

From this point in the discussion, the issue is not whether the transvestite is or should be self-conscious, but rather that she is unaware, unconscious, of herself, of her language. For example, Sarduy is very self-conscious of his language when he designs that graph that explains the operation of inversions that he sees; it is, at that unconscious moment, when he talks about inversion as a shifting of eroticism and desire, when he delivers his most profound insights that deconstruct any previous appeal to form, structure, closure (of the adjustable "Russian dolls," for example). Sarduy's multiple readings of *El lugar sin límites* confront each other, and create a tension, a dialectic that represents Sarduy's entrance and situation as a writer/critic at the nexus of different languages, cultures, theories. He uses and resists different and disparate critical theories, always wanting to make his own, which makes his work all the more difficult to read. It is at this threshold, which could be labeled the structuralism/deconstruction crux, that we can read how he signifies on himself and metaphorizes the difficulty of representing his life as an exiled Cuban, writing often in a different language, and as a gay man, writing with the metaphor of transvestism.[21]

In the opening epigraph, Derrida reminds us that the Mime, even in silence—in this case, just like the mere *presence* of the transvestite—puts "truth" into motion. He explains

> Not, of course, truth in the form of adequation between representation and the present of the thing itself, or between the imitator and the imitated, but truth as the present unveiling of the present: monstration, manifestation, production, *aletheia*. The mime produces, that is to say makes appear *in praesentia*, manifests the very meaning of what he is presently writing: of what he *performs*. He enables the thing to be perceived in person, in its true face. If one followed the thread of this objection, one would go back, beyond imitation, toward a more "originary" sense of *aletheia* and *mimeisthai*. One would thus come up with one of the most typical and tempting reappropriations of writing, one that can always crop up in the most divergent of contexts.[22]

Thus by showing at the most elementary level the means of (re)production, the transvestite (like the Mime) deconstructs the very idea of the "original." To apply and paraphrase Derrida, transvestism is not so much about imitation as it is about revealing how meaning is constructed. A truly revolutionary transvestite act is not replicating and thus confirming the authority of the "original," but rather it is showing how the "original" is a construction—or a "parody," to use an example elaborated in Butler. Sarduy will conclude his essay "Escritura/travestismo" with quite a Lacanian perspective: "El progreso teórico de ciertos trabajos, el virage total de éstos han operado en la crítica literaria nos han hecho revalorizar lo que antes se consideraba como el exterior, la apariencia." [The theoretical movement of some works, the complete turnaround (or twirl) of these works, which have affected literary theory, have made us revalorize what was before considering the exterior (the outside), the appearance.] Without a doubt, we can see that this new focus on surface and exterior looks a lot like Lacan's argument that meaning operates most importantly at the level of the signifier (a relation and deployment of signifiers, appearances) in "Le séminaire sur 'La Lettre volée'."[23] Furthermore, citing Jean-Louis Baudry, Sarduy adds that

> La aparente exterioridad del texto, la superficie, esa *máscara* nos engaña, "ya que si hay una máscara, no hay nada detrás; superficie que no esconde más que a sí misma; superficie que, porque nos hace suponer que hay algo detrás, impide que la consideremos como superficie. La máscara nos hace creer que hay una profundidad, pero lo que ésta enmascara es ella misma: la máscara simula la disimulación para disimular que no es más que simulación."[24]

> [The apparent exteriority of the text, its surface, that *mask* deceives us, "since if there is a mask, there is nothing behind it; it is a surface that does not hide anything more than itself; a surface that, since it makes us suppose there is something behind it, prevents us from considering it to be a surface. The mask makes believe us that there is depth, but what this mask masks is itself: the mask simulates a dissimulation in order to dissimulate that it is no more than a simulation."[25]]

The horror of the mask is the revelation that it masks nothing. Transvestism, then, reveals a proper subjectivity, not just an imposition or appropriation of the other. Sarduy: "El travestismo . . . sería la metáfora mejor de lo que es la escritura: lo que Manuela nos hace ver no es una mujer *bajo la apariencia* de la cual se escondería un hombre, [. . .] sino *el hecho mismo del travestismo.*" [Transvestism . . . would be the best metaphor of what writing is: what Manuela makes us see is not the *appearance* of woman under which a man would hide, [. . .] but *the very fact of transvestism.*][26] It is here that Sarduy finally comes to express his theory in its most radical form. Furthermore, the transvestite's subjectivity is (ac)claimed by showing the illegitimate claims of naturalness of the "original": the very event of transvestism is not simply a mimesis, but a performance that calls into question the "performance of the original," that signifies itself and, in so doing, mirrors the Other. Sarduy's notion of transvestism as a simulation reveals the structuration of meaning and its deconstruction; it also reminds us of discussions on performativity. It is also at this moment in his critical narrative where I find my own theoretical and political positionings most in line with Sarduy. What I would insist upon, then, is how Sarduy's articulation of a theory of transvestism moves and grows throughout this essay "Escritura/travestismo." He begins with a very structuralist understanding of transvestism as a series of turns and inversions before he finally arrives at a poststructuralist conceptualization of transvestism as a theory of the surface and appearances. It is very necessary to see this flow in his critical thinking because it gives us a greater appreciation of the ways in which he narrates literary theory. Sarduy's critical writing is an act of dynamism; thus, a *moment* in his writing cannot be frozen and made to represent his entire work; this would stall the act of reading and erroneously reduce theory to something hollow and empty. It is our imperative as critics to understand the contours and faults of how Sarduy arrives at theory, only then to begin a judicious theoretical engagement.

Sarduy's Symbolic Body in the (Transvestite's) Mirror

In his essay "Homographesis," Lee Edelman defines this very phenomenon as "the process by which homosexuality is put into writing through a rhetorical or tropological articulation that raises the question of writing as difference by constituting the homosexual as text. The process whereby the homosexual as subject of discourse, and therefore a subject on which one may write, coincides with the process whereby the homosexual as subject is conceived of as being, even more than as inhabiting, a body on which his sexuality is written."[27] So, Edelman displaces the question of the "homosexual character" in writing, an essentialist question that seeks points of reference to uncover or identify what is "homosexual"—indeed, a checklist that will answer, "¿quién es más macho?" [who is more macho?]; instead he asks whether or not it is more fruitful to look at how the process of writing constructs the homosexual. The notion of the "body" that Edelman puts forth is more complex than just the physical, but it includes the textual, political, and sexual, as well.[28] Transvestism, as I have shown throughout my analyses, represents an instance where the notion of the body is difficult to determine. Writing on the body is an uneasy as well as unstable activity.

One of the things that is most striking about the scholarship on Sarduy is the relative absence of reference to his homosexuality as an epistemology in his work. Critics have invested so much time trying to decipher Sarduy's *barroquismos* that they have forgotten to mention how gay he was. One interesting, though passing, mention of Sarduy's homosexuality comes from Roberto González-Echevarría. He writes that Sarduy is nearly bald now, though the face remains youthful. The mellow darkness of his skin and fullness at the lips give more than a hint that his Catalan ancestors did not disdain their African brethren in the Carribean. The eyes are deep and long, revealing traces of yet another faraway ancestor named Macao, one of the thousands of Chinese laborers brought to Cuba to work in the cane fields.

At moments he looks like a Buddhist monk or a retired Cuban lightweight boxer who has put on a pound or two, perhaps a cabaret dancer with a few moves left. Or, with a change of mood, he can become an effeminate gay, mimicking the put-on sexiness of a stereotypical Cuban mulatto [sic] woman. In Spanish he flavors his conversation with kitschy expressions drawn from Cuban popular culture of the '50s. His French, though unmistakably accented, is of precise Parisian purity. In France, where he has lived and worked for a quarter of a century, many think of him as a slightly exotic French writer. But he is far from it. Severo Sarduy is a *very* Latin American writer.[29]

González-Echevarría writes (on) Sarduy's body. The critic uses different facial characteristics to mark the nationalities that merge in the body of Sarduy: he is Catalan, African, Chinese, Cuban. The complex question of nationality is not only attributed to Sarduy's exiled body, but the body itself also embodies that question.[30] Not only is he a displaced body across the national, but also a national body (Cuba) circumscribed by displacement; this tension stretches the dimensions of what it means to be. The national displacement goes beyond space, it includes time: a history. González-Echevarría identifies or superimposes certain class and racial qualities on Sarduy's voice. The author already speaks in a code that is both "popular" and refined, "pure." His accent, his song, fools us. Finally, González-Echevarría tells us about the religious Sarduy, a Buddhist monk who is also a boxer and a dancer. Here the critic goes further to sexualize Sarduy's body, which becomes that of "an effeminate gay, mimicking the put-on sexiness of a stereotypical Cuban mulatto [sic] woman." I am stunned by the way in which Sarduy's body becomes so invested, so twirled out, with so many metaphors. It is interesting to see here how and to understand why Sarduy's body is so easily feminized; yet, when talking about Sarduy's work, critics, not just González-Echevarría, cannot talk *directly* about Sarduy's identity as a gay man—but then, again, perhaps neither could Sarduy, for whom at times everything seems metaphoric.

Sarduy's metaphoric gesture, in fact, inaugurates *La simulacion:* the opening narrative of Sarduy's text can be read as a sumptuous textual self-fashioning of himself as a *modernista* writer. He concludes his *modernista* allegory with a striking and powerfully queer "I" that disappears: "Y ahora, en medio de cojines rubendarianos y cortinajes, con fondo de biombos y valses—entre pajarracos y pollos—, sólo reino yo, recorrido por la simulación, imantado por la reverberación de una apariencia, vaciado por la sacudida de la risa: anulado, ausente." [And now, among Darian pillows and drapes, with a background of movable screens and waltzes, among ugly birds and chickens (or also, bad pieces of work and "fops"), only I reign, crossed by simulations, magnetized by the reverberation of an appearance, emptied by the jolt of laughter: anulled, absent.][31] Sarduy's self-fashioning with and disappearance into the language of *modernismo* allows him to circumvent essentialist body markings of gender and nation. So, if his project is to write "Cuba," he does so by always alluding to it through metaphor and the voice of his "masters"—José Lezama Lima, Carpentier, Wilfredo Lam, and the *modernista* writer, Julián Casal. He does the same when discussing his own homosexuality: he "reigns" supreme among birds and fops and the abject—all homographetic markings on his elusive body.[32] Moreover, Sarduy rejects the direct relationship between transvestism and homosexuality:

> Relacionar el *trabajo corporal* de los travestís a la simple manía cosmética, al afeminamiento o a la homosexualidad es simplemente ingenuo: esas no son más que las fronteras aparentes de una metamorfosis sin límites, su pantalla "natural".[33]

> [Relating the *corporeal work* of the transvestite to simple cosmetic mania, to effeminacy or to homosexuality is simply naïve: those are nothing more than the apparent borders of a metamorphosis without limits, their "natural" screen.]

Sarduy's commentary sounds *avant la lettre* surprisingly like Butler's criticism of the collapse between homosexuality and drag.[34] Clearly Sarduy is interested in pushing his theoretical intervention *à la limite,* a practice in and of theory that I accept; however, by placing "cosmetics," "effeminacy," and "homosexuality" on the same relative plane, he is ignoring that these "apparent borders" are sites of cultural contestation and political struggle, thereby he commits an ingenuous act of political violence on the queer body, which is more difficult to embrace altogether.[35]

Roberto González-Echevarría once told me a joke. He asked, "Do you know what Severo's enemies and mine call my book . . . ? (pause) *La puta de Severo Sarduy.*" Severo Sarduy's whore. Here we have a rather tasteless pun, but an interesting one nonetheless. Roberto and Severo's enemies have played with the title of Roberto's book, *La ruta de Severo Sarduy* [The Ways of Severo Sarduy].[36] This titular rewriting is problematic for other reasons: It seems to say that any effort to interpret Sarduy's work is, in fact, being subservient to the work, being a whore to a difficult and compulsory "masculine" text. This act attributes a crass and imprecise gender and sexual orientation to the *oeuvre*.

Sarduy's body is queer—and so is his writing. Again, we hear and sense this queerness in the first lines of *La simulación*:

> El travestí no imita a la mujer. Para él, *à la limite,* no hay mujer, sabe—y quizás, paradójicamente es [*sic*] el único en saberlo—, que ella es una apariencia, que su reino y la fuerza de su fetiche encubren un defecto.[37]
>
> [The transvestite does not imitate woman. For him, *à la limite,* there is no woman, he knows—and paradoxically perhaps, he is the only one in knowing—that she is an appearance, that the transvestite's kingdom and the strength of the transvestite's fetish hide a fault.]

This opening paragraph is a fine example of the complexity of Sarduy's texts, of how he writes on his body grammatically and critically the language of the "homosexual." I am certainly not talking about a simplistic autobiographical relationship that would equate and reduce the author as transvestite. In *La simulación* (again, 1982), a different Sarduy emerges, a Sarduy who has thought out many of the contradictions that we notice in "Escritura/travestismo." Sarduy has by this time already published several novels that include transvestites as major protagonists; I suspect that this reflection within the literary is responsible for bringing about a more fully developed conceptualization of what transvestism represents not only as a series of "inversions," but more thoroughly as an act of writing, a rhetorical mode. The Sarduy we read in *La simulación* talks about transvestites with much more breadth: their theatricality and/as death, and our culture. Here he also elaborates on his passion, rethinking the dimensions and complexity of *la cubanidad,* Cubanness, a topic which I take up later in my discussion on *De donde son los cantantes.* The author's writing borrows from the transvestite's performance skills (translating, recycling, re-presenting, etc.), but the author himself is always mediating a distance from that "transvestite" on whom he writes. This borrowing can be seen in the use that the author makes of the gendered and neuter Spanish pronouns to cause an effect, to simulate the blurring of the subject. Thus, Sarduy's transvestite narrative defines the homographetic markings in his work.

On an ideological level, the opening lines of *La simulación* reflect the idea that compulsory (male) heterosexuality could never have eschewed the idea of Woman, an idea upon which the whole of Patriarchy is mounted. Sarduy's writing is endowed and pregnant—mind the metaphors—with a succulent pleasure for debunking all expectation of normalization; his writing cannot be disciplined. This is a privileged position that the author enjoys; how, we might ask, would a critic who enjoys closure and unity—still in some circles, the hallmarks of "good" literature—explain this meditation:

> La erección cosmética del travestí, la agresión esplendente de sus párpados temblorosos y metalizados como alas de insectos voraces, su voz desplazada, como si perteneciera a otro personaje, siempre en *off,* la boca dibujada sobre su boca, su propio sexo, más presente cuanto más castrado, sólo sirven a la reproducción obstinada de ese ícono, aunque falaz omnipresente: la madre que la tiene parada y que el travestí dobla, aunque sólo sea para simbolizar que la erección es una apariencia.[38]

> [The transvestite's cosmetic erection, the splendid aggression of her lashes, trembling and metallic like the wings of voracious insects, her displaced voice, always *off* as if it belonged to another character, the mouth drawn on her mouth, her own sex, more present when most castrated, these only serve for the obsessive reproduction of that icon, though fallaciously omnipresent: the mother who has a hard-on and whom the transvestite doubles, even if it is only to symbolize that the erection is an appearance.]

Actually, a closer look at the structure of this particular passage would reveal a tightly arranged, unified argument around the trope of mirroring: that is, the transvestite's techniques double the mother's appearance, her own cosmetic erection; the transvestite privileges the phallic mother as a model, which is another way of saying that the transvestite constructs identity through a relation with a fetish.[39] Where the structure begins to fall apart is in the language itself: phallic mother, castrated transvestites, non-reproductive obsessive reproduction. Sarduy's metaphors are juxtapositions that are meant to create a tension, a gender fuck. Of the theoretical impulses that one can identify here, I would like to address one in particular: the mirror stage. Lacan writes that

> The *mirror stage* is a drama whose internal thrust is precipitated from insufficiency to anticipation—and which, manufactures for the subject, caught up in the lure of spatial identification, the succession of phantasies that extends from a fragmented body-image to a form of its totality that I shall call orthopaedic—and, lastly, to the assumption of the armour of an alienating identity, which will mark with its rigid structure the subject's entire mental development. Thus, to break out of the circle of the *Innenwelt* into the *Umwelt* generates the inexhaustible quadrature of the ego's verification.[40]

The mirror stage entails first and foremost a dramatic event of performativity. Through the mirror stage the subject negotiates her subjectivity as a specular (dis)figuration and redrawing of the limits of the *Innenwelt* (a subjective interiority) and the *Umwelt* (the subject's sense of reality). The mirror stage is also a process that stems from a sense of "lack," which, paradoxically, initiates the subject to reproduce himself, that is, a don Quijote not looking at himself in the mirror. This psychic phenomenon exceeds the limits of both time and space through fantasy and dream. Once the cycle of the mirror stage begins it can be as endless as exiting from and re-turning to the *Innenwelt;* it is a dynamic and generative event. Lacan notes that in "the deflection of the specular *I* into a social *I*,"

> [that] moment in which the mirror-stage comes to an end inaugurates, by identification with the *imago* of the counterpart and the drama of primordial jealousy, [. . .] the dialectic that will henceforth link the *I* to socially elaborated situations.
>
> It is this moment that decisively tips the whole of human knowledge into mediatization through the desire of the other, constitutes its subjects in an abstract equivalence by the co-operation of others, and turns the *I* into that apparatus for which every instinctual thrust constitutes a danger, even though it should correspond to a natural maturation—the very normalization of this maturation being henceforth dependent, in man, on a cultural mediation as exemplified, in the case of the sexual object, by the Oedipal complex.[41]

In other words, the mirror stage ends violently with the breaking of the mirror, and the seeing of the culture that opens up behind it, holding it; the end of the mirror stage also signals a narcissistic injury and forces the subject to identify with the *imago*, which Lacan compares to the witnessing of the primal scene. The resolution of the primal scene "tips the whole of human knowledge into mediatization through the desire of the other"; in other words, the "mediated" subject enters the constellation of the Lacanian Symbolic.

Appropriately the figuration of the transvestite pushes the mirror stage to the limits. Only the transvestite can understand the dimensions and ramifications of seeing herself in the mirror *ad infinitum:* More than quixotic madness, she sees survival and sanity. About this multiplying and fragmenting of the subject, Sarduy provides plenty of examples, most strikingly "a mouth drawn on her mouth," a re-inscription that permits the transvestite to speak. The transvestite, like the child who first sees himself in his mother's eyes, sees herself erecting and doubling the image of the (m)Other. I would even argue further that the transvestite subject never exits the mirror stage; (s)he appropriates, consumes, and enacts the mirror stage, and collapses the specular *I* and the social *I*. Since the mirror stage represents a structure (or style) for the subject's coming to terms with his (in)ability to give birth, the transvestite parodies this stylization by literally identifying with the mother, by radically calling into question her performance of femininity. The transvestite does not imitate woman, (s)he—and, in denying the mimesis, the pronoun is deconstructed—imitates—insofar as it is any longer possible "to imitate"—or effects the construction of woman. Ironically, the transvestite becomes the model *for* women to imitate, according to Sarduy.[42] The transvestite is an effect as well as an affect.[43] Another way to explain this affectation would be through the figure of anamorphosis. Slavoj Žižek relates "anamorphosis" to the introduction into the "phallic" stage: "'Phallic' is precisely the detail that 'does not fit,' that 'sticks out' from the idyllic surface scene and denatures it, renders it uncanny. It is the point of *anamorphosis* in a picture: the element that, when viewed straightforwardly, remains a meaningless stain, but which, as soon as we look at the picture from a precisely determined lateral perspective, all of a sudden acquires well-known contours."[44] The transvestite figure, who occupies the space of the "phallic"—Sarduy has already insisted on the transvestite's obsessive reading and comprehension of an "erection"—"does not fit in." The anamorphic relation of the transvestite to culture hinges on the fact that the transvestite stands in the position of the Symbolic; she is not suspicious of any danger because she knows too much.

Comparing the act of reading the figure of anamorphosis with the work of the analyst, Sarduy explains a Baroque, interpretative labor of anamorphosis thus,

> un primer movimiento, paralelo al del analista, asimila en efecto a lo real la imagen "difusa y rota"; pero un segundo gesto, el propiamente barroco, de

alejamiento y especificación del objeto, crítica de lo figurado, lo desasimila de lo real: esa reducción a su propio mecanismo técnico, a la teatralidad de la simulación, es la *verdad* barroca de la anamorfosis.[45]

[an initial movement, parallel to the analyst, in effect assimilates the "diffused and fragmented" image into the Real; but as a second gesture, a truly Baroque one, of distancing and specifying the object, as a critique of figuration, disassimilates the image from the Real: that reduction to its very technical mechanics, to the theatrics of simulation, is the Baroque *truth* of anamorphosis.]

While Žižek grounds his understanding of anamorphosis in its relation to the phallic, Sarduy sees it as the entrance and exit from the Real. An image is recognized—this act of recognition involves consuming and collecting ("fragments" of) a body—and lumped together; this uncritical lumping marks the entrance into the Real. The mechanics of "distancing and specifying the object," of constructing the object, involves the Imaginary; and what Sarduy reads as the awareness of this mechanism that suggests the "theatrics of simulation" marks the presence of the Symbolic. Sarduy reads and rewrites the Lacanian Real, Imaginary, and Symbolic as a figuration of the Baroque. The transvestite is a useful figure for this act of rewriting because her performance involves and puts into motion the Lacanian constellation.

The transvestite mirrors, simulates, duplicates an imperfect copy. Through the use of mirror(ing)s, the transvestite inhabits every space of the Oedipal triangle. This complex, which can unfold and cause deadly consequences, takes place and resolves itself *within* her body. This resolution "within" is why the transvestite can displace (forget) the physical pain of her transformations; why we can metaphorize or actualize her pain. The transvestite grabs the phallus and runs with it. She hides it—an act that is at once playful and painful, not to mention, performative.

Beyond Narcissus: The Homobaroque: A Lacanian Paradigm

Sarduy rereads and recasts Lacan's insights as the Baroque, by using the figure of the transvestite. The transvestite is a powerful figure, although not in and of herself, but when she holds a mirror. The metaphor of the transvestite's mirror—and, why not, the transvestite *as* mirror[46]—offers another reading of narcissism, and by extension, of the homosexual.

A homosexual relation can be thought as one of mirroring the body.

However, remembering Shoshana Felman's reading of Lacan, we know that projection and introjection are asymmetrical experiences, and thus this mirroring is uncanny.[47] Narcissism would, then, be an asymmetrical and non-corresponding relation of one body to another body. To that degree, what is the pedagogical value of the Narcissus myth, how does the myth make acts of reading and homographesis available to us?

Since the story of Narcissus is culturally well-known, I will skip to the end. One day Narcissus finds himself near a pool of water and sees an image reflected; he is so impressed by that image, so fully—or should I say "fooly"—mesmerized with and unaware of that image of himself, that he remains there completely wrapped in an unknowing desire for himself, that unreachable Other.[48] The story ends with Narcissus's recognition that that other is no Other but himself. He reaches to embrace his image and drowns. I interpret this act of drowning as a double negation: first, Narcissus takes one view or perspective; he is blinded. Second, Narcissus negates the Self and returns to the Father (his father was the river god Cephisus). What I am proposing is that the Narcissus story is not merely a representation of self-love, but an Oedipal desire to replace the father. Narcissus's deadly embrace repeats Cephisus's embrace of his mother, the nymph Liriope. In other words, Narcissus wants to return to his origins: he wants to reproduce, that is, to write himself as Other. He enacts the Oedipal narrative. In his effort to do this, he, too, not unlike Echo wanting to possess the unattainable, destroys his body and presence. Narcissus's obsessive desire to attain the place of the Father produces a *supplément* of images. The reflection of the narcissistic image is one that has been created and mediated by the Father (in this case, the chain of signifiers, water/Father/Symbolic). The reflection of the Other that Narcissus perceives is in effect one that has been constructed by the image and the name of the father (*nom-du-père*). Looking into the mirror, Narcissus enters the space of the homosocial; literalizing and desiring the image of himself structures the prohibited, incestuous, homosexual relation between son (Narcissus) and Father (water/river/Cephisus). Homosexuality is regulated by the Symbolic to the degree that the homosexual rewrites and literalizes (in actuality, debunks) the Symbolic as a reflection and deflection of the Father; this double process of the writing of the Symbolic (once by the Father; again by the son) involves Sarduy's rewriting of the Baroque as "neo-Baroque,"[49] what I would call the "homobaroque." I introduce this neologism not to displace the idea of the "neo-Baroque" as such, but rather to underline the specular and homographetic metaphors that lace the whole enterprise of Sarduy's reading the Baroque.

Emerging in the literalization of the (homosexual) image is a floating signifier or oxymoron (another figuration of the transvestite) that becomes a grander symbol of the Self. Our act of reading involves this narcissistic program of projection, figuration, and recognition of an oxymoron (or disfiguration). The image of the reader/writer floats on the water/mirror, constantly changing and displacing himself or herself. We hear echoes of this in the opening stanza of Xavier Villaurrutia's beautiful poem, "Reflejos" [Reflections]: "Eras como el agua / un rostro movido, ¡ay!, / cortado / por el metal de los reflejos." [You were like the water / a displaced face, oh!, / cut / by the metal of the reflections.][50] The desire to constrain or anchor that image, a symbolic disfiguration, leads to the death of the Self. This is the most important lesson that the Narcissus myth teaches us, that locking self-figuration within a discrete, almost self-indulgent discourse, within the Imaginary—for example, Valentín's Marxist figuration in *Kiss of the Spider Woman,* la Manuela's insistence that she still is adored, or any inaccessible projection of the Self— outside of the conditions of the Symbolic, represents a violent self-imaging that breaks through Narcissus's mirror and tears the flesh.

Hence, fixing transvestism too seriously or to the extreme contains a similar danger. Sarduy writes

> La puesta en escena del travestí tiene su reverso y su contrario—un triunfo de la ilusión—en lo que, aparentemente, más se le parece: la pasión— aun en el sentido cristiano de la palabra, es decir, corrección y sacrificio del cuerpo—del transexual que remodelando su físico, realiza lo imaginario.
>
> Para el travestí, la dicotomía y oposición de los sexos queda abolida o reducida a criterios inoportunos o arqueológicos; para el transexual, al contrario, esa oposición no sólo se mantiene sino que es subrayada, aceptada: simplemente el sujeto, tomando el "corte" al pie de la letra, ha saltado del otro lado de la barra.[51]

> [The transvestite's *mise-en scène* has its reverse and contrary side—a triumph of illusion—in that [event] which apparently most looks like it: the passion—even in the Christian sense of the word, that is, the correction and sacrifice of the body—of the transsexual who remodeling her physique, makes "real" (*realiza*) the Imaginary.
>
> For the transvestite, the dichotomy and opposition of genders is abolished or reduced to inopportune or archaeological criteria; for the transsexual, on the contrary, that opposition not only is maintained but it is underlined, accepted: simply, the subject, taking the "cut" literally (or to the letter), has jumped to the other side of the bar.]

This bar that divides the binarism male/female is the transvestite's mirror, the Symbolic. For the transsexual, going across the bar/mirror is not only an act of figuration but disfiguration; the transvestite suspends and blurs that (dis)figuration. The Symbolic location—like the bar itself—introduces a possibility of falling (apart) or uncertainty; nonetheless, it represents most clearly our privileged position as readers, as transvestites. Sarduy knows this: His writing represents a particular, readerly position with respect to Derrida and Lacan. Sarduy occupies the space of the "third"; this enables him to translate the forces or speech acts of deconstruction and psychoanalysis. This is why the transvestite is such a powerful and necessary figure for understanding Sarduy, the man, the text. Furthermore, this self-positioning or styling that gives Sarduy such critical maneuverability with respect to the French critics parallels a similar act of projection and reading when he names his literary precursors, Alejo Carpentier and José Lezama Lima. Specifically, it would be Lezama's Baroque that Sarduy would translate to his own writings.

A Lezamian Paradigm: Narcissus Reading

Although I have used a retelling of the Narcissus story to articulate a kind of Lacanian paradigm, I must look back—if only briefly—at the work of Lezama Lima, undoubtedly, the most influential figure (or mirror) in Sarduy's essayistic and novelistic body of work. In one of his earliest poems, "Muerte de Narciso" (1937) ["The Death of Narcissus"], he writes:

> Rostro absoluto, firmeza mentida del espejo.
> El espejo se olvida del sonido y de la noche
> y su puerta al cambiante pontífice entreabre.
> Máscara y río, grifo de los sueños.[52]

> [Absolute face, deceitful fixity of the mirror.
> The mirror forgets about sound and night
> and its door for the changing pontiff cracks ajar.
> Mask and river, griffin of dreams.]

Lezama sees the mirror as a figure of contradiction, one that frames or fixes an image and lies about it. Mirrors hold images. Sound and darkness cannot be captured: voice/language and blindness/death are metaphors of what a mirror "forgets" or must not desire. For Lezama, mirrors are metaphors; and metaphors, mirrors. This image and imagining are the privileged figures of the Lezamian poetic enterprise, which enable him to read for us. Lezama reads the obvious metaphor—that Narcissus's mirror is a mask of his dreams—as well as *the* obvious—that the mirror is a river, from which dreams pour out. A reading of the narcissistic fall appears in Sarduy's text: "No es asombroso que el cuerpo, el sacrificado de nuestra cultura, regrese, con la violencia de lo reprimido, a la escena de su exclusión." [It is not surprising that the body, the sacrificed of our culture, returns to the scene of its exclusion with all the violence of the repressed.][53] Sarduy understands the death wish inherent in any body as the desire for the ungraspable. I find more poignant still Lezama's reading of the end of the myth; it is a reading that is a closer reflection of Sarduy's understanding of the transvestite figure and space. Narcissus, the androgynous beauty, cannot survive the look of the staring mirror: "Así el espejo averiguó callado, así Narciso en pleamar fugó sin alas." [Like so, the mirror sought silently; like so, in high tide, Narcissus escaped without wings.] Playing with our expectation, Lezama tells us that the mirror tacitly "sought" or wanted to know Narcissus—very much in the same way that Narcissus wanted to know himself. The author seems to suggest that the image or meaning found in the mirror wants a body. This conceptualization can be applied to the figuration of the transvestite: the image in the mirror (in effect, an object) consumes the subject's body. This turn of events enacts the transvestite's deconstructive effect. Sarduy concludes by echoing Lezama with the following:

> Como los pintores hiperrealistas, el travestí y el autor de obras manifiesta e insolentemente narcisísticas . . . obedecen a una sola compulsión: representar la fantasía. . . . El travestí, y todo el que trabaja sobre el cuerpo y lo expone, satura la realidad de su imaginario *y la obliga, a fuerza de arreglo, de reorganización, de artificio y de maquillaje, a entrar, aunque de modo mimético y efímero, en su juego.*[54]

> [Like hyperrealist painters, the transvestite and the author of manifestly and insolently narcissistic works . . . are regulated by a single compulsion: to represent fantasy. . . . The transvestite and everyone who works on the body and exposes it, saturates reality with their Imaginary, and, through the force of arrangement, of reorganization, of artifice and of cosmetics, *they force reality to enter—though, in a mimetic and ephemeral fashion—into their game.*]

In so anticipating the structuration of subjectivity, where objects (mirrors) have a life of their own, Lezama's monumental "Muerte de Narciso" would then be an appropriate "preface"—with all the Hegelian connotations that this term implies—to Sarduy's work.

La cubanidad

A deliberate gap that I have left in this chapter thus far has been how the notion of *la cubanidad* is a motivating obsession in all of Sarduy's work. In a wonderful—at times, brilliant—interview with Emir Rodríguez Monegal, Sarduy explains how, as a student of art history in Paris, he became aware of Cuba:

> SS: [. . .] En el fondo quizás lo que hice fue empezar a recorrer el Louvre, visitarlo de verdad. Es decir, ir cada vez a ver un solo cuadro. El hecho de convivir con un cuadro no sólo revela la intensidad del arte, sino creo que de la vida también, porque como es sabido la vida imita al arte.
> ERM: Ya lo descubrió Wilde.
> SS: A partir de esas repetidas visitas al Louvre, me fui interiorizando con esta cultura al mismo tiempo que iba descubriendo mejor mi entronque con la cultura de mi país. Al distanciarme de Cuba comprendí qué era Cuba, o al menos me planteé con toda claridad la pregunta: *¿Qué es Cuba?*[55]
>
> [SS: [. . .] Basically what I did was to run around the Louvre, truly visiting it. That is to say, each time I would go see one work alone. The fact of sharing/living with (*convivir*) a work of art, not only reveals the intensity of art, but, I believe, also reveals life, because as it is known life imitates art.
> ERM: Wilde had already discovered that.
> SS: From those visits to the Louvre, I began interiorizing [French] culture, at the same time I was better discovering my rootedness with the culture of my country. By distancing myself from Cuba, I understood what Cuba was, or at least, I posed myself with complete clarity the question: *What is Cuba?*]

This exchange and moment of "complete clarity"—this insight—circumscribes a primal scene in Sarduy's writing. His visits to the Louvre as occasions for research became powerful autobiographical moments of (dis)identification: through his fascination with art, Sarduy internalizes French culture to discover the question of *cubanidad*. Earlier in this study, I suggest that a "question" is a textual fragment or a challenge to narrativity; also, it parallels the project of subject formation in that both—questions and subjects—seek completion. Sarduy's intellectual enterprise—his questioning in art—leads to the discovery of the question of the national Self. This paradox could be explained by thinking through that, when Sarduy tells us that he shares/lives with (*convivir*) a work of art, he is performing a (per)version of the Narcissus story. Also sharing/living with art produces a double relation: the inner working of the work of art, as well as the Self's structure of address in his relation to the artwork. These two systems are woven together or overlap or differ from each other. Overall, Sarduy's project is *the very question of (Cuban) identity*. His effort to understand his relation to that question involves supplying a whole series of narrative structures that are always already implicated and faulty for the project—thus, the need to conjure up new critical tools again. The question of Cuba is always retractable, becoming unknowable, at every turn. Therefore, the questioning itself is Cuba.

I insist that this short exchange between Rodríguez Monegal and Sarduy is a primal scene because it contains structurally and thematically the questions that regulate Sarduy's writing. Monegal's queer intervention about Wilde should not escape notice, especially as it is ignored or displaced by Sarduy. It almost seems that he "doesn't want to go there." Of course, he will return to homosexual and queer identities throughout his work, albeit through metaphoric engagement.

Transvestism, sexualities, identity, and nation: how are they linked Sarduy's literary narrative? Let us look in brief at his first important work, *De donde son los cantantes* [literally, *The Place from Where the Singers Come*] to understand how these connections are made.[56] The novel is a perpetual rehearsal (literally, a repetition of death) to capture an elusive Other. It brings together a series of narrative moments or literary *tableaux* that each gives us a Polaroid of the author's struggle to articulate an aesthetic of *cubanidad*. The final "Nota" describes the novel's project: "Tres culturas se han superpuesto para constituir la cubana—española, africana y china—; tres ficciones que aluden a ellas constituyen este libro." [Three cultures have been superimposed to constitute Cuban culture—Spanish, African and Chinese; these three fictions that allude to those cultures constitute this book.][57] Immediately we notice how culture is understood as a fiction; these fictions are laced together into another fiction called "Cuba." Sarduy continues that "[a] esas fábulas son comunes tres personajes—o temas—: Mortal, español rubio, de habla castiza, que detenta los atributos, siempre inciertos del poder; Auxilio y Socorro . . . " [Common to those fables are three characters—or themes: Mortal, a blond Spaniard, of pure speech, who unlawfully holds the ever-uncertain attributes of power; Auxilio and Socorro . . .][58] Each of the novel's narratives re-introduces these three characters; they are the unifying thread of the narrative, if one could possibly be identified. By saying that these characters can be thought of as "themes," the author suggests that the character's subjectivity is necessarily excessive because they do not represent just the Self, but something greater, a type, a culture, or a drive. These themes are then inserted in different fictions. What we have here is Sarduy's explaining again the process by which he constructs the "metaphor to the second power," a refunctioned metaphor of a metaphor as a neo-Baroque strategy, to begin telling his story of "Cuba." Of the three characters, let us look at the transvestites, Auxilio and Socorro.

From the opening accident to the General blindly enamoured of Flor de Loto, a transvestite singer in the Chinese opera; to la Dolores Rondón, a Black woman in search of power by any means necessary; to the final episode, "La entrada de Cristo en la Habana," a retelling of Fidel Castro's triumphal entrance to Havana; each narrative is bound by the continual and persistent appearance of Auxilio and Socorro. Their names are synonymous (meaning "help!"), thus they appear together as mirroring figures. Auxilio and Socorro's names also represent an apostrophe, a call to an absent other. Calling out "auxilio" and "socorro" demands a response. González-Echevarría argues that the transvestite characters are constantly changing, and that if any thing remains constant it is the relation between each of them in the text. Furthermore, he argues that, in *De donde son los cantantes*, filiation is no longer continuous; all family romances as metaphors for oneness, and other unifying themes, so visible in the novels of the "Boom," have been undone.[59] I would add that the family romances of the "Boom"—the Páramos (of *Pedro Páramo*), the Buendías (of *One Hundred Years of Solitude*), and so many more—can be read differently after Donoso questioned the very idea of "family" and domesticity, by introducing the González Asticas—la Manuela and la Japonesa. (After all, *El lugar sin límites* was published in 1966, a year before *De donde son los cantantes; El lugar* may well have been a model for Sarduy's text.) Donoso's textual family deals face to face with issues such as prostitution and homosexuality, and signifies on other dysfunctional family romances. Are Auxilio and Socorro "family"? Their relation to each other is never elaborated. Do these transvestites own a family romance? I propose that what Sarduy does specifically is write the drama of the family romance and then place that drama in a *mise-en-scène* of the body of the transvestite. *De donde son los cantantes* and *La simulación* capture this critical intervention. So, if the family romance is played on the body of the transvestite, let us look at one particular example of that dramatization.

In the opening chapter of *De donde son los cantantes*, "Curriculum

Cubense," a kind of prologue for the rest of the work, we encounter Auxilio and Socorro getting ready to go out. Getting ready for their day is quite a spectacular display of color and dress and feathers. There is an allusion to their having taken drugs and to having a spiritual moment. Hungry, they go to a cafeteria, the Self-Service, where they run into some problems. In the dessert section, Auxilio's orange-colored, nylon hair gets stuck in one of the General's uniform pins. Auxilio and the General struggle to get loose; however, this makes matters worse: "[a]llí estan los dos—serpientes emplumadas—cheek to cheek, pegados uno a otro, pegadas las bandejas. Hermanos siameses forcejeando. Murciélago de Bacardi, mancha de tinta, animal doble, ostra abierta, cuerpo con su reflejo; eso son Auxilio y el General." [(t)here they are the two—feather snakes—cheek to cheek, stuck one to the other, trays stuck together. Siamese twins struggling. The Bacardi bat, a stain of ink, a double animal, an opened oyster, a body with its reflection; those are Auxilio and the General.][60] The proliferation of (mirror) images in this passage is astounding: the subjects, though linked, begin to unfold in a series of narrative attempts to define their new status. This is quite emblematic of Sarduy's own effort to define *cubanidad:* the label "Cuban" brings disparate parts together—and the effect it produces is one of naming, a dissemination of names. This proliferation of names is a *centrifugal* gesture, which is followed by a *centripetal* one:

> Pues nada, que esa cosmogonía en ciernes atrajo, chupó mundo. Como un imán debajo de un río de anzuelos, o como un aspirador en un pollero las plumas, así el binomio Auxilio-General chupó todo lo que había alrededor, y claro está, chupó a una negra y a una china: así se completó el curriculum cubense.[61]

> [Well nothing, that cosmogony in bloom attracted, sucked up the world. Like a magnet under a river of hooks, or like a vacuum cleaner in a chicken coop to the feathers, thus the binomial Auxilio-General sucked everything that was around, and of course, sucked up a Black woman and a Chinese woman: in that fashion, the curriculum cubense was completed.]

Again, we see the double movement: a blooming cosmogony (outward) attracts (inward). This figure becomes complete when it gathers the Black and the Chinese into the web of identity. Sarduy calls it "curriculum cubense," the course or history of Cuba. It is imperative to recognize that he is not identifying this image of Auxilio tangled up with a Spaniard, a woman of African descent, and a Chinese woman, as a final stage, but rather a course, a movement. The image is fixed long enough to be captured in the psyche, but it continues to move, to proliferate. It is worth remarking on the recurrence of mirror images, projection and introjection, a desire for symmetry, uncontrolled drives, and other tropes in the novel as in Sarduy's essays. Like in his discussion of transvestism, Sarduy maintains that the national(ist) project is ongoing, that it should not stop transforming itself again and again. That is Sarduy's lesson is about how national identity is assumed, the lesson he discovered, absorbed looking at paintings, while exiled at the Louvre. It is important to note here that whether discussing the transformative pulsion of transvestism, which Sarduy resists to anchor in the "apparent borders" of cosmetics, effeminacy, or homosexuality, or whether he is discussing the project of nation formation as an ever-lasting project of definition and redefinition, that in either case, Sarduy is consistent in his *theoretical* project, but not necessarily in tune to the social, cultural, and political effects of each. While I am sympathetic to Sarduy's reading of Nation, I am critical of his dismissal to link the project of transvestism and homosexuality, especially. Although a parallel, theoretical exercise of transvestite and national figurations exists, each enterprise has a different value. That is, the relationship between the transvestite/homosexual and the national projects is not one of sameness; indeed, there has been a long history of struggle between the national project, which too often gets articulated and promoted as part of the Nation and State, and a homosexual project of identity politics, which is always local and often diffuse in Latin America, as elsewhere. As we saw with the "41," the Nation was implacable to suppress queer difference; while my reading of the "41" seeks to recuperate that event as a site and sight of resistance. I am not willing to collapse these different histories of oppression and resistance. It is important to see how each—literary analysis and cultural theory—informs the other, although I want to weigh the *analytic* strategies and specificity of literary and cultural practices.

Earlier I suggested that this opening chapter of *De donde son los cantantes* was a kind of prologue to the other four. This chapter encapsulates a narrative and an *ars poetica,* a lesson in reading. If it is to be taken as prologue, I do not want to suggest that it gives a "face" to the rest of the novel; that would be a misrepresentation. The novel disobeys linear narrativity and temporality, so by promoting a certain fixity to the "prologue," one would be imposing a structure that does not belong there. Rather, as an opening to the novel, "Curriculum Cubense" should be read alongside the other chapters, always establishing relations among the chapters, creating a new set of tangled themes and metaphors, and watching what happens. It is here that we can uncover one of Sarduy's most exciting literary contributions to the Latin American novel, endorsing a new way of reading, a *relational* practice of reading, that demands a particular set of cultural and social crossings and identifications—reading across gender, race, and nation. In other words, Sarduy wants us to reflect on what it means to be.

Final Reflection

I would like to conclude by reading a fragment of one my favorite poems, which serves as an epigraph to this book. From Villaurrutia's "Nocturno en que nada se oye" [Nocturne where nothing can be heard]:

> Y en el juego angustioso de un espejo frente a otro
> cae mi voz
> y mi voz que madura
> y mi voz quemadura
> y mi bosque madura
> y mi voz quema dura
> como el hielo de vidrio
> como el grito de hielo[62]

> [And in the anguished game of a mirror in front of another
> my voice falls
> and my voice that matures
> and my voice, a scar
> and my forest grows thicker
> and my voice burns hard
> like the ice of glass
> like the screaming of ice]

Villaurrutia's game with language—using the homophone, "y mi voz que madura," to represent the "all" of voice and echoes, like the projected voice and figure of a transvestite that have fallen in the *ad infinitum* reflections of facing mirrors—traces to a degree the difficulty of writing about transvestism. Sarduy writes that the transvestite is a "hyper-woman"; he adds, however, that "Lacan diría que se trata de una fantasía si se trata de ser *toda* la mujer, ya que según él la mujer no existe, justamente, más por el hecho de no ser ese todo."[63] [Lacan would say that it is a fantasy to try being an *all-out* woman because, according to him, woman does not exist any longer, precisely for the fact that she cannot be that "all."] This idea of wanting to be "all," which emerges over and over as a motif in transvestite texts, takes on a strange tone in Sarduy's uses of Lacan above. First, Sarduy ventriloquizes Lacan ("Lacan would say . . . "); then, he quotes Lacan directly ("according to him, . . . "). There is an uneasy sense of how Sarduy rehearses and echoes the French critic's ideas; this uneasiness stems from the unsettling issues involved in identification and repetition.[64] It may appear that Villaurrutia also wanted to broach that concept of the "all"—although not with questions of genders, but of language. This desire to define the "whole" is actually quite important in Sarduy's own effort to define "Cuba" in *De donde son los cantantes* and his other texts. The project is both a desire and an impossibility, also too much an impossibility to desire. Sarduy's search for *la cubanidad,* also Villaurrutia's homophone, seeks to articulate, yet fails to produce a "complete" voice or language. In his search for Cubanness, Sarduy has offered us *De donde son los cantantes.* The title of the novel is constructed as an answer "de donde son los cantantes" [(a nameless place) from where the singers come]. Sarduy performs yet fails in his search for Cuban identities in a novel, whose very title is supposedly an answer to a homophonic question: "De dónde son los cantantes?" [Where are the singers from?] [65] That place that must necessarily remain nameless may be here or there or Cuba. Performance and failure go together in the effort to exact and fix an identity. Perhaps the homophonic title is telling us something: that the very question as well as the answer are inarticulable, unknowable, just twirling approximations.

The homophonic performance and failure to achieve that desired "all" also signifies on the transvestite's desire for "real" feminine voice and persona. Here I am also talking about the fact that an unforced, "feminine" voice is one of the most difficult things for a transvestite to simulate. Transsexuals or transvestites can only change their voices with much work and training. It is the irony of "a mouth drawn on [a] mouth." As Sarduy puts it, the transvestite's voice is always *off.* Likewise, writing about transvestism has been such a difficult project to articulate: gender, pronouns, voice, identification, sexuality, everything about the transvestite's world is a reconstruction or a repetition of our world. Just when I thought I had been successful in describing what I heard or saw, I knew that I, too, had slipped. However, now only the reader of this book who stands in the much-decorated position of the "third" subject—in relation and opposition to my effort to write a transvestite narrative—can truly look back and be critical of my theoretical and political voice that has matured—at times, agitatedly, at others, calmly.

Chapter 5

Kissing the Body Politic: Engendering Heterosexuality / Screening the Homosocial

> *Si quieres besarme . . . besa,*
> *—yo comparto tus antojos—*
> *Mas no hagas mi boca presa,*
> *¡Bésame quedo en los ojos!*
> —from *"Al oído,"* Alfonsina Storni

> *La noche ya es más noche en la arboleda,*
> *en los follajes ha anidado el rayo,*
> *vago jardín a la deriva*
> *—entra, tu sombra cubre esta página.*
> —from *"Como quien oye llover,"* Octavio Paz

> *Wer auf dem Kopf geht, meine Damen und Herren,—wer auf dem Kopf geht, der hat Himmel als Abgrund unter sich.*
> —Paul Celan[1]

Manuel Puig's *El beso de la mujer araña* [*Kiss of the Spider Woman*] (1976) is truly a magical text that not only reinvents the possibilities of gender, subjectivity, and passion, but reinvents narrative itself to seduce us into new modes of identification. The text's history—from novel to play to Hollywood film to Broadway musical—is a dazzling example of genre crossing. Each textual moment gives us new stories to read, to contemplate, and to rehearse identification. In this final chapter, I will focus on Puig's novel, a *tour de force* in Latin American literature, that represents a *summa* of the author's *oeuvre*, as well as a culmination of the literary movements and tendencies in which this work has been canonized. The novel's structure follows many of Puig's previous narrative experiments. For instance, the text's structure resembles a film script or the text of a play. The story of Valentín and Molina—the former, a political prisoner who is accused of anti-government activities, also of being a Marxist; the latter, a very feminine, gay man accused of "corrupting youth," also a political prisoner—unfolds as an ongoing scripted dialogue, sometimes friendly, sometimes bitter. At times it is difficult to figure out who is talking, since the author does not give us the usual notations that reference action in the prison space; he occasionally uses footnotes to supply useful information and textual gaps to signal that nothing much might be happening. As with other works, Puig borrows and samples other narrative styles to tell his story—here he adapts the language of film into literary space.[2]

Again, the signature of Puig's literary work remains in his bold and provocative approach to sexuality in his texts. More than any Latin American author, Puig openly presents and addresses sexual identities, pleasures, and problems: adultery, rape, premarital sex, virginity, erection dysfunction, female sexual desire, and a long list of other issues in the realm of sexuality.

Writing Sexual Culture

In *Kiss of the Spider Woman* Puig has a particular goal in mind: that of writing about how a particular form of femininity believes and creates the super man. He writes rather poignantly about this matter:

> Me interesaba un personaje femenino que creyese todavía en la existencia del macho superior, y lo primero que se me ocurrió fue que hoy ese personaje no podía ser una mujer, porque una mujer de hoy día, de alguna manera ya duda; a estas alturas ya duda que exista ese *partner* que la va a guiar en todo.[3]

> [What interested me was a feminine character who would still believe in the existence of a superior man (*macho*), and the first thought I had was that today that character could not be a woman, because a woman nowadays doubts in some manner; at this level, she doubts that that partner who will guide her in everything exists.]

Thus Manuel Puig introduces his literary project and vision of *Kiss of the Spider Woman*.[4] What is important to notice is that, for Puig, women are not believers in the superior macho, they "doubt." Furthermore, they are no longer able to support or maintain the ideology of an overwhelming patriarchy. It is a huge and essential project to describe that ideology and its subject, because it gives us a more precise understanding of the contours and dynamics of power relations at many levels—social, sexual, and cultural. Puig's project gives us a perspicacious insight into the subjectivity of the superior man, while it takes into account the Symbolic order of the novel and the mechanisms of power that constitute and regulate the scene of writing.[5] So, the author continues,

> En cambio, un homosexual, con fijación femenina, sí, todavía, puede defender esa ideología, porque, como desea ser mujer, pero no puede realizar la experiencia de ser mujer, no puede llegar a desengañarse y sigue el engaño, en el sueño de que la realización de la mujer está en encontrar un hombre que la va a guiar y que se va a ocupar de ella, lo cual es buscar un padre y no un compañero.[6]

> [However, a homosexual with feminine fixations, indeed, still can defend that ideology (of the super man), because, since he wishes to be a woman, but cannot perform (*realizar*) the experience of being a woman, he is unable to disabuse himself (*desengañarse*) and continues the deception (or trick) of the illusion that becoming a woman lies in finding a man to guide her and to take care of her; this means finding a father and not a partner.]

Here Puig continues his articulation of the subject of his novel. What is most striking is how he identifies that the purveyor of a patriarchal ideology is not a woman, but a notion of femininity itself is the bearer of such an ideology. That is, woman as subject does not produce the superior macho; rather, femininity (in the Spanish neuter, *lo femenino*) as a construct held by a homosexual man is what promotes that *macho* subjectivity. In other words, Puig is suggesting that the conceptualization of the superior macho happens as a relation or liaison between men, that is, the homosocial. Puig subtly unfolds another aspect of his project: writing about a homosexual. It does not stop surprising us how or why this aspect of his writing has to be grounded with a certain reluctance, with an explanation "beforehand." That is, by first framing the homosexual character of the novel, Molina, as "a feminine character who still believed in the existence of a superior man" and, then, as a "homosexual, with feminine fixations," Puig is showing us a certain anxiety regarding homosexuality in his writing—he moves toward the subject of homosexuality slowly. Puig's presentation of Molina appears to be almost an excuse. I underline this particular moment in the author's reluctant explanation (or excuse) for the homosexual subject because, after presenting such a brilliant feminist reading of the homosocial valorization of the superior *macho,* he almost obsessively and uncritically positions the homosexual in terms of the heterosexual matrix. How do we reconcile both of the author's positions? On the one hand, his more challenging perspective informs the construction of masculinity as the fantasy of the homosocial. On the other hand, he reductively and misogynistically reads male homosexuality as a desire to become and appropriate the "feminine."[7]

When we consider the question of sexuality in the text, we must look not simply at writing about homosexual themes or a homosexual character in a "popular" novel, but—and more importantly—also at the author's own gayness. A consideration of sexual difference as epistemology illuminates our critical reading of a text.[8] I want to pause and explain the importance of establishing a dialogue between my work on Latin America and current gay and lesbian studies. Understanding the possible inflections of gender and sexuality in the Latin American scene is imperative. By asking what different representations sexuality and gender take on in Latin America, how these re-presentations manifest themselves in the formation of a subject, what differences and similarities between a Symbolic vision of the sexual and the Imaginary exist, and how these differences figure prominently in discussions of cultural superiority, we perform a double reading of different literary texts alongside critical statements about post-structuralism, psychoanalysis, and gender studies, thus evaluating the universality of the claims made by authors in such disciplines.[9]

Along these lines, a reading of *Kiss of the Spider Woman* must not only focus on the construction of Molina's sexual identity, the homosexual "with feminine fixations" as a performer of transvestism, but, also, analyze the reenactment of Marxist ideology by Valentín as a performance that doubles transvestism. In the Donoso chapter, I argued that Pancho Vega's "masculinity," a deliberately symptomatic response of his homosexual panic, was as much a performance of gender as la Manuela's transvestite subjectivity. In this chapter, I will show that ideology—in this case, oppositional revolutionary politics—signals a particular performance that is transvestic, and, that this ideological transvestism necessarily sublimates the homoerotics of any heterosexual male encounter. That is, every male "event" connotes a hidden homosexual embrace. The politics of denying this embrace shamelessly produce the language of sexism and homophobia. This chapter can be roughly divided into two parts: the first deals with the heterosexual body and its relation to the language of political ideology;

the second part shows how the homosexual body becomes resignified through the gestures and performance of heterosexuality.

The Prison of Narration; or, How to Read like a "Real" Man.

The structure of the *Kiss of the Spider Woman* is simple: Valentín, a political prisoner, and Molina share a cell where Molina's retelling of B-movies helps pass the time they spend there. Before looking at some of the stories told by the prisoners, I would like to evaluate the importance that the prison takes as a site for narration. One cannot help thinking of an Arçipreste de Hita or a Cervantes who wrote his masterpiece in/from prison. The architectural design of a prison influences Molina's fantastic story telling: the close walls must be transcended with complex narratives and performances.[10] On the question of the text's narrative complexity, I am not concerned with the intertextual relationship between film and text,[11] but rather I am interested here in reading indirectly several aspects of these films in the text: first, how does Molina's retelling of these films refigure in a written adaptation, how do cinematic strategies, such as *film noir* techniques become writing; second, how is the narrative projected onto/limited by the prison walls, what are the possibilities of success or failure in escaping these walls through language; and, third, how do the men's *identification* with different characters in the films reveal their subjectivity? I will not pretend to answer all of these questions head on, but rather make proposals along the way to begin understanding the very questions' significance as mirroring spaces or fragments—strategies that capture a new formulation of subjectivity.

If spaces can be labeled "heterosexual," "lesbian," "educational," and the like, what has come to define a male "homosexual" space most would be its marginal and underground nature—the bar at night, the alleyway, the staircase between the seventh and eighth floors, the park (again?) at night, the rest stop, the "tearoom," the piers, the elevator, to name a few. I would also add that the prison is the homosexual space *par excellence:* the prison marks the periphery of the homosocial, and becomes forcibly (perhaps, violently) a homosexual space. Paradoxically, Molina and Valentín's cell mirrors the structure of the perfectly "heterosexual" family. In a (classical) dinner table scene, we can hear both men's nervous manners. Valentín is happy to eat well-prepared food, however he complains that Molina is going to "spoil him," and that can hurt him. Molina tells him not to think about the food as a luxury and " . . . ¡viví el momento!, ¡aprovechá!, ¿te vas a amargar la vida pensando en lo que va a pasar mañana?" [. . . live the moment! Enjoy! Are you going to make your life bitter thinking about what will happen tomorrow?]¹² Again, Valentín's initial compliment of Molina's cooking is followed with a note of caution: that he might become spoiled. What Valentín claims might hurt him is not the food itself (which is poisoned by prison officials later in the text), but rather the *pleasure of eating* good food that would somehow spoil him by associating him with the pleasures of the bourgeoisie, therefore, contaminating his Marxist persona. Valentín insists at length that

> —Yo no puedo vivir el momento, porque vivo en función de una lucha política, o bueno, actividad política digamos, ¿entendés? Todo lo que yo puedo aguantar acá, que es bastante, . . . pero que es nada si pensás en la tortura, . . . que vos *no* sabés lo que es.
> —Pero me puedo imaginar.
> —No, no te lo podés imaginar . . . *Bueno, todo me lo aguanto* . . . porque hay una planificación. Está lo importante que es la revolución social, y lo secundario, que son los placeres de los sentidos. Mientras dure la lucha, que durará tal vez toda mi vida, no me conviene cultivar los placeres de los sentidos, ¿te das cuenta?, porque son, de verdad, secundarios para mí. El gran placer es otro, el de saber que estoy al servicio de lo más noble, que es . . . bueno . . . todas mis ideas . . .
> —¿Cómo tus ideas?
> —Mis ideales, . . . el marxismo, si querés que te defina todo *con una palabra*. Y ese placer lo puedo sentir en cualquier parte, acá mismo en esta celda, y hasta en la tortura. Y ésa es mi fuerza.¹³

> [—I cannot live the moment, because I live in the context of a political struggle, or, let us better say, a political activity, do you understand? Everything that I put up with over here, which is a lot, . . . but it's nothing if you think about torture, . . . you do *not* know what it is.
> —But I can imagine.
> —No, you cannot imagine it . . . Well, I will put up with anything (*me lo aguanto*) . . . because there is a plan. There's what's important, the social revolution, and what's secondary, the pleasures of the senses. While the struggle lasts, and it will probably last all of my life, it is not convenient for me to cultivate the pleasures of the senses—are you aware of that?—because they are truly secondary for me. The grand pleasure is another, knowing that I am at the service of the most noble things, that is . . . well . . . all of my ideas . . .
> —What do you mean your ideas?

—My ideals, . . . Marxism, if you want me to define everything for you *with one word*. And I can feel that pleasure everywhere, here in this cell, and even in torture. And that is my strength.]

Pleasure of the senses becomes a distraction Valentín cannot afford—literally (in the Marxist sense) and figuratively—because it disassociates him from his struggle. He cannot "live the moment" because he has constructed an identity *outside* the body that limits and stifles him. Ironically, this fictional identity or being is defined or constructed around a *central* plan. Indeed, this idealized Self is both a transvestism and, if you like, a travesty of Marxism. However artificial, the "one word" signifier is a powerful invention: Valentín is subordinate to "Marxism." What matters here is to understand the *performative* relation that defines Valentín as a Marxist; What really defines his ideological view are his actions, not the "one word" that he claims. I agree with Butler's discussion of the totalizing gesture revealed by a claim such as "I am a Marxist": in showing the limitations that the "lesbian-signifier" imposes on her subjectivity, she argues that

> To claim that this [a lesbian] is what I *am* is to suggest a provisional totalization of this "I." But if the I can so determine itself, then that which it excludes in order to make that determination remains constitutive of the determination itself. In other words, such a statement presupposes that the "I" exceeds its determination, and even produces that very excess in and by the act which seeks to exhaust the semantic field of that "I." In the act which would disclose the true and full content of that "I," a certain radical *concealment* is thereby produced. [. . .] [That] is to say that the copula is empty, that it cannot be substituted for with a set of descriptions. And perhaps that is a situation to be valued.[14]

Butler's sharp critique clearly signifies on Valentín's blindness. What reveals his Marxism is a performance of it, not the mere label. His "one word" definition or self-portrait of a man paradoxically *conceals* the complexity of his own defense (performance) of the values and goals of the Revolution. Valentín's naming of "I" a Marxist "exhaust[s] the semantic field of that 'I'"—to recap Butler. Furthermore, the closure of the semantic field produces that "radical concealment," a manifestation of transvestism at an ideological level. Transvestism not only presents a new subjectivity but conceals others. The effects of this transvestism are manifested, of course, in Molina's "failure" to get the point of Marxism: for him, the Revolution translates as a prohibition. Again, Molina's sexuality (anyone's sexuality, for that matter) is concealed or blurred specifically in the Marxist re-vision. The possibility of erasure would categorically explain Molina's resistance to accept the Marxist vision; a resistance misread by Valentín, who is constantly asking, "do you understand?" or "are you aware of that?" Or, Molina's understanding of the situation is constantly denied by Valentín: "you do *not* know what it is" and "[y]ou do not seem convinced." Valentín deprives Molina of the possibility of response, because only he empathetically knows and understands Marxism. In other words, there is only one brand of Marxism, Valentín's. Furthermore, Valentín has situated within his romanticized ideal of Marxism a greater, more productive pleasure that inhabits his body and extends to every part of his life. Sublimation, then, is required to become a "good" Marxist.[15] Now, if Marxism were to assume the place of all sexuality, (Molina's) homosexuality would represent a *supplément*. Then, Molina, appropriately, goes on to ask Valentín about his girlfriend. Valentín immediately answers that "Eso también tiene que ser secundario. Para ella también soy yo secundario." [That also has to be secondary. For her I am also secondary.][16] This answer, of course does not convince Molina.

The totalizing impulse of the Marxist-signifier—that is, claiming that "I am a Marxist"—perversely erases sexuality, leaving some traces, however. For example, to bring up Valentín's girlfriend is a way in which Molina resists Marxism. Otherwise, privileging Marxist discourse over the "sexual" would welcome a repressive epistemology that dismisses all configurations of sexuality and gender, and would annihilate Molina's homosexuality. Molina's "Yes . . . " shows that he can understand Marxism, all right, but his tentative manner signals that he *does not want* to take it in and understand it. Another way to say this: a strongly "male" perspective inscribes Marxist discourse. Valentín's own words reveal this inscription of the "masculine": "*Bueno, todo me lo aguanto . . .* " *Aguantar(se)* literally means to bear, to hold on, to tolerate, to be strong, to contain (oneself); culturally, it means to be in control, to have a hold of oneself; not to fall apart; by extension, to be a "man." Valentín must suggest that Marxism enables him to bear (*aguantarse*) the torture given to him. Marxism enables him to be strong, that is, to be a man. Marxism functions, then, as a masquerade of masculinity that constantly shifts and disguises any inadequacies that Valentín perceives about his "true" Self.

Let us examine the traces and perversions of sexuality that are left after a sweeping Marxist dismissal of sexuality. If Marxism, as suggested by Valentín, can deliver us to a *plaisir,* what kind of sexual pleasure might it be? As I have discussed above, homosexuality is an excess that in its own supplementarity challenges the perversion of "compulsory asexuality" articulated by the Marxist. I say "perversion" because it is an "unhealthy" heterosexuality, full of repression, barren of pleasure. Valentín's notion of sexuality appears as the necessary, literal, and critical *absence* of sexuality; literally, because the prisoner feels that the presence of a woman is always "secondary." (Poignantly, if Valentín's "girl" is secondary: she, too, is a *supplément*. Her supplementarity can be articulated along the lines of sexuality, and also along gender.) And it is a critical absence of sexuality because Valentín's Marxist tendencies ignore or avoid its discursive importance. However, the sexual is always present; it is present even in its dismissal.

Let us try to imagine what "sexual relation" Valentín may have with Marxism. First and foremost, it is a relation that goes beyond the Self, it is not autosexual; there is the presence of the Other that gives enjoyment. This Other does not necessarily have a penis. A phallus? If the penis is replaced by a phallus, then, Valentín strokes, elevates, and excites Marxism's phallus, which endows all bearers with power. However, we all know that after such an orgasmic dissemination or circulation, the phallus, like most penises, becomes limp; consequently, more stroking is required. If this description of Valentín's sexual relation with Marxism (or Marx's "ism") sounds queer, it is. Every relation between men, that is, every institution—patriarchal institution would seem redundant—is marked by a repressed homosexual discourse; this repression delimits the "homosocial."

Valentín's subjectivity is informed by a strong homosocial behavior found in Marxism. Valentín seems to identify with the "masculine" in his ideological reading or construction of Marx; therefore, the "masculine" imprint that he finds in Marx is but a spectacular projection of the Self. Again, the copula remains empty: very much like saying "I am who I am," Valentín's subjectivity is tautological. Valentín is simply an uncritical reader of Marx. Aside from this, it is important to understand that "to be a 'man'" demands that he read in such a narrow manner: being a "revolutionary" has meant flagrantly reproducing the same gendered structures of power against which he is fighting.

Masculine Men and Anal Eroticism

All of a sudden, Valentín's affirmation of his masculinity, "*Bueno, todo me lo aguanto . . .* " explicitly states his homosexual panic as well as a homosexual desire. "I can take it all . . . " There is an innuendo in this phrase that is too provocative to go unnoticed: I am talking about the threat and the withstanding of sodomy as a way to prove contradictorily his masculinity. What defines a "man" most, according to Valentín, is his cunning and valor to "take it all," whether that "all" is torture or humiliation. Without fail, the greatest humiliation that Valentín's manhood can suffer is becoming a "woman." Additionally, castration as a threat to normative, heterosexual masculinity can be matched with the threat of sodomy. Hence, "taking it all" can be read as an act of accepting sodomy, which in turn can be interpreted as a shifting sign for masculinity. Once more, it is crucial to emphasize that masculinity can be asserted by the very act of calling it into question or threatening it.

If sodomy is too strong a sign to mark masculinity, perhaps it is best to think about a precursor, a prelude, to penetration that would be more "acceptable," say anal eroticism. Freud uses his discussion on anal eroticism to establish some masturbatory practices among children, hence, the very notion of infantile sexuality.[17] Freud locates the importance of anal eroticism as follows, "[l]ike the labial zone, the anal zone is well suited by its position to act as a medium through which sexuality may attach itself to other somatic functions."[18] Freud carefully begins his explanation of the anal zone by looking and privileging the anus's *proximity* to the genitalia— and not the anus itself—as a site of sexual activity. He impresses upon us that "[i]t is presumed that the erotogenic significance of this part of the body [the anus] is very great from the first."[19] And Freud rhetorically joins our surprise when he adds that

> We learn with some astonishment from psycho-analysis of the transmutations normally undergone by sexual excitations arising from this zone and of the frequency with which it retains a considerable amount of susceptibility to genital stimulation throughout life. The intestinal disturbances which are so common in childhood see to it that the zone shall not lack intense excitations. Intestinal catarrhs at the tenderest age make children "nervy," as people say, and in cases of later neurotic illness they have a determining influence on the symptoms in which the neurosis is expressed . . . [20]

Furthermore, Freud argues that "Children who are making use of the susceptibility to erotogenic stimulation of the anal zone betray themselves by holding back their stool till this accumulation brings about violent muscular contractions and, as it passes through the anus, is able to produce powerful stimulation of the mucous membrane. In so doing it must no doubt cause not only painful but also highly pleasurable sensations. [. . .] Educators are once more right when they describe children who keep the process back as 'naughty'." [21] Freud is skilled at relating the psychoanalytic with the commonplace: he manages to convince his readers that what psychoanalysis is promulgating can be found in the quotidian. This critical gesture does not surprise us since infantile sexuality is one of his most radical contributions. What is most interesting about the passages that I have cited—from the section entitled "[4] Masturbatory Sexual Manifestations: Activity of the Anal Zone"[22]—is Freud's shifting of his subtle and uncritical suggestion of the anal zone as a "misreading" to normal genitalia to understanding the anal zone as an erotogenic site on the order of the "normal." His tacit shift allows him to "read" the anal zone as erotogenic and to deconstruct the privileged erection of the penis as the site for "normal" sexuality. This expansion of sexuality is of paramount importance for Freud for within it he is able to begin articulating or orchestrating different possibilities of the sexual, of subjectivity. Freud writes about the body, on the body, and also from the body. For example, sexual dysfunction would then involve more activities than just impotence ("not getting it up"), but also constipation ("not getting it out"), likewise premature ejaculation or diarrhea ("getting it out too fast"). This interrelation between sexuality, language, and subjectivity produces a network of paramount gravity in Freud's *oeuvre* that underlines the conceptualization of "process" as "meaning," or further, process as identity.

In any event and along these lines, Freud uses his seductive rhetoric to establish our trust because, later, he can really surprise us:

> The contents of the bowels, which act as a stimulating mass upon a sexually sensitive portion of mucous membrane, behave like forerunners of another organ, which is destined to come into action after the phase of childhood. But they have other important meanings for the infant. They are clearly treated as a part of the infant's own body and represent his first "gift": by producing them he can express his active compliance with his environment and, by witholding them, his disobedience. From being a "gift" they later come to acquire the meaning of 'baby"—for babies, according to one of the sexual theories of children, are acquired by eating and are born through the bowels.[23]

This passage that follows immediately after the more general, previous one was added in 1915; like most of his work, we can see that, although the "original" version of "Infantile Sexuality" was written in 1905, he constantly renews and challenges his previous assumptions. This rewriting illustrates the complexity of Freud's thought.[24] What is important to see here is that Freud pushes his interpretative skills to the extreme—feces represent babies. This interpretive breach puts into motion and supports questions of free association and dream interpretation, which are central to psychoanalytic practice.

Returning to Valentín's affirmation of his masculinity, "*Bueno, todo me lo aguanto* . . . ," let us read this differently: "Well, I can hold it all . . . " I want to advance that "holding it all" (versus the earlier translation "I can take it all . . . ") describes the act of Valentín's "keep[ing] the process back," that is, it can be read as a pleasurable foreplay of anal eroticism. It is too easy and perverse to reread some of Valentín's lines. However, we must read Valentín within the anal stage for he has placed the genital stage as "secondary." His relation to genital process has been displaced as a "secondary pleasure." In a footnote as it were, Freud maintains that this is "the first occasion on which the infant has a glimpse of a hostile environment to his instinctual impulses, on which he learns to separate his own entity from this alien one and on which he carries out the first 'repression' of his possibilities of pleasure. From that time on, what is 'anal' remains the symbol of everything that is to be repudiated and excluded from life."[25] In the case of Valentín, then, sexuality has been reassigned to the anal, rather than the genital, stage. What follows from this displacement is a repression of other pleasures, primarily, the social. At the anal stage, his revolutionary struggle sounds different now. Listen again to Valentín's words, "While the struggle lasts, and it will probably last all of my life, it is not convenient for me to cultivate the pleasures of the senses—are you aware of that?—because they are truly secondary for me. The grand pleasure is another, knowing that I am at the service of the most noble, that is . . . well . . . all of my ideas . . . " The ideas of Marxism developed by Valentín can be read as a strained or, better, constrained "gift" that he is holding dearly. Holding on to his idea(l)s as an act of anal eroticism is what gives Valentín pleasure. Perhaps, this is why he cannot share his ideas and convince Molina of their value because to give them to another would mean their loss. To give up his ideas means to lose control of his body and, by extension, his subjectivity. But what does it mean to lose control? How is control lost? What happens when control is lost?

As much as I have quoted Freud so far, I have limited myself to a detailed passage of his essay on infantile sexuality. Although the argument developed in the preceding discussion seems fairly straightforward—if one can say that about Freud's complexity—the last paragraph from his analysis of the anal zone seems out of place; it appears almost extraneous: "Actual masturbatory stimulation of the anal zone by means of the finger, provoked by a centrally determined or peripherally maintained sensation of itching, is by no means rare among older children."[26] Up to this final comment, Freud has been arguing and explaining provocatively the interpretive possibilities of anal eroticism: He has raised questions about pleasure and temperament; of anxiety and its relation to the body; and, he alludes to the resolution of the Oedipal complex in his discussion of the "gift." That he leaves this final passage unexplained should be of no surprise to us; and, perhaps, this uninterpreted observation of digital play should be privileged as a opening—if you prefer, as a *coda*—to further the discussion of anal eroticism. It is good to tinker with or probe into some of the scintillating and itching questions that this closing passage presents. I want to make several observations: There is no explanation whatsoever about the meaning of anal stimulation—not only that but Freud does not know whether this stimulation is caused by an itch or that the itch is simply an excuse for something else. Moreover, by broadening the space of the sexual to include the anal zone, we can read Freud's sympathy toward male homosexuality.[27] I also want to submit that Freud's revolutionary awareness of the "sexual" connotations of the anal zone has implications not only for the homosexual, but for the heterosexual. By this, I mean, that heterosexuality has been limited or circumscribed to a topology of the genitals and reproduction. That we read heterosexuality outside the confines of reproduction alone permits the possibility of rethinking such questions as rape, domesticity, abortion, maternity leave, while it broadens our notions of fantasy, working women, surrogacy, and paternity leave. An open-minded "heterosexual" erotic imagination also allows us to understand different figurations of sexuality. And is that not Valentín's problem, not understanding other sexualities? Indeed, Valentín, whose moral rigidity constipates his developing identities, admits, "Si estamos en esta celda juntos mejor es que nos comprendamos, y yo de gente de tus inclinaciones sé muy poco." [If we are going to be in this cell together it is best that we understand each other; I know very little about people of your inclination.][28] This is a particularly important moment because not only does the Marxist express his ignorance about the homosexual but, paradoxically, the acknowledgment of ignorance itself creates a textual space of difference in which the homosexual may represent himself. Furthermore, this confession of unawareness inaugurates the writing of a central subtext in the novel, the footnotes. I want to postpone the discussion of these momentarily; it is enough to say that they are a *supplément* that addresses the etiology of homosexuality and desire. What interests me, now, is how Valentín begins accepting his own limitations and how this initial losing of control, so to speak, culminates in a terrible, yet insightful, scene that reenacts anal eroticism. My goal is to show the relation between anal eroticism and writing: how Valentín moves from being a dogmatic politician to becoming a poet, in effect, from reader to writer.

Anal Eroticism as Ecriture; or The Problem of the Digital

In chapter six of the novel, Valentín gets sick from eating poisoned food. Molina had already fallen ill and recovered from a bout of indigestion (in chapter five); now Valentín suffers from similar pains. The opening of each scene of illness is strikingly similar. First, Molina gets sick and Valentín warns him that perhaps something he ate affected him. However, Molina disregards Valentín's rather accurate hypothesis, and simply sighs, "Qué ganas de ver a mamá, hoy sí no sé qué daría por verla un rato." [How badly I want to see my mother, today I don't know what I'd give to see her awhile.][29] Unknowingly, Valentín is responsible for Molina's illness because, as we later learn, the homosexual is collaborating with the prison official to draw information from Valentín. The other scene, when Valentín falls ill, begins with a broken promise by Molina,

—Había jurado que no te iba a contar otra película. Ahora voy a ir al infierno por no cumplir la palabra.
—No te imaginás cómo me duele. Son brutales las puntadas.
—Así igual me dio a mí antes de ayer.
—Cada vez parece que me da más fuerte, Molina.
—Pero entonces tendrías que ir a la enfermería.
—No seas bruto, por favor. Ya te dije que no quiero ir.[30]

[—I had sworn that I wasn't going to tell you another movie. Now, I'm going to hell for not keeping my word.
—You can't imagine how it hurts. The pain is brutally sharp.
—That's how it hit me two days ago.
—Each time it seems that it's stronger, Molina.
—So then you should go to the infirmary.
—Don't be stupid, please. I've already told you that I don't want to go.]

"*No cumplir la palabra,*" not to keep one's promise, literally, not to fulfill the word: to narrate a film, then, represents a literary speech act. This insight has enormous repercussions in reading the novel versus the film. In the novel, when Molina narrates a film, he must remember and recreate each scene: Earlier he had explained that "[n]o, yo no invento, te lo juro, pero hay cosas que hay que redondeártelas, que las veas como las estoy viendo yo, bueno, de algún modo te las tengo que explicar." [No, I don't invent, I swear to you, but there are things that I have to give shape to them for you (*redondéartelas*), so that you can see them as I am seeing them—well!— somehow I have to explain them to you.][31] Molina is not narrating what he saw at the movie-houses but rather what he is seeing now. He wants to give Valentín a sense of what he is experiencing at the moment of narration. This is quite a different experience than the one in Hector Babenco's film because the movies that Molina narrates are presented in the movie itself, rather than "remaining" in the mind of Molina—a displacement that means that the subjectivity that is identified in the film is not necessarily that of Molina, it may be the imagination of Valentín, the director, or another who is *seeing* the Nazi propaganda film.

Molina's breaking of a promise—his recounting of another film which, in turn, is another way of talking about himself—is immediately interrupted by Valentín's complaints. So, Molina recommends that Valentín go to the infirmary. The men's attitudes about going to the infirmary are quite different: Molina is almost cavalier that he does not have to go there because "[he]'ll get better soon"; his only wish is to see his mother. Differently, Valentín is fiercely against going there since he sees the infirmary as a torture chamber where prisoners are given drugs: "Le pasó a un compañero, que lo acostumbraron [a seconal], y lo ablandaron, le quitaron la voluntad. Un preso político no debe caer a la enfermería nunca, me entendés, nunca." [It happened to a partner; they got him used to [seconal[32]], and they softened him, they stole his will. A political prisoner must never fall into the infirmary, do you understand, never.][33] The infirmary is a space of torture and, more importantly, of social and political rehabilitation. There, by continuous repetition, political prisoners are made used to (*acostumbrar*) other ways of thinking and living. It is impossible not to notice here the reemergence of the word *acostumbrar*. Valentín had used it before to accuse Molina of making him accustomed to eating well. Repetition is seen by the Marxist as a threat to subjectivity, hence Marx's "first tragedy, second comedy" statement. Of course, repetition is regarded differently by the homosexual; repetition is an affirmation of subjectivity. Remember: Molina does not have a problem with heterosexuality; as a matter of fact he wants to emulate it.

About the trope of repetition, I would like to reread it in a word: *acostumbrar(se)* means more than a mere "getting used to or accustomed to something"; it introduces the notion of repetition, hence, the ironic possibility of sameness; for Valentín, it means that such a behavior must be avoided under certain circumstances. In the strange case of the stomach pains, Valentín succeeds in making himself not seem the same as Molina. For example, the stomach pain suffered by Valentín is contrasted as quite different than Molina's. Valentín's pain is greater ("Each time it seems that it's stronger"), something else that Molina cannot understand again. Valentín's attitude to differentiate his pain from Molina's is almost infantile—it sounds like a little boy's bragging "My daddy makes more money than yours" or, "My daddy is bigger than yours." A perverse, although nonetheless asserted, restatement of this back and forth crowing would be "My penis is bigger than yours." But is it? We remember the men of Estación El Olivo's great surprise when they saw la Manuela's gargantuan penis—hers should have been small? Why it is that Valentín cannot have a pain "just like" Molina's can be explained by the whole notion of identification. The denial of sameness expressed here as an ideological contradiction (or as a lie) by Valentín is necessary to avoid the psychological nesting with the homosexual; that is, here we have yet another expression of the homosexual panic that clearly underlies the Marxist's discourse. Homosexual panic—caused, first, by a fear of losing control and, then, as a crisis of identification—is not the only way to refer to the "panic" present in Valentín's words, it is also that epistemological panic that regulates his social position as a revolutionary. Homosexuality is a difference of epistemology. *Différance* becomes, then, the epistemology of the homosexual; by this, I mean that there is another way of conceptualizing sexuality and subjectivity. How then do we read "heterosexuality"? Is it possible to "know" what it means to be a "heterosexual"?

Let us pause for a second and tie up some loose ends. First there are the different valences of panic; then, anal eroticism; and, finally, repetition and writing. In *Kiss of the Spider Woman,* heterosexual desire is a complex or fixation of these three things—panic, anal eroticism, and repetition. In one of the most traumatic scenes in the novel, Molina is recounting the story of a Latin American playboy in France when Valentín loses control:

—Y también se siente mal de haber dejado a la madre. Y todo eso se lo cuenta a la tipa. Sabés una cosa . . . nunca nunca me hablaste de tu mamá.
—Sí, como no.
—Por Dios, te lo juro, nunca nunca,
—Es que yo tengo nada que contar.
—Gracias. Te agradezco la confianza.
—¿Por qué ese tono?

—Nada, cuando te compongas hablaremos.
—Ay . . . ay . . . perdoname . . . ay . . . qué he hecho . . .
—No, con la sábana no te limpies, esperá . . .³⁴

[—And he also feels bad about leaving his mother behind. And he confesses all this to the girl. You know something . . . you never ever spoke to me about your mother.
—Yes. Of course, I did.
—In God's name, I swear it, never ever.
—It's that I have nothing to tell.
—Thank you. I appreciate your trust.
—Why that tone?
—Oh nothing, when you get better, we'll talk.
—Oh . . . oh . . . forgive me . . . oh . . . what have I done . . .
—No, don't clean yourself with the sheet, wait . . .]

This scene affords us an original moment of anal eroticism. It is not accidental that the discussion revolves around Valentín's mother when he loses control. Each man's attitude about whether Valentín has or has not told Molina about his mother shows their adamance: "you never ever spoke to me" "of course, I did" "never ever" "I have nothing . . . " This back-and-forth bickering repeats the constant struggle between both men; it is not a struggle to determine "who is telling the truth or not," but rather, a fight about whose position as Subject is more central, more valid. The response by both to Valentín's accidental fecal evacuation is equally provocative. Molina becomes practical and immediately starts to clean up and return things to order; Valentín can only wonder "what have I done." His response can be read both ways: as a surprise, a shock of his (mis)behavior, as well as a literal questioning. "What have I done" radically calls into question his subjective integrity; it also casts doubt on his availability "to read" the event. To cite Barbara Johnson again: "[t]he surprise of otherness is that moment when a new form of ignorance is activated as an imperative."³⁵ The importance of this scene of anal eroticism is that it forces Valentín to reevaluate his positionality. That is, when Valentín is caught up in the urgency of a process that literally evacuates him of his subjectivity—the shit stains and interferes with his sense of integrity—he becomes alienated from himself. This accident opens up for Valentín a space of wonder, of Otherness.

I stated earlier that it was not by accident that Valentín was resisting conversation about his mother when he defecated; this assertion was made because without delay after being cleaned up, Valentín begins talking about his mother, "una mujer muy ... dificil" [a woman, a very ... difficult woman] who "siente que todo lo que tiene se lo merece, la familia de ella tiene dinero, y cierta posición social" [feels that she deserves everything she owns, [since] her family has money and a certain social position.][36] Valentín, though in disagreement with his mother, identifies unconsciously with her strength, with her dogmatism. I speculate that his question, "what have I done," ventriloquizes his mother's accusation of his lifestyle as a revolutionary, that is, her reproach "what have *you* done." Certainly, anal eroticism enables Valentín to talk about his mother, better yet, to talk *as* his own mother would, thus revealing "negative" Oedipal desire.[37]

What is absolutely fascinating in *Kiss of the Spider Woman* is that Valentín becomes "disconcerted" after remembering his family romance, and asks Molina to finish the film about the playboy. We learn that the playboy's father is kidnapped and he must return to his home country; he makes a deal with the guerrilla members who have kidnapped his father and his father is liberated, but then killed anyway. The French girlfriend follows the playboy back to his country, but she cannot stay with him there because each belongs to a "different world." End of story.[38] Not really. Molina then remembers a pertinent detail: "y me olvidé decirte que cuando al final lo sueltan al padre hay un tiroteo con la policía, y lo hieren de muerte al padre, y la madre reaparece, y quedan juntos, el hijo y la madre te quiero decir, porque la otra mujer no, la que lo quiere se vuelve a Paris." [and I forgot to tell you that at the end when they release the father there is a shooting with the police, and the father is fatally wounded, and the mother reappears, and they remain together, the son and the mother, that is, because the other woman didn't stay, the one who loved him returns to Paris.][39] I am most interested in the precipitous manner in which Molina retells the end of the story when the playboy's mother returns. The awkward and hurried syntax seems to recuperate more than just the true ending of the story. I want to reconsider Molina's outpouring of words as an outrage against Valentín's anal eroticism and, also, as itself another scene of anal eroticism—in other words, there exists a direct relationship between anal eroticism and *écriture*. Let me begin by saying that the narrated film's family romance is different from Valentín's. In Molina's film, we have a positive Oedipal construct, that is, (as in Sophocles's myth itself) the father dies and the son remains blindly with his mother. The son takes the reconciliatory position with and as the father, which is different from what Valentín did. Valentín is uninterested in being with the mother because of their social disagreement, but this disagreement nonetheless structures and signifies on his identification with and as the mother. That the "homosexual" man articulates the positive Oedipal, thus reaffirming heterosexual centrality and that the "heterosexual" performs the negative Oedipal (where the son wants to be like the mother to seduce the father) is important here because it shows brilliantly Puig's understanding of the *complex* and its implications in the construction of gender. In other words, each man speaks unconsciously the language of the other.

If we accept Freud and that "what is 'anal' remains the symbol of everything that is to be repudiated and excluded from life," then what is "anal" must also be repressed and controlled outside the body. For Valentín, the uncontrolled release of the feces, or the "gift," symbolizes more than just the pestilence of his penal condition, the feces come to represent and to remind him of his attachment to his mother; they also represent the "messiness" of language—the "arbitrariness of the sign," to recall a cliché. Tellingly, the release itself gives significance to the difficulty of pinning down a tightly articulated subject, and performs and deconstructs the illusion of "control."

Speaking about control, I am still troubled by an earlier quotation in which Freud observes that "[a]ctual masturbatory stimulation of the anal zone *by means of the finger* . . . is by no means rare among older children." I want to revisit this line by asking, what is the finger doing? Whose finger—or, perhaps, whose hand—is under there?

The word "digital" means literally something pertaining to or involving the finger; it is also related to the act of counting. Technological advances have specialized the meaning of "digital," referring to a technique of copying a wavelength and marking it to reproduce an exact, discrete copy of an original; indeed, it is a process of exact repetition or duplication. "Digital" reminds me also of a type of communication, the telegraph as digital writing. With this in mind, it is easy to read Freud's observation thus: masturbatory stimulation of the anal zone is a digital event. For the masturbating child, the finger represents the possibility of repetition and reproduction; the finger is the fantasy of a penis. This metaphor can be taken further: like the writer who dips the pen into the inkwell, the child uses the finger to write the Self—and others.

It is not surprising to learn that only after Valentín has released his furious attack against his mother, can he then begin to write; he ceases to maintain the "controlled" notion of subjectivity, and escapes into the dream world of writing.[40]

Messy Boys

I have argued that the question and representation of heterosexuality in the text should not be reduced merely to a shifter that undoes homosexual desire, for not only is heterosexuality often complicated by its own instability *qua* dogmatism, it is something that is in and of itself resisted. Let us say, then, that there is another kind of "panic" for Valentín: heterosexual panic. The panic of heterosexuality displayed in giving women a "secondary" position in Valentín's life will help us locate and define the importance that the construct "woman" has in the text, a construction that we have already seen expressed in Valentín's desires and dreams: *"una mujer europea, una mujer inteligente, una mujer hermosa, una mujer con conocimientos de política internacional, una mujer con conocimientos del marxismo,"* and so on. [*a European woman, an intelligent woman, a beautiful woman, a woman with an understanding of international politics, a woman with knowledge of Marxism* . . .][41]

The different valences or manifestations of "panic" provide the text's complexity, which I insist on calling "messiness." Earlier I mentioned that the prisoners constantly fought and that this fighting was not necessarily to establish who was right or wrong, but rather to decide who controls the conditions of discourse. Sometimes the conversations are reflexive and subtle; other times, brutal. Like a "true" intellectual, Valentín insists that all discussions be made with a level of dignity and intellectual rigor. This attitude is certainly motivated by his confidence and conviction in the "scientific method" that defines and is defined by Marxist thought. While Molina may want a simple conversation, Valentín will not have it. This "rigor" strangely explicates some of the unaccounted and unresolved contradictions found in Valentín's position. Interestingly, we can begin to see that his theoretical method itself veils or screens some of these contradictions. And here, I am referring to the most obvious contradiction, the presence of Molina, and to the not-so-obvious breaks in Valentín's logic. Notwithstanding, Molina's "messy" discussion ("por las ramas"[42]) bothers Valentín. The Marxist is disturbed by the different ways they talk about things. This difference is not simply ideological but rhetorical, which are related modes because the *ideological* program of Valentín depends on a *rhetorical* contract between himself and others. Not agreeing to such a contract (or linguistic/literary pact) disables the seductive power of Marxism. We are reminded of an earlier question: Can you negotiate with the Other in a language other than its own? Indeed the discursive and political matrix laid down by Marxism is needed for a dialogue between Molina and the heterosexual.

Another structure that governs the (possibility of) dialogue between the prisoners is the heterosexual matrix that fixes the limits of the binarisms male/female, masculine/feminine, politics/pleasure, where the "important" first term negates the second; it is an important relational structure because within it we are able to find the "woman" (the Spider Woman) in the text. Valentín tells us that his girlfriend was always a "revolutionary," that she initially formed part of the sexual revolution. He adds that, although she came for a well-to-do family, she spent her childhood and youth destroyed by her parents' fighting:

—Su padre engañaba [a su madre] al no decirle que necesitaba de otras relaciones. Y la madre se dedicó a criticarlo delante de la hija, se dedicó a ser víctima. Yo no creo en el matrimonio, en la monogamia más precisamente.
—Pero qué lindo cuando una pareja se quiere toda la vida.[43]

[—Her father deceived her mother by not telling her that he needed other relationships. And the mother dedicated herself to criticizing him in front of the daughter, she dedicated herself to becoming a victim. I don't believe in matrimony, more precisely, in monogamy.
—But how beautiful when a couple loves each other their entire life.]

Although the "feminine" is restrained as the (dis)articulation of the "masculine," a unique "feminine" eloquence, which resembles "feminism," can be heard in this exchange, if only as an echo. Valentín suggests that the "origin" of the girlfriend's revolutionary activities is her dysfunctional family, with a cheating father and a nagging mother. By joining the "sexual revolution" she resolves or escapes the family problems. It is significant to underline that what is meant by "sexual revolution" is an inchoate feminism. Historically and socially, the sexual revolution is characterized by sexual freedom and permissiveness; so, in becoming part of this "revolution," Valentín's girlfriend is simply duplicating the promiscuous behavior of her father.[44] It seems strange then that Valentín, who does not believe in monogamy, would be so bothered by his girlfriend's unscrupulous activity. Now there are too many conflicting ideologies and poses available to rendering a precise portrait of Valentín, who previously had declared himself, in one word, a Marxist. The self-naming is too dogmatic, hence too unstable. Going back to the issue of "heterosexual panic," we cannot help but notice Valentín's misgivings about marriage: his reluctance to accept marriage (read: institutionalized heterosexuality), specifically monogamy (perversely read: heterosexuality), signals latent queer desires and narratives that have been culturally and socially attributed to the homosexual—and confirms the unnatural demands of heterosexual constructs.

I do not want to make this point casually. Valentín begins talking about his girlfriend on the condition beforehand of changing her name. He uses the pseudonym of "Jane Randolph," one of the stars of a movie that Molina has been narrating. The substitution of names protects her identity in case the prison officials want to extort the name from Molina. This switching of names also changes narrators. Now, Valentín has taken the place of Molina, thus creating a complicated discursive economy. Valentín's retelling of the new "Jane Randolph"'s family romance is highly impersonal, thus producing a text that is (dis)affected like Molina's movie narratives. Interestingly, it is during his repetition of the failed "family romance" that Valentín reveals a subjectivity outside the ideological imposition of Marxism: "I don't believe in matrimony, more precisely, in monogamy." It is perhaps banal—and too late—to even mention that the heterosexual repeats the insubordination of marriage and monogamy that has been Homerically attributed to the homosexual subjects; once again, the inversion of terms problematizes heterosexual subjectivity. It is interesting to hear what Puig himself has to say about the institution of heterosexuality:

> En la novela (*The Buenos Aires Affair*) hay descripciones sobre la práctica de la sexualidad con el propósito de desmitificar todo lo que hay de tenebroso, de tabú en la sexualidad. Yo creo que la sexualidad es la inocencia misma. Mientras haya respeto de la pareja, no hay perversidad. Leí mucho de lo último que se ha investigado sobre esto, porque esas son las zonas del comportamiento humano que se querían dejar en la penumbra, así deliberadamente, en las tinieblas totalmente para que asustase y la gente actuase a ciegas. Saber más a qué corresponden nuestros impulsos. Para mí, por ejemplo, me parece una monstrosidad el casamiento de una virgen, como era de rigor, esa unión "para siempre" de dos seres que no sabían si se iban a complementar bien.[45]

> [In the novel (*The Buenos Aires Affair*) there are descriptions about sexual practice with the intention of demystifying everything dark, the taboo in sexuality. I believe that sexuality is innocence itself. While there is respect between a couple, there is no perversity. I have read a lot on the latest research on this because those are the areas of human behavior that people want kept in the dark, almost deliberately in the shadows so that it would be frightening and people would act blindly. To know more to what our impulses (cor)respond. To me, for example, the marriage of a virgin, which

used to be *de rigeur,* seems a monstrosity—that union "forever" of two beings who did not know if they were going to complement each other.]

Although Puig is speaking about a different novel, there are some interesting commentaries that can be elaborated from this passage to contrast to the heterosexual's preoccupations. First, we notice the importance that Puig places on sexuality and its unknowing. Puig's interest in the perversity of sexuality and the monstrosity of virginity stresses that sexual performance is more important in subject formation, rather than in the labels "heterosexual" and "homosexual," which are empty, incapable of informing the reader of the sexual practice of the subject. In other words and to echo Butler, to say that I am a "heterosexual" says little or nothing about my subjectivity, but to say that I enjoy certain practices (or fantasies) with certain people addresses specific issues about the configuration of the semantic field of the "I" and the deployment of that "I": power, gender construction, desire, and the like. This means that when Molina, as a gay man desiring to achieve the traditional heterosexual aphorism, says "But how beautiful when a couple loves each other their entire life," he is somehow articulating a desire to be a heterosexual or, at least, like a heterosexual. Already a "problematic" category. The "homosexual, with feminine fixations," thus, begins to embody a complex of contradictions that parallels those of the "heterosexual" in the novel.

It would be commonplace to discuss sexuality and gender in *Kiss of the Spider Woman* and to look at Molina as the character that assumes both the "masculine" and the "feminine" in the text. I have resisted taking such a route because such a reading is too facile, too wrong. The construction of gender and sexual desire is far too complex to be so mechanical in reading *Kiss of the Spider Woman*. A reading of the construction and contradictions of heterosexuality is perhaps more interesting. Certainly, a reading of male heterosexuality signifies on the complexity of narrative through the end of the novel. A dying Valentín becomes the storyteller:

> . . . no puede moverse, ahí en lo más espeso de la selva está atrapada, en una tela de araña, o no, la telaraña le crece del cuerpo de ella misma, de la cintura y las caderas le salen los hilos, es parte del cuerpo de ella [. . .], no, está llorando, o no, está sonriendo pero se le resbala una lágrima por la máscara, "¿una lágrima que brilla como diamante?"[46]

> [. . . she cannot move, there she is trapped in the thickness of the jungle, in a spiderweb, or no, the spiderweb grows from her own body, the threads come

out from her waist and her hips, the web is part of her body [. . .], no, she is crying, or no, she is smiling but a tear runs down her mask, "a tear that shines like a diamond?"]

Although delirious under the influence of morphine, Valentín struggles to tell us one last narrative to make time and life go by easier. Unfortunately, his fantastic narrative of the Spider Woman, like his earlier one of Marxism (and gender), does and undoes itself. Valentín wants to tell a particular story but he cannot because it is he who is trapped in the web of the narrative. He is the spider woman.

Scattered Notes on Homosexuality

The question of the subject constantly troubles the reader of *Kiss of the Spider Woman* because it is not as simple as any cavalier reading would render it. Turning to the other subject in the novel, Molina's subjectivity—as I began to show—is equally complex. As narrator of classical Hollywood films, he can be seen as a translator or interlocutor of the cinematic frame into written text. Nevertheless, I am afraid that once more this assigned role of the "homosexual" with an obsession for Hollywood divas is too facile and reductive to describe Molina. How do we read Molina's homosexuality *outside* the "diva drama"-filled movie theater, *outside* of Hollywood? I want to explore further whether or not we can read the "homosexual question" *outside* the Oedipal drama?[47]

Although I will argue later that the fracture (a catachresis) in the Oedipal triangle facilitates the (double) articulation of a transvestite figure, a reading of male homosexuality *outside* Oedipal complex—although, such a project is not without grounds—remains virtually impossible in *Kiss of the Spider Woman*. I imagine that Puig struggled with the same question; signs of this interrogation are found abstrusely in the layerings of gender with sexual orientation and sexual practice; explicitly, in the footnotes. Without a doubt the incorporation of these footnotes that deal so proficiently with the issue of homosexuality and its debates produces a dialectic between them and the "main" text.[48]

Dennis Altman's work—one of the historians or critics of sexuality in the footnotes[49]—has been popular among Latin American gay intellectuals in the seventies and even today; many readers of Altman have used his *Homosexuality, Oppression and Liberation* as a kind of initiation into the gay rights' movements throughout Latin America. So, an awareness of Altman's writing well informs a reader (or locates the writer) of *Kiss of the Spider*

Woman in the context of a gay political debate. On one level, Puig uses the footnote as a literal sub-text that conflates the textual (inside) and political (outside); on another level, Puig locates and privileges in the footnote the deconstruction of an inside/outside binary. This symbiotic relationship established by the author, to use such an "academic" figure as the footnote to supplement—or, better, as *supplément* to—his "popular" writing, parallels (although, inversely, in this case) Puig's shift of popular culture *as* high culture in his work.[50] In this instance, we could say that the "high" (academic) literary form takes the place *within*—not *of*, as if it fails to subvert—the "popular" context. Undoubtedly the terminology itself—"popular," "high," "heterosexual," and the like—becomes useless to describe the process of recontextualization.

I am thinking about the "glossary," another textual "supplement" that functions similarly to the footnote. The glossary has been used by many Latin American authors to supply fundamental information and vocabulary in the *novelas de la tierra* (Spanish American regionalist novels); however, the footnote is a much more radical literary device than the glossary. The footnote takes on a different process of signification than the glossary within the novel. I would argue that the glossary serves as an archetypal screen that, like the prison walls, delimits the mobility of language. Puig's footnotes become an "unconscious" (always there influencing and substantiating an "event," although not always being read fully) that deconstructs the main text's conscious effort to ignore.

By defining both the "homosexual" and the "footnotes" as *supplément*, I do not want to risk proposing that homosexuality is performed as somehow a "footnote" to heterosexuality (the "main" text); if anything, the converse could be easily argued, that heterosexuality is an excess that "bothers"—to use one of Valentín's favorite words—homosexuality: By insisting on its own centrality, heterosexuality becomes the "supporting" structure or "piece of evidence" that argues and maintains a particular design of the "homosexual." Inverting the terms can be fun, but can also be petty. I made a very conscious effort to rethink and deploy "heterosexuality" as an unstable notion for the sheer reason that it occupies such a dominant, Symbolic role in our cultures. That dominance often goes unquestioned, freely flattering its own centrality. Furthermore, discussions about the origin of homosexuality (which is really what is debated in the infamous footnotes) are tiresome: To care where homosexuality "really comes from" repeatedly lies at the heart of a homophobic act of displacing it, of putting it back. That is why the Oedipal complex can be so limiting to the discussion of sexual orientation; already hetero-/homo-sexuality as well as gender are moments of identification within the complex; furthermore, what comes after that very moment of identification, the here and now, must be theorized.

Now, following the discussion of the footnotes as a space for the debate about different theories of homosexuality, the debate itself suggests a performance. Homosexuality is constructed in *Kiss of the Spider Woman* as an anxiety of authority, of authorship. In other words, the footnotes, rather than establishing a synthesis of the different positions regarding the "homosexual question" where the most "powerful" theory wins, the motion of the competing homosexualities generates an anxiety about the unavailability of a singular, totalizing theory. That is why I would like to investigate the "homosexual question" as an autobiographical trope: as its "eccentricity" produces the subject, it also, replaces the subject. Molina does not simply define his homosexuality by the "shame" that he feels because of his "crime," nor by the embarrassment it causes his mother, nor by his desire to find that perfect man, nor by his desire to be a *dama burguesa,* a bourgeois lady; but, instead, his gay persona is constituted by all of these "moments."

Perhaps one of the most obvious yet most ignored aspects of the novel is its "dialogic" style. The novel could be seen as an extended drama or a film script; both of these genres are applicable and feasible. However, I would like to underline a feature of the dialogue; that is, it presents and stresses a very "strong" subject. Whether Molina and Valentín are describing a scene from a film or talking about themselves, direct speech creates a theatrical illusion of intimacy between the prisoners and the readers. Moreover, it allows for the articulation of an autobiographical "I;" for example, "Look, that's how I am . . ." I want to argue that this autobiographical "I" permits a new reading of gay subjectivity, for it gives Molina a personal eloquence or fluency with which to talk about himself—different from the more "scientific" discussions of homosexuality. The autobiographical "I" presented in the novel is presumably—although, not necessarily—"more fictional" than the one we find, say, in José Vasconcelos's *Ulises criollo* or elsewhere in Spanish American autobiography. For example, by reading Valentín's "I" as an autobiographical gesture, we could nicely apply what Sylvia Molloy says about self-figuration and national identity to the character of Valentín:

> The "I" speaks from more than one place. Reliance on either view—the text as national essence or national allegory—cuts critical reflection short instead of encouraging it and channels the text into one exclusive reading. What

seems more profitable, instead, is to allow the preoccupation with national identity (undeniably present in Spanish American self-writing) to reverberate in the text as an ever renewed scene of crisis necessary to the *rhetoric* of self-figuration; to see it as a critical space, fraught with the anxiety of origins and representation, within which the self stages its presence and achieves ephemeral unity.[51]

The reader can see clearly the relevance that a critical staging of the autobiographical "I" has to reading Valentín's nationalism. More advantageous still would be to discern and imply what Molloy calls a "scene of crisis" in (as) the self-writing of the homosexual. Here, I would like to turn to the question of Puig's own homosexuality. Although it is no great secret that Puig was gay, it was often rarely talked about beyond "gossip." It would be simplistic to guess that the author was gay because he had such an interest with the homoerotic in his work, or flatly because Molina is Puig's alter ego. However, the latter point can be made rather successfully. In the text of the novel in 1976, Valentín tells Molina that his girlfriend is twenty-four years old. Two years younger than he. To which Molina replies, "Thirteen younger than I."[52] Four years later, Puig adapts the novel into a play; this same scene remains in the play but now Molina comments, "Thirteen younger than I—no, I lied—seventeen years younger."[53] This revision seems to suggest that the homosexual got older and the heterosexual and his girlfriend remained the same age. A provocative interpretation of this "update" would be that the author confirms the status of the "ageless heterosexual"—heterosexuality remains permanently the same, it does not change. In any event, in the novel the homosexual is thirty-seven; in the play, forty-one years old. It is not surprising to learn that Puig himself was thirty-seven in 1969, a remarkable year at the global scale. And in 1973 at forty-one, Puig personally "had felt some hostility from the Peronista Government and [he] left, thinking that it would be for a few months. Four years went by and [he] still ha[d] not returned. A bit later [his] novel *Buenos Aires Affair* was banned, and it became clear that there were problems with the regime. [He] settled in Mexico, where [he] wrote that fourth novel, *El beso de la mujer araña*."[54] It is not by accident that the author's autobiographical moments of political repression, persecution, and exile can be traced literally over the aging Molina. The trope of the scene of writing is an exile; to write about his own homosexuality necessitates that Puig write it outside the Self, with somewhat jarring and limiting stereotypes, always approaching the configuration of a gay subject, never fully realizing it.

In her study about Spanish-American autobiography, Molloy proposes the term autobiographeme, to mean "recurring units that would signify in a manner sufficiently stable so as to establish, if not a model for autobiography, a continuity in autobiographical discourse."[55] Homosexuality, then, is an autobiographeme that, when used to represent the Self, becomes a central and regulating epistemology. The situation of the Self within/as the autobiographeme of homosexuality represents the spectacular configuration of the "closet" and its exit. More importantly, the shifting between moments of critical awareness decide the personal and/or political sensibility of the gay subject. In the following pages I would like to look closer at specific moments (or "events") to see how Molina's homosexuality confirms and subverts political affiliations as well as personal filiations.

Foucault postulated that "[b]y speaking about it [sex] so much, by discovering it multiplied, partitioned off, and specified precisely where one had placed it, what one was seeking essentially was simply to conceal sex: a screen-discourse, a dispersion-avoidance."[56] To speak about sex in this context produces up to a certain point the illusion of a discourse that is true. In other words, any articulation (or confession) about sex—if sex is possible to represent—performs a rupture from that tendency to "conceal" sex; this sexual representation conjures up the spirit of truth, thus giving it a soul, a signified. In other words, a confession of sex symbolizes its baptism and purification; to talk about sex or to confess produces a "pure" discourse of the sexual. Furthermore, confession and discussion gives "sex" an objective nature; paradoxically, sex becomes de-sexualized when it is submitted to a whole series of scientific, moral, and political discourses. We could say that talking about sex can only be done inadvertently. Sexual truth can only reveal itself accidentally, never completely. Perhaps, sex, like truth, can only be found in the dark, as a function of ignorance or blindness: was this what Paul de Man meant by "insight"?

I am interested in the relationship between sex and confession. This relation could not be clearer than in the case of homosexuality. "To come out of the closet" offers us an interesting discursive model to examine confession—both its liberatory and terrorist aspects. Let us speculate: what does it mean to confess one's sexual desire in order to operate within a gay or lesbian context? This utterance "I am gay" that facilitates inclusion is also an act of exclusion, because "to confess" has traditionally meant "to ask for forgiveness." What does it mean that lesbians and gays have to "confess" their desire as an act of authorization? And, moreover, what does it mean that their confession reminds us of a search for an excuse from another? Foucault notes that

> The confession is a ritual of discourse in which the speaking subject is also the subject of the statement; it is also a ritual that unfolds within a power relationship, for one does not confess without the presence (or virtual presence) of a partner who is not simply the interlocutor but the authority who requires the confession, prescribes and appreciates it, and intervenes in order to judge, punish, forgive, console, and reconcile; a ritual in which the truth is corroborated by the obstacles and resistances it has had to surmount in order to be formulated; and finally a ritual in which the expression alone, independently of its external consequences, produces intrinsic modifications in the person who articulates it: it exonerates, redeems, and purifies him; it unburdens him of his wrongs, liberates him, and promises him salvation.[57]

Foucault is right; we learn to talk about sex *in other words;* rarely do or can we confront the subject directly since we have constructed a system of communication for sex, a science of sexuality. We do not speak about sex, but rather speak about how to talk about it.

Back to the question of confession and homosexuality, how does the notion of confession pervert gay identity? To say "I am gay"—those three words that seem to connote a discrete, inherent characteristic of a locutor function once again as a search for acceptance, for penance—to say "I am gay" says little about who I am. Gay subjectivity obviously suffers before this inscribed violence in and of confession. Especially within the social context of "machismo," to hide, rather than say those three words, appears to be an "easier" and "safer" project. I do not want to suggest so narrowly that a gay man or a lesbian should not affirm his or her sexuality however he or she pleases; what I want to uncover are strategies to define gay experience *outside the judgement boundaries of confession and the identity politics that follow confessional modes.* I am interested in the autobiographical moment and how it is performed and recorded. How can autobiography be subversive? What are the relational boundaries between confession and performativity? These questions regarding how the structure of confession signifies on sexuality are central not only to the project at hand but to the larger effort of writing a "history of sexuality" in Latin America: since (homo)sexual discourse is largely suppressed, where, then, we locate voices of sexual (and gender) difference to write that history becomes an imperative.

To clarify let us go back to the prisoners: after Valentín has explained to Molina why he cannot "live the moment" and how Marxism enables him to endure many hardships, Molina feels slighted and complains that he shared his food, and that Valentín just threw the favor back in his face.

Valentín just says that Molina is "demasiado sensible" [too sensitive].[58] Their "domestic" squabble prominently distinguishes and elucidates both men's sensibilities: Valentín, preoccupied with the "distant" repercussions that eating may have on his life's struggle; Molina, upset over the deprivation of the senses. What is of interest is Molina's assertion ("this is how I am"), for he explains that "things hurt [him]." Of those things that hurt him are Valentín's words. Molina takes Valentín's verbal abuse as a literal slap in the face. This exchange shows the degree to which the gay man sees the force and performance of language; for him, language is not merely for communication. Language for Molina is the stuff of which dreams are made, of which fantasy becomes reality, of an uncontrollable force (a speech act) that cannot be reduced, but that is dynamic. The argument continues with an elaboration of Molina's excessive sensitivity,

—Qué le vas a hacer, soy así, muy sentimental.
—Demasiado. Eso es cosa . . .
—¿Por qué te callás?
—Nada.
—Decílo, yo sé lo que ibas a decir, Valentín.
—No seas sonso.
—Decílo, que soy como una mujer ibas a decir.
—Sí.
—¿Y qué tiene de malo ser blando como una mujer? ¿por qué un hombre o lo que sea, un perro, o un puto, no puede ser sensible si se le antoja?
—No sé, pero al hombre ese exceso le puede estorbar.
—¿Para qué?, ¿para torturar?
—No, para acabar con los torturadores.
—Pero si todos los hombres fueran como las mujeres no habría torturadores.
—¿Y vos qué harías sin hombres?
—Tenés razón. Son unos brutos pero me gustan.[59]

[—What are you going to do about it, that's how I am, very sentimental.
—Extremely. That's for . . .
—Why do you stop?
—Nothing.
—Say it, I know what you were going to say, Valentín.
—Don't be dumb.
—Say it, you were going to say that I am like a woman.
—Yes.

—And what's wrong with being soft like a woman? Why can't a man or whatever, a dog or a faggot, what can't he be sensitive if he feels like it?
—I don't know, but for men that excess may get in the way.
—What for? For torturing?
—No, to end with torturers.
—But if all men were like women there wouldn't be any torturers.
—And what would you do without men?
—You're right. They are brutes but I like them.]

This is one of the most "messy" and difficult passages in the text because it laces different questions of "masculinity" and "femininity," sexual orientation and performance, erotic imagination and sexual practices, while it (dis)articulates a theory of homosexuality that serves as a counterpoint to those theories presented in the footnotes. Here the heterosexual warns, at the same time that the homosexual accepts, that he is acting like a woman. However, more than just a representation of the gay man is made here, the differentiation of the sexes along the lines of the emotional is also established: "women" are sensitive, they perpetuate an excess; for insensitive "men," this excess is a nuisance, it gets in the way. Again, Valentín assures us that "sensitivity"/"femininity" is a *supplément*. On the one hand, the negation of the "excess" paradoxically defines "masculinity"; I say "paradoxically" here because classical psychoanalytic theory has taught us that the negation of the penis, what is essential, defines woman. On the other hand, the deployment of that "excess" clothes the homosexual. In both cases, though, the figuration of "woman" is being used, which makes for a problematic and misogynistic relationship to define both male hetero- and homosexuality. To avoid such a troublesome construction of the homosexual, it behooves us to try possibly to understand the gay male subjectivity in his terms, outside the binary "male"/"female."

Let us turn to the psychoanalytic mechanics of how Molina's subjectivity relates to the Oedipal complex. Within the frame of the "negative" Oedipal complex, Molina's mother becomes the "feminine" figure with whom he can identify, the men with whom he identifies in writing himself into his narratives are phantasmagoric. "Positive" Oedipal identification requires a father (or a father figure), which in this case has been absented *a priori*. So the relationship of the positive and negative Oedipal identifications that constitute the complex are always incomplete. The *nom-du-père* is erased, creating a lawless subject, the homosexual. The argument that can be made against such a calculated construct would be that the gay man's fantasies for a "perfect partner" signifies on the ever-lasting quest for the father, as Puig suggested in his interview. But the loss of the "original" father calls for a greater intervention and manifestation of the Symbolic (to replace the lost father), as well as awakens a greater desire to know the Real. There is a fracture in Molina's Oedipal triangle; the absent father reifies the positive Oedipal. Hence, I am arguing that transvestism, or "acting like a woman," permits the child to (ex)change gender so as to make the Oedipal triangle complete, to repair that fracture. Another way of saying this, Molina can affirm his incestuous love for his mother; his absent father facilitates the process of maternal identification. What is striking here is the shame that Molina acknowledges—even, insists upon—that he has brought to his mother. It is important to understand that his shame is not referring or limited to the realization of the incest taboo for this aspect of the positive Oedipal is often a source of blindness: incest remains consciously unknown, denied. Molina's shame is a certain result of his homosexuality. Shame must be read as the *objet petit a,* an elusive surplus or a rhetorical articulation of difference within the space of sameness, homosexual desire. We have a particular instance here where the construction of male homosexuality is reduced to a "man who is 'like a woman'," hence this construction conjures up the importance of epistemological difference; the homosexual as transvestite permits a virtual representation of the negative Oedipal, through which the gay man identifies with the mother figure and establishes a male love-object, the father. It is significant that in the case of Molina, the negative manifestation of the complex in the classical sense will remain fully *un*realized, given that the father is already absent; however, what the absence of the father does (perversely) explain is the search for that idealized, aestheticized, and "perfect partner" that lives in Molina's fantasies. Molina's desire impacts our definition of fantasy: it is not simply desire, but rather fantasy is the act of being caught desiring. Fantasy involves more than a child witnessing the primal scene; it requires that the child get caught in the act of fantasy as the struggle to reconstruct the event of the primal scene.

While a full description of the Oedipal complex advances etiological and psychoanalytic dimensions of the question of male homosexuality, to wit, the unique (mis)representation of the homosexual as a transvestite (in the specific case of Molina), the complex fails to derive an adequate epistemological paradigm beyond that of attributing an already essentialist "femininity" to the homosexual man.[60] In other words, the homosexual's subjectivity when reduced to "a man who is *like* a woman" can only be captured and defined as that of a "woman"'s subjectivity—with all the dangers that category implies. This reductive move avoids difficult questions of the complexity of fractured gender identity and sexual fantasy.

Sexuality and Autobiography

Puig seems to suggest the impossibility of theory to define homosexuality from the outset. We might remember that the first footnote in which he addresses D. J. West's discussion of three theories of the "physical origin of homosexuality"[61] follows Valentín's statement of his own ignorance regarding homosexuality, "yo de gente de tus inclinaciones sé muy poco" [I know very little about people of your inclinations.][62] The footnote on West's work, of course, seems superfluous since Puig writes that the researcher "*refutes* all three [theories]"[63] What follows in the main text, however, is Molina telling Valentín about meeting the love of his life, and it is an "autobiographical" alternative to the discussion of homosexuality in the footnotes. This is a major *split* in the text's narrative. Valentín's ignorance—"I know very little about people of your inclinations"—is answered in two ways. On the one hand, Valentín's ignorance is answered by West's discussions on homosexuality and, on the other hand, by Molina's personal story about falling in love. It is this autobiographical moment that I find most challenging and central to the writing of a history of Latin American sexualities.

Earlier I mentioned reading the subversive intent of autobiography. Paul de Man argues "that the distinction between fiction and autobiography is not an either/or polarity but that it is an *undecidable*." He continues with a question "But is it possible *to remain* [. . .] *within an undecidable situation?*"[64] In *Kiss of the Spider Woman,* homosexuality functions explicitly as that "undecidable situation" to which de Man alludes; however, the dilemma that homosexuality presents is not a simple question of "coming out" or not, but rather homosexuality is a presence that becomes a sort of radical otherness that cannot be fully expressed in the text, hence the need for footnotes. Furthermore and as we have seen, homosexuality introduces that destabilizing element that deconstructs any either/or polarity. The autobiographeme of homosexuality empties any pretension on the part of the heterosexual to absolute authorship (or authority), that is, Valentín's claim to originality or to control the prison-house of language.

At no time is this homosexual autobiographical presence more striking in its deconstructive power than in the touching moment when the gay man recounts his visit to the restaurant where he met that "perfect" lover. I should mention immediately that this beloved man is "straight"; Molina will try to convince him of the possibility of love between them but "con la amistad de él me conformé." [his friendship was enough for me.][65] Furthermore, an analysis between Molina and his "perfect" lover, a waiter, can be done along the lines of class difference that only increases their incompatibility socially. I will not go into the richly intricate retelling of the encounter and the relation between Molina and his nameless subject, except to highlight some important moments in this particular narrative.

What a wonderful moment when Valentín asks what the other man's name is and Molina replies, "Es lo único de él que me puedo guardar, adentro mío, en la garganta lo tengo, y me lo guardo para mí. No lo suelto. . . ." [(His name) is the only thing that I can keep to myself, inside me, I have his name in my throat, and I keep it for me. I will not release it. . . .][66] Molina zealously protects the identity of the perfect lover, although ironically it slips out just before falling asleep and, again later, in the official investigation following Molina's release we learn that his name is Gabriel Armando Solé. In any event, it is important that the homosexual initially keeps the other man's name to himself for such privacy enables and continues the gay man's fancy. By this I mean that the perfect man cannot have a name because, to some degree, he becomes idealized in the Molina's description:

> —Al verlo por segunda vez me pareció más lindo todavía, con una casaca blanca de cuello blanca de cuello Mao que le quedaba divina. Era un galán de película. Todo en él era perfecto, el modo de caminar, la voz ronquita pero por ahí con una tonadita tierna, no sé como decirte, ¡y el modo de servir! Mirá, eso era un poema, una vez le vi servir una ensalada, que me quedé pasmada.[67]
>
> [—When I saw him a second time, he was still more precious, wearing a white jacket with a Mao collar that fit him divinely. He was a leading man. All about him was perfect, his way of walking, the low voice that had also a tender tone, I don't know what to say, and his way of serving! Listen, it was a poem, once I saw him serve a salad that left me breathless (*pasmada*).]

The salad as poetry comparison makes one snigger. But seriously, this hyperbole makes the reader suspicious of the gay man's claim and account. That the homosexual refers to the star-quality of the waiter, that the love of his life is a "leading man," makes us suspect that the perfect lover is merely cast in another of his fantastic narratives. Nonetheless it is here that de Man's more extensive definition of autobiography mysteriously captures the narrative structure and desire found within the prison walls: "Autobiography, then, is not a genre or a mode, but a figure of reading or of understanding that occurs, to some degree, in all texts. The autobiographical moment happens as an alignment between two subjects involved in the process of reading in which they determine each other by mutual reflexive substitution. The structure implies differentiation as well as similarity, since both depend on a substitutive exchange that constitutes the subject."[68] The narrative alignment operates not only between the text and a reader but also *within* the text. This intratextual narrative can be seen with astonishing results between both prisoners; to wit, I have shown that the specular narratives, their need for differentiation and similarity constitute each man's subjectivity. The autobiographical moment permits such a fruitful exchange, whether through identification or resistance, from which subjectivity is born; autobiography delineates a scene of *différance*—what de Man calls a substitutive exchange constitutive of the subject—for authorial presence.

Molina's Body Politic

One of the most powerful (ex)changes that we witness in *Kiss of the Spider Woman* is the process of politicization that Molina goes through when he leaves prison. Molina assures Valentín that "voy a hacer todo lo que me digas." [I am going to do everything you tell me to do.][69] That is the last time that we hear Molina's voice, that is, the dialogue between the two men has ended. The following chapter is a different kind of narration: It is a report and transcript of all of Molina's actions and whereabouts, "*Informe sobre Luis Alberto Molina, procesado 3.018, puesto en libertad condicional, etc. . . .*" [Report on Luis Alberto Molina, prisoner 3,018, set free on parole, etc. . . .][70] Molina's "conditional release" suggests to us that there has been a degree of negotiation and collaboration between himself and the police.

The actual report language is most revealing for the dialogue of the prisoners has been supplanted by the official discourse of the law; for instance, the language is quite programmatic in recording some of the things Molina does:

> Llamó por teléfono a las 10.16 preguntó por Lalo, y cuando éste atendió hablaron varios minutos, en femenino, dándose nombres diferentes que se intercambiaban a lo largo de la conversación, por ejemplo Teresa, Ni, China, Perla, Caracola, Pepita, Carla y Tina. El nombrado Lalo ante todo insistió en que el procesado le contara sus "conquistas" en el penal. El procesado contestó que eran todas mentiras las cosas que se contaban

sobre las relaciones sexuales en los penales y que no había tenido ninguna "diversión".[71]

[At 10:16 he phoned and asked for Lalo, and when this man answered they spoke for a few minutes, using feminine forms, giving each other different names that changed throughout the phone conversation; some of these names were, for example, Teresa, Ni, China, Perla, Caracola, Pepita, Carla, and Tina. The so-called Lalo insisted more than anything for the former prisoner to tell him about his "conquests" in prison. The prisoner answered that everything that they had been told about sexual relations in prisons was a lie and that he had not had any "fun."]

The police's response to this initial call signals their extreme care to understand everything that is said; they acknowledged "the need to study attentively the possible code hidden in the feminine names."[72] Two days later, Molina talks with Lalo again and they continue their name game—this time using the names of Hollywood movies stars "Greta, Marlene, Marilyn, Merle, Gina, Jedi (?)." The police end this report entry affirming that "No daban la impresión de tratarse de un código, sino broma corriente entre ellos, se repite." [We repeat that they did not give the impression of these names' being a code, but a cheap joke between themselves.][73] And nine days later, the two men spoke on the phone again: "Se dieron nombres diferentes, pero no creemos que constituyan código alguno. Esos nombres fueron Delia, Mirta, Silvia, Niní, Líber, Paulina, etc., referidos casi con seguridad a actrices del cine argentino de años atrás." [They gave each other different names, but we do not think that they represent any code. Those names were Delia, Mirta, Silvia, Niní, Líber, Paulina, etc., referring almost with certainty to actresses from Argentine films from years past.][74]

If I have gone on too long, it is to emphasize several things that this report shows. First, there is the paranoia on behalf of the police that the gay men's playful naming is part of a secret code, with which the men are exchanging valuable and secret information to each other. In effect, all that is happening in each of these cases is that the men are using these names or signs of women and divas so to identify with them. I would not be at all surprised that the men were acting out different lines from some of their favorite movies. The policemen "have obviously never have been gay"—to echo Margo Channing. Second, the policemen read the law to the letter; they do not see the bigger picture. In other words, the police, listening in to Molina and Lalo's conversation, are incompetent to hear what the men are doing because they lack the point of reference, the old Argentine and Hollywood movies that the gay men share. Interestingly, during the second conversation when the gay men use names of actresses (Greta, etc.), the police were reticent to assert that they had broken the code; they write that they "suppose" that what they are hearing are the names of Hollywood actresses. Their shying away from the most obvious explanation can be read paradoxically as the police's effort to impose a code rather than to break it; they want to dictate the terms of language. Their momentary vacillation calls into question their very authority. The police's reluctance also reminds us of how in the case of the "41," the police did not want to bear or handle the sign of homosexuality for fear of being implicated. It is only two weeks into the report (nearing its end) that the police are actually able to accept that the renaming between the men as just a game. Molina has started a new job at a boutique and has called his friend Lalo to thank him for the recommendation. Again, they playfully use women's names to refer to each other. The police note again: "Cabe señalar que el modo en que constantemente cambian nombres hace pensar que es todo no premeditado, juego que no oculta código." [It is worthwhile mentioning that the ways in which they constantly change their names makes one think that everything is unpremeditated, a game that does not hide any code.][75] This is a moment of blindness of major proportions, yet it marks the official way of knowing. In the report, the police write that they quote "palabras textuales" [word-for-word].[76] Knowledge is recorded "word-for-word" without any pretense or desire to paraphrase or change the words of the speaker, hence, the quotation marks. The police are happy to understand finally the gay game of renaming and re-gendering. However, what the police understand to be the reason behind this "unpremeditated" game of naming is that the men desire to be women, and not the fact of transvestism. That these men might be drag queens and that their names, the roles they perform are those of movie actresses (Marlene, Marilyn, Silvia, Líber, etc.) means nothing to the police; for them, it is "a game that does not hide a code." For the police, transvestism is a game without rules. What the police want is to occupy the place of the Symbolic, the Law. It is for this reason as well, then, that the police are so ready to include one of Molina's lies in the report, that is, "everything that they had been told about sexual relations in prisons was a lie and that he had not had any 'fun'."

This denial of homosexuality would also affirm the prison system's success in disciplining and normalizing "degenerative" sexualities. One could observe then that Molina entered prison a child molester and left it a "normal" man. Of course, Molina's new "normality" is contingent upon obeying the letter of the law. While Puig does not say this explicitly he does show us how heterosexuality reads and breeds "heterosexuality." I am talking about how the political crusade that Molina takes differs both in substance and interpretation. We know that the gay man has decided to help Valentín, to do everything the Marxist wanted; this action is taken by the gay man not necessarily to further the causes of Marxism, but rather to express his love for the other man. Here we also learn that the gay man has decided to collaborate with the police to obtain his liberty; however, this act is read differently by everyone. On the one hand, Valentín will suppose that Molina's act is one of concern for the revolutionary cause. On the other hand, Molina has accepted the role of "intelligence agent," a role that the police have assigned to him "officially." Molina's body becomes politicized at the moment he becomes a booby trap for the Marxist "extremists." Even though the police have decided to erase any attributes of "official" (read: heterosexual) valor, Molina's body politic is certain because he has secretly contacted Valentín's allies. The police ignore until the very last minute that Molina is getting in touch with the revolutionaries behind their back. He has already accepted the dangers of the mission—not the mission as defined by the police to gather information from underground forces, but rather as defined *by his love for Valentín*. This is how Molina's body becomes politic.

Molina performs his kamikaze mission without realizing that he is being watched by the police. When he arrives at the meeting place, it is too late. The revolutionaries consider him a traitor and kill him. In the text of the report, however, the police write about a different Valentín:

> Además, la acción previa del procesado concerniente a su cuenta bancaria, indica que él mismo temía que algo le podía suceder. Más aún, si estaba a sabiendas de que era vigilado, su plan, en caso de ser sorprendido en actitud comprometida por las fuerzas del CISL, pudo haber sido uno de los siguientes: o pensaba escapar con los extremistas, o estaba dispuesto a que estos lo eliminaran.[77]

> [Also, the previous action by the prisoner concerning his bank account shows that he himself was afraid that something could happen to him. Furthermore, if he were aware that he was being watched, his plan, in case that he were surprised by forces of the CISL, could have been one of the following: he planned to escape with the extremists, or he was willing to be killed by them.]

The police are ready to offer explanations of the murder of Molina. First, we can see that any affiliation that Molina had with the police has been erased from the record, thereby exculpating the officials of any wrongdoing. Second, the police explain that Molina's financial arrangement (he had taken his money out of the bank and put it in an envelope for his mother) showed that he himself was conscious of a dangerous plan. What is unsettling, given the previous misreadings that the police have made, is the police's explanation of a plan of escape that Molina had somehow imagined in case all else failed: he would either run away with the extremists or he would be sacrificed by them. Molina's body is inscribed with a narrative of letting things follow their "natural" course, that is, submitting to a greater power or ideology. This moral masochism reminds us of the very pretenses of compulsory heterosexuality.

I suggest differently: For Molina, adopting the role of film star, a transvestitic gesture, means he is able to perform one of as many roles as he desires. In his final days, he was living, re-enacting, in effect, performing a performance of Leni Lamaison,[78] the beautiful chanteuse, who died for her loved one. For, if Molina was going to please Valentín, he was going to take on the role that most coincided with the one the Marxist projected as triumphant, the role that most matched the mission or event.

Without observing any political or historical relations, Molina imagines his life differently. He takes on the role of Leni and imposes the role of her Nazi lover onto Valentín. The Nazi Werner, representing the other face of Valentín, tells Leni that Hitler

> "[a]rriesgaba su vida una y otra vez, porque por las calles cundía el sanguinario terror marxista." Leni escucha fascinada, pero quiere saber más, como mujer le interesa saber el íntimo secreto de la fuerza personal del Conductor. Werner le responde, " . . . el Conductor se manifiesta a sí mismo en cada una de sus palabras."[79]

> ["[r]isked his life time and over again, because in the streets loomed the bloody Marxist terror" Leni listens fascinated, but she wants to know more, as a woman she is interested in knowing the intimate secret of the personal strength of the Conductor. Werner answers, " . . . the Conductor manifests himself in each one of his words."]

This script of the "fictional" film *Destino* [Destiny] guides Molina's actions; he had already confessed that it was his favorite film, regardless of the fact that it is a Nazi propaganda movie, he "liked it because it was well-made, besides it is a work of art."[80] Of course throughout the text, Molina had at numerous times expressed his indifference and distaste for politics. What mattered to him was art and performance. So, when he goes out on his mission, he is imagining that he is someone else; he is Leni following the example of her beloved, seeking to understand the *strength* of the great Conductor—whether it is Hitler or Marx makes no difference. When he is shot, Leni dies again. Molina performs Leni's death again. He dies. The different figurations of transvestism allow the Eternal Homosexual to survive.[81] He survives heroically performing in the last moments of Valentín's delirium: "... yo creo que se dejó matar porque así se moría como la heroína de una película, y nada de eso de una causa buena, eso lo sabrá el solo, y hasta es posible que ni el lo sepa..." [... I think that he allowed himself to be killed because that way he would die like a heroine from a movie, and not because of a good cause, he alone will know that, and it's even possible that he doesn't even know it...][82] Molina dies performing as he performs dying.

Kissing Good-bye

Kissing involves contact between individuals—contact implies, at the very least, tampering; to the extreme, contamination. I should mention that I have been somewhat reluctant in using the idea of "contamination" as a regulating trope since I feel it fails to adequately address or approach the complexities and powers of difference and recontextualization that I have tried to illustrate throughout this chapter. It is valuable, however, to rethink at this time the whole trope of contamination as it relates specifically to the metaphor of kissing.

The final kiss between Molina and Valentín is orchestrated as a culmination of the novel. What makes kissing a useful metaphor is that it sets up the relationship of encounter and exchange, of seduction. *Kiss of the Spider Woman* is precisely about a spectacular encounter with the Other and seducing him; it is about a radical exchange, about wrestling with language and setting the signifiers of a difficult discourse. No language remains pure in prison—or outside it. When we look closely at the turn of events, we realize that when Molina asks Valentín for a kiss, the gay man also asks whether or not he is "repulsed" or "disgusted" by the idea. The straight man does not address the question directly. What is particularly shocking is that before Valentín finally kisses Molina, they have sex "como el otro día, déjame levantar las piernas... sobre los hombros." [like the other day, (Molina adds,) let me raise my legs... over your shoulders.][83] Intercourse happens as a prelude to a kiss. How do we account for this turn of events that breaks the linearity of courtship and seduction? Why is kissing something that is left for the end?

That Valentín has had sex, he has penetrated Molina before[84] may surprise us; however, what is of utmost interest here is the fact that the men never kissed. I suspect that the only thing this could mean is that kissing involves an emotional commitment, an expression of love, which Valentín does not wish to face. This expression of love is a union with the other that the homosexual been spoken about earlier: "Por un minuto sólo, me pareció que yo no estaba acá, . . . ni acá, ni afuera . . ." [For a single minute, it seemed that I wasn't here, . . . not in here, nor out there . . .] And, "Me pareció que yo no estaba . . . que estabas sólo." [It seemed to me that that I wasn't present . . . that you were alone.] Finally, "O que yo no era yo. Que ahora yo . . . eras vos." [Or that I wasn't I. That now I . . . I was you.][85] This mirroring that becomes so vivid for the gay man after the first sexual encounter is one that is resisted by Valentín. And, because Valentín is stubborn, it will take more than a kiss to come to terms with his love. It will take dying, that moment of back and forth delirium—this happened, or no, that happened, etc.—which will fully identify Valentín with the gay man, to admit (inadvertently) his love for the other man.

Notes

Introduction

1. Paul de Man, "Criticism and Crisis," in *Blindness and Insight: Essays in the Rhetoric of Contemporary Criticism*, 2nd rev. ed., intro. by Wlad Godzich (Minneapolis: University of Minnesota Press, 1983), 3.
2. For an excellent overview of the complexity and promiscuity of the concept of "performance" as it pertains to theater, performativity, and cultural politics, see Elin Diamond, "Introduction," *Performance and Cultural Politics* (New York: Routledge, 1996), 1–12.
3. For a nuanced analysis of the film's cultural, sexual, aesthetic, and political "conservatism," see José Quiroga's reading in his *Tropics of Desire: Interventions from a Queer Latino America* (New York: New York University Press, 2000), 131–144.
4. Gabriel García Márquez, *Crónica de una muerte anunciada* (Buenos Aires: Sudamericana, 1981), 106. Unless otherwise noted, all translations are mine.
5. I use the term "homosexual" deliberately, and am cautious not to use "gay" so readily, since it is a term which has a particularly powerful history of social, cultural, and political struggle in the context of the United States. For a discussion of a wide-range taxonomy of terms to identify male-male sexual practices and social relations in Latin America, as well as the social and political identifications that stem from these relations, see Matthew Gutmann, *The Meanings of Macho: Being a Man in Mexico City* (Berkeley: University of California Press, 1996); Roger Lancaster, *Life is Hard: Machismo, Danger, and the Intimacy of Power in Nicaragua* (Berkeley: University of California Press, 1992); Stephen O. Murray, ed. *Latin American Male Homosexualities* (Albuquerque: University of New Mexico Press, 1995); and Rafael Ramírez, *What It Means to Be a Man: Reflections on Puerto Rican Masculinity*, trans. by Rosa E. Casper (New Brunswick: Rutgers University Press, 1999).

6. García Márquez, *Crónica*, 107.
7. Judith Butler's and Eve K. Sedgwick's work has been enormously influential in the theoretical scaffolding of this project. I agree strongly with both critics' theoretical discussions on performativity and how it relates to gender figuration. I insist on talking about the body in what verges on being essentialist ways because I hypothesize that the place and awareness of the body in Latin American culture, as well as in narrative, emerges in rather imposing ways. I would even argue that the making of a gendered identity happens through bodily writing. The mechanics of this identity construction are as follows: the Self recognizes a body as one's own and then it is transformed, rewritten, and recycled. The simplicity of this practice is almost too obvious and may seem reductive; however, it is a cultural practice that appears over and over again in Latin American writing. For example, I am thinking about bodily representations such as José Ingenieros's psychological treatises; Puig's initial gender stereotyping that becomes "contaminated" by other gender stereotypes; Fuentes's Artemio Cruz looking at his shriveling body and imagining it healthy again; García Márquez's re-presentation of Bolívar's body, and the debate that broke out among traditional historians for whom Bolívar was more like a "spirit." Then there is Molloy's narrator in *En breve cárcel* (*Certificate of Absence*), who seeks "words that have skin"; Clarice Lispector's masochistic bodies in *A hora da estrela* (*The Hour of the Star*); Rulfo's ghosts and Pedro Páramo becoming a bunch of stones; and Azuela's Demetrio Macías, who starts off as a bodiless "white shadow," becomes a "decorated General," and finally, is a mythical figure of the Revolution. I am also thinking about Vasconcelos's body becoming a body politic or the body of the Nation; in addition there is Jesusa Palancares's ascetic body, not to mention Delmira Agustini's poetic violence on the body, or Alfonina Storni's disappearing body ["tu me quieres blanca"], and Sor Juana's magnificent body. Also, the body in Paz's essays is one that undergoes castration and violence. In Latin American writing, a body is always sought after and claimed as one's own: this act of possession and incorporation is quite powerfully displayed in many literary texts. What follows is a complex process of bodily transformations. Although I understand that these bodily transformations are of different registers, what is again important to underscore is that the very physicality of the body becomes the *materia prima* for sexual and gender representation. Prior to a philosophical engagement with the body, there is an attachment and possession between body and subjectivity. The prior moment or prior bodily cognition and claim is what I am stressing here. I don't want to discard performative gender constitution, but rather I want to understand the prevalence of this model that establishes subjectivity prior to bodily attachment and recognition. The theoretical works that I cite to understand gender performativity are the following: Judith Butler, "Performative Acts and Gender

Constitution: An Essay in Phenomenology and Feminist Theory," in *Performing Feminisms: Feminist Critical Theory and Theater,* ed. Sue-Ellen Case (Baltimore: The Johns Hopkins University Press, 1990), 270–282; Butler, *Gender Trouble: Feminism and the Subversion of Identity* (New York: Routledge, 1990); Butler, *Bodies That Matter: On the Discursive Limits of "Sex"* (New York: Routledge, 1993); also, Eve Kosofsky Sedgwick, *Between Men: English Literature and Male Homosocial Desire* (New York: Columbia University Press, 1985); Sedgwick, *Epistemology of the Closet* (Berkeley: University of California Press, 1990); and, Sedgwick, "Queer Performativity: Henry James's *The Art of the Novel,*" *GLQ: A Journal of Lesbian and Gay Studies* 1, 1 (1993): 1–16.
8. I discuss these Paz and Molloy texts in fuller detail in chapter 1.
9. Marjorie Garber, *Vested Interests: Cross-Dressing and American Cultural Anxiety* (New York: Routledge, 1990), 10.
10. Ibid., 11.
11. Molloy, unpublished manuscript.
12. Israel Zeitlin [Clara Beter, pseud.], "Versos de una . . . ," in *Poesías completas de César Tiempo* (Buenos Aires: Stillman Editores, 1979), 1–41.

Chapter 1

1. Sor Juana Inés de la Cruz, "En reconocimiento a la inimitables plumas de la Europa," *Obras completas,* Vol. I, ed. Alfonso Méndez Plancarte (Mexico: Fondo de Cultura Económica, 1951), 158–161.
2. Judith Butler, *Excitable Speech: A Politics of the Performative* (New York: Routledge, 1997), 47.
3. The date of the dance was Sunday, November 17, 1901; however, newspaper reports of the event, as well as José Guadalupe Posada's prints, suggest November 20th as the date.
4. Shoshana Felman proposes that "[t]he scandal consists in the fact that the act cannot *know what it is doing,* that the act (of language) subverts both consciousness and knowledge (of language)." See Shoshana Felman, *The Literary Speech Act: Don Juan with J. L. Austin, or Seduction in Two Languages,* trans. Catherine Porter (Ithaca: Cornell University Press, 1983), 96. In other words, the scandalous act is not aware of its beginning; it can only be known (retroactively) as such by the other.
5. Daniel Cosío Villegas, *Historia moderna de México, Vol. IV, La vida social* (Mexico: Editorial Hermes, 1955), 409–410.
6. Ibid., 410.
7. On the ways in which "posing" gets refigured in Latin American culture as a political gesture that exceeds "mere imitation," see Sylvia Molloy, "Too Wilde for Comfort: Desire and Ideology in Fin-de-Siècle Spanish America," *Social Text* 31/32 (1992): 187–201; and also her later elaboration in

"The Politics of Posing," *Hispanisms and Homosexualities*, eds. Sylvia Molloy and Robert Irwin (Durham: Duke University Press, 1998), 141–160.
8. Michel Foucault, *Discipline and Punish: The Birth of the Prison*, trans. Alan Sheridan (New York: Vintage Books, 1979), 170–171.
9. For a general commentary on how national and homosexual identities inform one another in the articulation of the Latin American subject, see my essay "National Fantasies: Peeking into the Latin American Closet," *Queer Representations: Reading Lives, Reading Cultures*, ed. Martin B. Duberman (New York: New York University Press, 1997), 290–301.
10. Francisco L. Urquizo, *Símbolos y números* (Mexico: B. Costa-Amic, 1965), 67.
11. Carlos Monsiváis, "El mundo soslayado," introduction to *La estatua de sal*, by Salvador Novo (Mexico: Consejo Nacional para la Cultura y las Artes, 1998), 15.
12. Urquizo, *Símbolos y números*, 67; italics mine.
13. Molloy, "Politics of Posing," 147; italics mine.
14. It is important to keep in mind that transvestism does not always necessarily mean "crossing the divide" of gender difference. In some cases, transvestism is about "affirming" gender by performing one's own; in the case of beauty queens and fearless *machos*, for instance, these types take the act of transvestism in the "other" direction, so to speak. I discuss this phenomenon in greater detail in chapters 4 and 5.
15. In *How to Do Things with Words* (2nd ed., edited by J. O. Urmson and Marina Sbisà [Cambridge: Harvard University Press, 1975]), Austin goes to great pains to describe a whole series of performative speech acts. For a discussion of Austin's categorizations and Benvéniste's modifications of Austin's theory (esp., the exclusion of illocutionary forces), see chapter I, "Between Linguistics and Philosophy of Language," of Felman, *Literary Speech Act*, 11–22. Sedgwick and Parker note that "[a] variety of critiques of agency . . . have begun to put interpretative pressure on the relations between the individual and the group as those are embodied, negotiated, or even ruptured by potent acts of speech or silence. Viewed through the lenses of a postmodern deconstruction of agency, Austin can be seen to have tacitly performed two radical condensations: of the complex producing and underwriting relations on the 'hither' side of the utterance, and of the no-less-constitutive negotiations that comprise its uptake" (6–7). See Andrew Parker and Eve K. Sedgwick, "Introduction," *Performativity and Performance*, eds. Parker and Sedgwick (New York: Routledge, 1995), 1–18. As part of the effort to unpack the performative, they suggest a more nuanced understanding of "text" and "context" (15). It is important to understand Sedgwick and Parker's point that the performative works in at least two directions: inwardly, the "hither" side of the enunciation, to produce new identities, as well as outwardly, to project and affect other identities. Calling someone "41" possibly marks a queer subject, but also and importantly signifies something about the speaker. Further-

more, some performatives behave differently depending on context: Above, with the discussion of "official" versus "social" speech acts, I want to emphasize the role of "context." What is fascinating about "41" as performative is that it is so thorough in its signifying force.
16. Felman, *Literary Speech Act*, 75.
17. Ibid., 76.
18. Ibid., 76–77.
19. Ibid., 77.
20. Ibid., 77.
21. Ibid., 77–79.
22. Ibid., 82.
23. Ibid., 84.
24. Eve K. Sedgwick, "Queer Performativity: Henry James's *The Art of the Novel*," *GLQ: A Journal of Lesbian and Gay Studies* 1, 1 (1993): 4.
25. *El Imparcial*, November, 23, 1901.
26. Quoted in Luis Mario Schneider, "La novela de tema homosexual en la nueva narrativa mexicana," *La novela mexicana entre petróleo, la homosexualidad y la política* (Mexico: Editorial Patria, Nueva Imagen, 1997), 67; no date given.
27. Monsiváis, "El mundo soslayado," 15.
28. *El Imparcial*, November 23, 1901; italics mine.
29. It is important to note that most articles reporting the incident were quite short, usually no longer than two paragraphs.
30. *El Imparcial*, November 20, 1901.
31. For a good presentation of Posada's place in Mexican history, see Jesús Gómez Serrano, *José Guadalupe Posada: Testigo y crítico de su tiempo* (Aguascalientes [Mexico]: Universidad Aútonoma de Aguascalientes, SEP, 1995). Also, useful background information about Posada's work and politics can be found in Ron Tyler, ed., *Posada's Mexico* (Washington: Library of Congress [in cooperation with the Amon Carter Museum of Western Art, Ft. Worth, Texas], 1979).
32. Cosío Villegas, *Historia moderna, Vol. IV,* 408.
33. Ibid., 408.
34. Ibid., 408–409.
35. It is difficult to determine who was the author of the *corridos;* some were written by Vanegas Arroyo, the publisher of many of Posada's etchings and prints.
36. It is believed that there were originally 42 men; however, one of them "escaped" unmarked. It has been suspected that the forty-second man was Ignacio de la Torre, the son-in-law of Mexico's dictator, Porfirio Díaz. In popular usage, "42" refers to a closeted homosexual.
37. Eduardo Castrejón, *Los cuarenta y uno. Novela crítico-social* (Mexico: Fondo Rafael H. Valle, 1906). It is my evaluation that this is the first work written

in Spanish America that deals with the question of homosexuality. The only work prior to this one in Latin America was the Brazilian novel *Bom Crioullo* by Adolfo Caminha in 1896.
38. Felman, *Literary Speech Act,* 96.
39. José González Castillo, *Los invertidos* (Buenos Aires: Argentores, Ediciones del Carro de Tespis, 1957).
40. Hinojosa's texts represent one of the few and earliest contemporary demonstrations and efforts to debunk the cultural stronghold that medical and religious institutions have on the realm of gay and lesbian lives in Latin America, particularly in Mexico. See Claudia Hinojosa, "Confesiones de una mujer de costumbres raras," *fem.: 10 años de periodismo feminista* (Mexico: Fascículos Planeta, S.A. de C.V., 1988), 215–217; also her essay "Una perspectiva lesbiana del lesbianismo" in the same collection, 149–153.
41. Cosío Villegas, *Historia moderna, Vol. IV,* 410.
42. For a fuller discussion of the important role that positivism plays in Mexican culture during the Porfiriato, please refer to Zea's *El positivismo en México: Nacimiento, apogeo y decadencia* (Mexico: Fondo de Cultura Económica,1968), especially useful is the "Introducción," sections II (28–38) and IV (46–52).
43. Castrejón, *Los cuarenta y uno,* vi.
44. Ibid., ii.
45. Ibid., 1.
46. The best studies on Latin American *modernismo* include the following: Gerard Aching, *The Politics of Spanish American* Modernismo: *By Exquisite Design* (Cambridge: Cambridge University Press, 1997); Gwen Kirkpatrick, *The Dissonant Legacy of Modernismo: Lugones, Herrera y Reisig, and the Voices of Modern Spanish American Poetry* (Berkeley: University of California Press, 1989); and Julio Ramos, *Desencuentros de la modernidad en América Latina: Literatura y política en el siglo XIX* (Mexico: Fondo de Cultura Económica, 1989).
47. Judith Butler comments on the revalorization of the term "queer": "The possibility for a speech act to resignify a prior context depends, in part, upon the gap between the originiating context or intention by which an utterance is animated and the effects it produces." Butler, "On Linguistic Vulnerability," *Excitable Speech,* 14.
48. *La bohème* was first performed in Mexico City in August 22, 1897.
49. Castrejón, *Los cuarenta y uno,* 1.
50. Ibid., 3.
51. Koestenbaum argues that "[the] rushing intimation of vacuity and loss [produced by opera] isn't a solely gay or lesbian experience, but unsaid thoughts and unseen vistas particularly shaped gay and lesbian identities in the closed years of the nineteenth and twentieth centuries, the dark ages, when the shadow world of the opera queen flourished." Thus, the melodramatic space of opera served as a conduit for gay identifications. See Wayne

Koestenbaum, *The Queen's Throat: Opera, Homosexuality, and the Mystery of Desire* (New York: Poseidon Press, 1993), 44.
52. Castrejón, *Los cuarenta y uno,* 6.
53. Ibid., 6.
54. Interestingly, in Spanish, *puto,* faggot, is the male form of the word *puta,* slut.
55. Krauze outlines Porfirio Díaz's political program for Mexico: peace, order and progress. It was through Díaz's insistence on "order," through his doctrine of "pan y palo" ("bread and bludgeon"), that he seduced the nation and maintained his position as dictator for over 30 years. See Enrique Krauze, *Mexico: Biography of Power* (New York: Harper Collins Publishers, 1997), esp. his discussion on Díaz, 1–11 and 205–237.
56. Judith Butler, *Bodies That Matter: On the Discursive Limits of "Sex"* (New York: Routledge, 1993), 235.
57. Ibid., 235; italics mine.
58. Castrejón, *Los cuarenta y uno,* 23.
59. Octavio Paz, "Máscaras mexicanas" *El laberinto de la soledad,* edited by Enrico Mario Santí (Madrid: Cátedra, 1993), 175; italics mine.
60. Castrejón, *Los cuarenta y uno,* 47.
61. Ibid., 48.
62. Ibid., 48–49.
63. Ibid., 59.
64. For a thoughtful reflection on how Mexican culture looks at gay subjects, see José Joaquín Blanco's important essay "Ojos que da pánico soñar," *Función de medianoche: Ensayos de literatura cotidiana* (Mexico: Ediciones Era, 1981), 181–190.
65. Vasconcelos is one of Mexico's most important performance artists and cultural critics. I want to thank him for his generosity in sharing his work on the "41," and contributing to my understanding of gay life in Mexico.
66. Michael Moon, "Flaming Closets," *A Small Boy and Others: Imitation and Initiation in American Culture from Henry James to Andy Warhol* (Durham: Duke University Press, 1998), 76.

Chapter 2

1. Barbara Johnson, *A World of Difference* (Baltimore: The Johns Hopkins University Press, 1989), 16. Johnson also uses this epigraph to preface her comments on the de Man "scandal" (xi-xviii).
2. Walter Benjamin, "The Task of the Translator," in *Illuminations* (New York: Harcourt, Brace & Ward, Inc., 1968), 69.
3. Despite sensationalist discussions that have suggested that transvestism has been an "in-vogue" literary and academic preoccupation, earlier studies on transvestism include not only theoretical meditations, but historical (or new historical) interventions as well (esp. see works by Newton, Rekker, Wood-

house, and Hotchkiss). As mentioned earlier, the design of this study has been influenced by works such as Marjorie Garber's *Vested Interests: Cross-Dressing and Cultural Anxiety*, and Judith Butler's *Gender Trouble: Feminism and the Subversion of Identity*. Both Garber and Butler have discussed transvestism as a theory that transforms a body (of knowledge), more than just a phenomena that is applied to describe a gender change.

4. Sarduy has been a major exponent of a theory of transvestism as a metaphor for literature. I discuss his critical essays more thoroughly in chapter 4, Transvestite and Homobaroque Twirls.
5. Severo Sarduy, *La simulación* (Caracas: Monte Avila Editores, 1982), 13. All translations are mine.
6. Roberto González-Echevarría inaugurates a reading of the uses of the "artificiality" of masculinity in Sarduy's *Cobra*. See his "Plain Song: Sarduy's *Cobra*" in *Contemporary Literature* 28, 4 (1987): 437–459.
7. Sarduy, *La simulación*, 13.
8. There is a long tradition of male authors contributing to women's fashion magazines; the most famous case being Stephane Mallarmé who published in *La dernière mode;* in Latin America, there is the case of Juan Bautista Alberdi, whose articles have been collected *La Moda, Gacetín semanal de música, de poesía, de literatura, de costumbres,* volumes 1–23, prologue and notes by José A. Oría (Buenos Aires: Guillermo Kraft Ltda., S.A., 1938).
9. González-Echevarría provides a clear discussion of the importance of Carpentier's work for other Latin American authors; see his *Alejo Carpentier: The Pilgrim at Home* (Ithaca: Cornell University Press, 1976). Of particular relevance is the introductory chapter, "Preamble: A Post-Carpenterian Reflection" (15–33).
10. Throughout the essay and at specific junctures, I try carefully to place the name "Jacqueline" in quotation marks to remind myself and my readers of the constructivist nature of her appearance and presence in Carpentier's writing.
11. I introduce the concept of a coded writing for/by/about women as *gynographesis,* a neologism that echoes Lee Edelman's term "homographesis." See his essay by the same title in *The Yale Journal of Criticism.* 3, 1 (Fall 1989): 189–207. An example of a gynographetic text would be Gabriela Mistral's poetry, especially her *canciones de cuna;* the lullaby is a text that has inscribed within it certain values of maternity and womanliness.
12. Enumeration and chronology as rhetorical forms impose certain limitations and are paradoxically liberatory: what I refer to as a "approximation," "staging" or "tendency" in these articles is a highly arbitrary selection and listing, since many of the aspects within a particular "staging" may be re-produced simultaneously at others.
13. Alejo Carpentier ["Jacqueline"], "De la moda femenina" *Social* X, 10 (August 1925): 51.

14. For an insightful reading of how an idealized figure and voice of Woman gets appropriated as a practice of "voice snatching" among the *modernista* masters, see Sylvia Molloy, "Voice Snatching: *De sobremesa*, Hysteria, and the Impersonation of Marie Bashkirtseff," *Latin American Literary Review* XXV, 50 (1997): 11–29. What is important to note here is that Carpentier is not necessarily "snatching" a "real" woman's voice, rather he is projecting or imagining another entirely new one. His "model" is not a woman, but discourse itself.
15. Roberto González-Echevarría, *Relecturas: Estudios de literatura cubana* (Caracas: Monte Avila, 1976), 21; translation mine. Although González-Echevarría mentions specifically Colonial literature in this quote, this is perhaps the most succinct articulation of his "decolonization paradigm" of Latin American literature. In addition, González-Echevarría notes that the process of re-writing takes place using hegemonic authorial texts; that is, re-writing implies writing with(in) the same language of the Master in order to proceed with the subversion of the Master. For a full discussion of this theory of Latin American literary production or re-production, see his *Myth and Archive* (Cambridge: Cambridge University Press, 1990).
16. "Signifyin(g)" is a term proposed by Henry Louis Gates to mean a process by which the speaker in a position of powerlessness talks to/about another with authority. Slave and master relations require that the slave in a "lower" position create a (secret) language of survival. See Gates, *The Signifying Monkey: A Theory of African American Literary Criticism* (Oxford: Oxford University Press, 1988).
17. I am alluding to Lacan's Symbolic constellation; I provide a fuller discussion of the relationship between Latin American writing and the Symbolic in the following chapter.
18. Susan Sontag, "Notes on 'Camp'," in *Against Interpretation* (New York: Dell, 1967), 105.
19. Ibid., 106.
20. Ibid., 107.
21. Ibid., 107.
22. Ibid., 108–109; italics mine.
23. Carpentier's anonymity (read: depoliticization) should be contrasted with Andrew Ross's politicization of "camp." See Ross's essay "The Uses of Camp," in *No Respect: Intellectuals and Popular Culture* (New York: Routledge, 1989), 135–170.
24. These passages, in which Jacqueline sketches vignettes of several cities—even though at times gratuitous—follow and continue a long tradition of texts that talk about the city. I am thinking about the city as the subject in Baudelaire's *Le spleen de Paris,* Borges's *El fervor de Buenos Aires,* and those produced by avant-garde movements at the beginning of the last century—German Expressionism and Marinetti's Futurism. In fact, Jacqueline makes

specific reference to "los edificios de Marinetti." *Social* X, 10 (August 1925): 51. Another literary situation that is conjured up here is the travel chronicles at the turn-of-the-last-century.

25. See Molloy's *At Face Value: Autobiographical Writing in Spanish America* (Cambridge: Cambridge University Press, 1991), 97, 105–106.
26. *Social* X, 10 (December 1925): 55; italics mine.
27. Darío's *modernista* manifesto of *Las prosas profanas* states his resistance to creating such a model project, saying that only *celui-que-ne-comprends-pas* need the manifesto and explanation; though seemingly reluctant at first, Darío gives us nonetheless a (pre)text to understand Spanish American *modernismo*. See Rubén Darío, "Palabras Liminares," in *Prosas profanas* 11th ed. (Mexico: Colección Austral, Espasa-Calpe, 1985), 9–12.
28. These images remind me in particular of one of Darío's most beautiful sonnets, "De invierno" from *Azul* . . , 20th ed. (Madrid: Colección Austral, Espasa-Calpe, 1984), 146–147: "En invernales horas, mirad a Carolina. / Medio apelotonada, descansa en el sillón, / envuelta con su abrigo de marta cibelina / y no lejos del fuego que brilla en el sillón. [. . .] como una rosa roja que fuera flor de lis; / abre los ojos; mírame, con su mirar risueño, / y en tanto cae la nieve del cielo de París."
29. Although anachronistic, the concept of "reading" in contemporary U. S. Black and Latino transvestite and gay culture in Harlem is important. "Reading" is a more subtle form of "signifyin(g)" that places the speaking subject in a position of authority about a particular event. Please refer to Jennie Livingston's 1987 film, *Paris is Burning,* and the critical debate that followed by hooks, Butler, Fusco, and Phelan about the question of cultural appropriation and resignification.
30. *Social* X, 10 (September 1925): 51; italics mine.
31. The equation "acting like a woman = homosexual" is one that is predominant in the construction of male homosexuality in Latin America. I shall provide an expanded discussion of this epistemology in chapters 3 and 4.
32. I use this term as defined by Eve K. Sedgwick in *Between Men: English Literature and Male Homosocial Desire* (New York: Columbia University Press, 1985).
33. Marjorie Garber quotes Stoller in her essay "Fetish Envy," *Vested Interests,* 118.
34. In his "Introducción" to Carpentier's *Los pasos perdidos,* González-Echevarría notes that "Carpentier's collaboration with *Social* was assiduous and of high quality. Through this magazine, Carpentier had contact with Cuban high society. *Carteles* [a successful Cuban weekly which Carpentier helped edit] gave him economic stability; *Social* gave him class." (Madrid: Cátedra, 1985), 21. In other words, Carpentier's affiliation with *Social* shows his desire to belong: he, too, is a "wannabe."
35. *Social* X, 10 (November 1925): 49.

36. For a discussion of this point, see González-Echevarría's *Alejo Carpentier: The Pilgrim at Home*. The question of history and representation are articulated by González-Echevarría as a repetition: "The persistence of the structure and thematics of fall and redemption, of exile and return, of individual consciousness and collective conscience, stems from the constant return to the source of modern Latin American self-awareness within the philosophical coordinates of the transition from the Enlightenment to Romanticism" (27). González-Echevarría locates in this philosophical shift the historiographical bases that dictate the writing of Latin American narrative. My point here is that this same historiographical perspective affects Carpentier's performance as a woman writer; he must seek and incorporate "feminine" writing in the familiar forms of narrative.
37. Shoshana Felman, *Writing and Madness (Literature/Philosophy/Psycho-analysis)*, translated by M. N. Evans and the author (Ithaca: Cornell University Press, 1985), 12–13.
38. Ibid., 13.
39. Sarduy, *La simulación*, 19.
40. Rather than dealing with the question of the place of knowledge head on, Sarduy looks to "the East" where "knowledge itself is a condition of the body" (*La simulación*, 19). While this provocative insight is useful to articulate an epistemology of transvestism, Sarduy's Orientalist (or rather, Orientalizing) perspective locates transvestism *outside* Westernness.
41. *Social* X, 10 (December 1925): 57.
42. I mean that some of the pictures from a particular article have little or nothing to do with the fashion details about which Jacqueline writes. The text and photography seem unrelated one to the other.
43. *Social* XI, 1 (January 1926): 69.
44. *Social* XI, 2 (February 1926): 63; italics mine. I have chosen to reproduce this article (*Social* XI, 2 [February 1926]: 63–65) in its entirety to show an example of the magazine's pages, e.g., typography, photography, etc.
45. For a full discussion of the relationship between gender and Marxist discourses in Latin America, please refer to chapter 5, Kissing the Body Politic. Let me just state for the time being that there is an obvious performance of masculinity articulated in Marxist discourse that seeks to exclude gender as a social consideration. Within this discourse, woman's role is limited to reproduction; that is, her participation in the production of History and Knowledge can only go so far as an assimilation into the masculine persona. The ramifications that this assimilation has for transvestism is great.
46. *Social* XI, 2 (February 1926): 63.
47. Ibid., 63.
48. Ibid., 63–64.
49. Lucie Delarue Mardrus was the author of many texts, including romance novels like *Comme tout le monde* (1910), *L'inexpérimentée* (1912), *Le château*

tremblant (1920), and a myriad of others like these. I have been unable to find a text by the title of *Séduire;* the closest text to the one that Jacqueline describes in her column is *Embellissez-vous! dessins de Lucie Delarue Mardrus* (Paris: Les Éditions de France, 1926 [which is about the right time])—a handbook full of fashion tips like the ones presented by the Cuban author.

50. Shari Benstock notes that "[c]ertain socially prominent Paris women made their sexual preferences public in these years [at the start-of-the-century], however. Among them were the courtesan Liane de Pougy..., actress Sarah Bernhard..., Lucie Delarus Mardrus, and many others" (48). Later, she adds that "[i]ncluded in [the ranks of the burgeoning feminist movement] were lesbian writers who preserved the record that we now have of women—and lesbianism—of this era; in addition, literary aspiration itself became a subject of lesbian literature." Among those lesbian writers of the belle époque listed is the name of Delarue Mardrus. (59) See Benstock, *Women of the Left Bank: Paris, 1900–1940* (Austin: University of Texas Press, 1986).
51. *Social* XI, 7 (July 1926): 68.
52. *Social* XI, 6 (June 1926): 67. González-Echevarría once told me that Carpentier liked using ellipses at the end of sentences as a "wink" to the reader.
53. See Paul de Man, "Shelley Disfigured," *The Rhetoric of Romanticism.* (New York: Columbia University Press, 1984), 93–123.
54. Ibid., 94.
55. *Social* XI, 9 (September 1926): 67.
56. I introduce here the notion of the "epistemoerotic" as distinct from "gender" or "sexual orientation." By "epistemoerotic," I understand the possibility of creating an identity out of an erotic imagination and practice that do not necessarily prescribe certain normative and normalizing sexual practices to men vs. women, or heterosexuals vs. queers.
57. Active/passive; domination/submission; penetrator/penetrated; cutting/to be cut; fisting/to be fisted; writing/to be written; fundamental/controversial; *plaisir/jouissance*. These dichotomies are fundamental to sadomasochism.

Chapter 3

1. José Donoso, *El lugar sin límites*, 4th ed. (Barcelona: Editorial Seix Barral, S.A., 1987), 80. Donoso's text has been translated as *Hell Has No Limits* by Hallie D. Taylor and Suzanne Jill Levine, and is found in a collection entitled, *Triple Cross* (New York: E. P. Dutton & Co., Inc., 1972.) However, given the specific questions of gender that this chapter takes up, all translations are mine.
2. I am referring here to Barthes's discussion on the structure of the cliché as an interminable chain of signifiers/signifieds.
3. See Diana Palaversich's "The Metaphor of Transvestism in *El lugar sin límites*

by José Donoso"; here the author argues that the presence of the transvestite gives the novel its carnivalized discourse, in other words, the transvestite only serves to illuminate, dramatize and explain the narrative difficulty of the text. For a structuralist—or rather, "structured"—analysis of the carnivalesque in the novel, see Myrna Solotorevsky's *José Donoso: Incursiones en su producción novelesca* (Valparaíso: Ediciones Universitarias del Valparaíso, 1983), 69–80. Or, also see chapter 3 of Ricardo Gutiérrez Mouat's *José Donoso: Impostura e impostación* (Gaithersburg: Hispamérica, 1983). While all three authors discuss the transvestite's importance, it is almost a red herring to address narrative structure. For example, when Palaversich talks about la Manuela it is only to discuss her ambiguity, thus ignoring that transvestite's insistence that she is a woman. It is her very insistence that should trouble critics. However, Palaversich will ignore this demand and conclude that "the transvestism of Manuela does not only imply the sexual inversion and psychological and physical duality of the main character, but, *understood in its metaphorical function,* extends to the novel as a whole through the disruption it creates in the relationship between signifier and signified." Furthermore she argues that "it is possible to draw a parallel between a carnival in general, the brothel and the novel. In all of these three spaces *the social and cultural norms are suspended temporarily and through the play of disguise and imposture the protagonists can invert their sexual roles or relationships of power*" (163; italics mine). First, transvestites are more than metaphors, they are subjects, and how they (and we) articulate their subjectivity is a difficult but rather pedagogical project, insofar as their presence forces us to look at issues and inflections of gender. (Marjorie Garber refers to this reflection as a "crisis of category.") Second, to relate transvestism and the carnival is to impose and designate the transvestite as a scapegoat, for her presence redefines the "permissiveness" of any context; this collapsing of Bakhtinian near-anarchy with transvestitic restraint and composition is dubious to say the very least.
4. Refer to Hernán Vidal's discussion in his *José Donoso: Surrealismo y rebelión de los instintos* (Gerona: Ediciones Aubí, 1972), especially chapter 3.
5. I was amazed to discover that only one article discusses—though, not very thoroughly—the relationship between transvestism and homosexuality: Bernhardt Roland Shultz, "La Manuela: Personaje homosexual y sometimiento," *Discurso Literario* VII, 1 (1990): 225–240. The article's main problem lies in the fact that it uncritically merges homosexuality and transvestism; as a matter of fact, it insists on placing *El lugar sin límites* in the context of "recent gay narrative" (225) without really exploring the critical and theoretical dimensions of that literary historical situation and troping. It is only necessary to mention that transvestites are not always homosexual—and vice versa. Furthermore, it is important to underscore (again) that sex, sexuality, gender, erotic imagination, sexual orientation, and preference, all of these categories correspond to different discursive practices and con-

structions that are related but remain rather independent from each other; any effort to rally them (uncritically) only provides for a shallow perspective into the complexity of the sexed self.
6. Donoso, *El lugar sin límites,* 80–81.
7. Ibid., 79.
8. Ibid., 79.
9. Magnarelli argues that the place without limits is language, "the locus of the logos"; *Understanding José Donoso* (Columbia: University of South Carolina Press, 1993), 67–68. I hasten to add that the place without limits is also the body and the articulation of *genders* and *sexualities* as a function of desire in language.
10. Donoso, *El lugar sin límites,* 64.
11. Ibid., 82; italics mine.
12. Ibid., 83.
13. Ibid. 84–85.
14. I have taken the liberty of translating "*loca*" as "queer." It is important before I continue, however, to note that the word in Spanish means "crazy woman" and is also a derogatory term for a gay man, like "faggot," "queen," and other similar invectives.
15. I do not ignore the fact that la Manuela uses in Spanish the feminine form of "one," "*una.*" She does this as part of her ongoing project of representing herself always as a woman; however, I have taken the liberty again of blurring the translation to show effectively the subtle way in which the transvestite implicates us by her performance, revealing our own performances of gender. Though in his study of "gay and lesbian themes" David William Foster attempts to give an all-encompassing view of alternative representations of sexuality, he fails to consider the complexity of la Manuela's *locura*. He observes narrowly that "La Manuela does not rise above being a stereotypical *loca*: hysterical, ludicrous, alternately sentimental and viper-tongued, coquettish." See Foster's *Gay and Lesbian Themes in Latin American Writing* (Austin: University of Texas Press, 1991), 91. He rather wants to describe transvestism as a "disruptive" element to patriarchy: it is why, in his opinion, transvestism must be eliminated by characters in the novel to normalize the social order (92–93). For Foster, the place without limits is don Alejo's land and world as metaphors for patriarchy (88). I argue that the place without limits is la Manuela's body and her *locura*.
16. Donoso, *El lugar sin límites,* 85.
17. Ibid., 85.
18. Sigmund Freud, "From the History of an Infantile Neurosis" in *Standard Edition* XVII: 37. My interest here is the section "The Dream and the Primal Scene" (29–47) where Freud reveals or unravels the significance of the primal scene as an original fantasy of witnessing the parents during intercourse and interpreting this event as one of violence and pleasure, of contradiction.

19. Ibid., 45.
20. Peter Brooks argues in "Fictions of the Wolf Man: Freud and Narrative Understanding," that "in the place of a primal scene we [. . .] have a primal phantasy, operating *as* event by deferred action." See *Reading for the Plot* (New York: Vintage Books, 1984), 264–285. He adds that Freud "consider[ed] that such primal phantasies may have a phylogenic inheritance through which the individual reaches back to the history of mankind, to a racial 'masterplot'." In other words, Brooks concludes that the primal scene signifies "at [a] crucial moment in the case history [of the Wolf man] an apparent evacuation of the problem of origins, substituting for a founding event a phantasy of fiction on which is conferred all the authority and force of a prime mover" (276).
21. Donoso, *El lugar sin límites,* 89.
22. Ibid., 106–109.
23. Ibid., 107.
24. Ibid., 107–108.
25. For an excellent discussion of the relationship between the Lacanian Symbolic, Imaginary and Real, see Shoshana Felman, *Jacques Lacan and the Adventure of Insight* (Cambridge: Harvard University Press, 1987). Specifically relevant is chapter 5, "Beyond Oedipus: The Specimen Story of Psychoanalysis," (98–159). Felman argues that "[i]n this symbolic constellation, the mother's function differs from the father's function. The mother (or the *mother's image*) stands for the first object of the child's narcissistic attachment (an object and image of the child's self-love, or love for his own body—for his own image), inaugurating a type of mirroring relationship that Lacan calls 'the Imaginary'" (104). Hence, we can see that the shifting within the symbolic structure registers an epistemological crisis in subjectivity for la Manuela; she is being asked to perform as a man as another would (op)press her to be. La Manuela sees this oppression as a form of discipline, in the Foucauldian sense: the men want to control and "normalize" her phallus.
26. Marjorie Garber discusses the position of the transvestite as the Symbolic: "The transvestite makes culture possible, that there can be no culture without the transvestite because the transvestite marks the entrance into the Symbolic." See *Vested Interests,* 34.
27. Donoso, *El lugar sin límites,* 108.
28. Refer to my discussion in the section "Transvestism and Performance" in the Introduction where I conclude that "transvestism also reveals the 'falseness' (that is, the construction) of the other. Stated simply, transvestism makes something out of nothing, as well as nothing out of something. More specifically, transvestism recycles something out of nothing (production), as well as nothing out of something (consumption)."
29. Donoso, *El lugar sin límites,* 108.

30. This donjuanist attitude is located within the narrative of the West and explodes in David Henry Hwang's *M. Butterfly* (New York: New American Library, 1986) when the transvestite protagonist Song Liling testifies at the tribunal: "Okay, Rule One is: Men always believe what they want to hear. So a girl can tell the most obnoxious lies and the guys will believe them every time—'This is my first time'—'That's the biggest I've ever seen'—or *both,* which, if you really think about it, is not possible in a single lifetime. You've maybe heard those phrases a few times in your own life, yes, Your Honor?" And, later, she continues, "Rule Two: As soon as a Western man comes in contact with the East—he's already confused. The West has sort of an international rape mentality towards the East. Do you know rape mentality?" (III, 1; 82) I have provocatively chosen this critical example of the ever-charming Western figure of don Juan rather than lines from Tirso de Molina's *El burlador de Sevilla,* Mozart and da Ponte's *Don Giovanni,* and many others, which would have also shown this quality of the tireless seducer. However, what makes Hwang's play particularly appropriate to compare with la Japonesa is precisely the implications that her name acquires through this comparison. I believe that *El lugar sin límites* articulates a complex racial relationship; it is sufficient to say that a close analysis is quite revealing, especially about the women's race: Misia Blanca, don Alejo's wife, is "una rubia muy linda" [a beautiful blonde] (74); la Manuela likes wearing her flamenco dress because "como [es] tan negra el colorado [l]e queda regio" [since (she is) so black the red looks fabulous] (72). These are but a few references to color that, nonetheless, suggest a deeper awareness of race in the novel.

31. I am borrowing and adapting this term based on Michael Warner's discussion of "reprosexuality"; he states that "[r]eprosexuality involves more than reproducing, more than compulsive heterosexuality; it involves a relation to self that finds its proper temporality and fulfillment in generational transmission. Queers often find themselves in transgression not simply of a commandment to be fruitful and multiply, but more insidiously of the self-relation that goes with it." See "Introduction: Fear of a Queer Planet," *Social Text* 29 (1991): 9. By "repronarrativity," then, I want to underline the normalizing discourse that accompanies the pretension of compulsive heterosexuality: to boot, I am talking about the expectations and, indeed, the assurance of happiness that "marriage, children and a house in the suburbs" brings. By "repronarrativity," I also am referring to the situation familiar to many queer men when they mention their "friend," and the listener will inevitably ask, "what's *her* name?" Repronarrativity is the graphetic inscription of heterosexuality. I use this very formulation in my essay "The Swishing of Gender: Homographetic Marks in *Lazarillo de Tormes,*" *Hispanisms and Homosexualities,* ed. by Sylvia Molloy and Robert Irwin (Durham: Duke University Press, 1998), 133.

32. Donoso, *El lugar sin límites*, 108–9.
33. A note on translation: I have translated the name "la Pecho de Palo" as the "Ice Princess" to connote the figurative meaning of her name—cold, detached, also wretched. However, it is worth mentioning that *pecho de palo* may also mean "flat-chested," and from this I am tempted to speculate that she too was a transvestite.
34. Donoso, *El lugar sin límites*, 109.
35. Ibid., 109.
36. Ibid., 109.
37. Ibid., 15.
38. Butler, *Gender Trouble*, 31.
39. Donoso, *El lugar sin límites*, 73.
40. Ibid., 10.
41. Ibid., 73.
42. I am also thinking of another novel, José Joaquín Blanco's *Calles como incendios* (Mexico: Ediciones Océano, S.A., 1985) where the transvestites are always nearby, surrounding the politically powerful and the police. Or, we find another similar situation between the sexual outcast and the police in Manuel Puig's *El beso de la mujer araña;* I shall discuss this suspicious relationship in fuller detail in the final chapter.
43. Donoso, *El lugar sin límites*, 68.
44. Ibid., 113.
45. Ibid., 111.
46. Ibid., 48.
47. Ibid., 111.
48. Ibid., 111–12.
49. Ibid., 112; italics mine.
50. Ibid., 126.
51. Ibid., 126.
52. I borrow this term from Juliet Mitchell's essay "From King Lear to Anna O and Beyond: Some Speculative Theses on Hysteria and the Traditionless Self," *The Yale Journal of Criticism* 5, 2 (1992): 91–107. Mitchell argues that "Between the repression of an idea unacceptable to the conscious ego and conscious acknowledgement of that idea there is a halfway house: negation. A 'no' is the minus sign that allows an idea into consciousness. A hysteric's refusal of all meaning through the denial of death and castration was a 'no' to a 'no.' This minus sign introduced 'nothing.' The conversion symptom enabled a forbidden fantasy to come into play, allowable in the perverse sexuality that was denied." (104) This insight can be traced neatly over Pancho's negation of his homosexuality. For him, homosexuality is literally "nothing," a nothingness that regulates, however, his every move.
53. Mitchell, "Speculative Theses on Hysteria," 104.
54. Ibid., 104.

55. Donoso, *El lugar sin límites*, 129.
56. Ibid., 130.
57. Ibid., 130.
58. Ibid., 130.
59. Ibid., 132–33.

Chapter 4

1. Jacques Derrida, "The Double Session," in *Dissemination*, trans. Barbara Johnson (Chicago: The University of Chicago Press, 1981), 205.
2. "Escritura/travestismo" originally appeared in *Mundo Nuevo* 20 (February 1968): 72–74. It later forms part of Sarduy's collection of essays, *Escrito sobre un cuerpo* (Buenos Aires: Editorial Sudamericana, 1969), a text that approaches Latin American literature and authors from a structuralist angle. This approach accentuates his deep involvement at the time with the Tel Quel group. A translation of this text has been done by Carol Maier, *Written on a Body* (New York: Lumen Books, 1989). Another translation of the particular passage that I have chosen to analyze exists, it is by Alfred MacAdam, "Writing/Transvestism," *Review* 9 (Fall 1973): 31–33. The other collection of essays with which I will deal is *La simulación* (Caracas: Monte Ávila, 1982). The French edition of this text was published a year earlier under the title *La doublure* (Paris: Flammarion, 1981). The first essay in *La simulación* appears as an epilogue to Maier's translation of *Escrito*. Sarduy has brought together both texts, *Escrito* and *La simulación*, in an important edition entitled *Ensayos generales sobre el barroco* (Mexico-Argentina: Fondo de Cultura Económica, 1987): *Escrito* appears on pages 223–317; *La simulación*, on pages 51–142. All quotations from *La simulación* are from the 1982 Monte Ávila edition; quotations from "Escritura/travestismo" are from the 1969 *Escrito*. For the sake of consistency and close reading, all translations are mine.
3. What follows is a discussion that looks at the manner in which Derridean deconstruction and Lacanian psychoanalysis affect Sarduy's writing. For a good analysis that considers how Sarduy's writing affects French critical theory, see Mary Ann Gosser's "*Conversación en la Catedral* and *Cobra*: (Per)versions of French Narrative" (Ph.D. Dissertation, Department of Comparative Literature, Yale University, 1990), which looks "to study Severo Sarduy's French intertexts, in order to explore instead Phillipe Sollers' Sarduyan intertexts" (20).
4. Sarduy, "Escritura/travestismo," 44.
5. For interesting discussions of Sarduy's literary production, and how this production is influenced by French psychoanalytic and poststructuralist currents, see Roberto González-Echevarría's "Prologue" to Suzanne Jill Levine's translation of *Maitreya* (Hanover: Ediciones del Norte, 1987), xii; also his *La ruta de Severo Sarduy* (Hanover: Ediciones del Norte, 1987); and,

René Prieto, "The degraded body in the work of Severo Sarduy," in *Body of Writing: Figuring Desire in Spanish American Literature* (Durham: Duke University Press, 2000), 135–172.
6. De Certeau's main argument is that "literature is the theoretical discourse of the historical process" (18), a point that he uses to show how Freud's case history narratives necessarily take on a novelistic form to provide a theoretical structure and complex. The novel—like Freud's case histories—is an object of affect and the construction of a melancholic and narcissistic language. See Michel de Certeau, "The Freudian Novel: History and Literature," *Heterologies: Discourse on the Other,* trans. Brian Massumi (Minnesota: University of Minnesota Press, 1986), 17–34.
7. Ibid., 25.
8. Sarduy introduces this concept of the "metaphor to the second power" in his reading of Góngora's poetics in *Escrito,* 55–60.
9. Undoubtedly one of Sarduy's most lucid theoretical explanations of the relationship between the Baroque and his neo-Baroque is found in his article, "El barroco y el neobarroco" in César Fernández Moreno's influential *América en su literatura* (Mexico-Paris: Siglo XXI-UNESCO, 1972), 167–184.
10. Freud's work dealing with homosexuality as "sexual inversion" can be traced to his *Three Essays on the Theory of Sexuality, Standard Edition* VII, 123–245, to which I make reference in the Puig chapter. What is important to keep in mind here is that this notion of homosexuality as "inversion" presupposes a compulsory heterosexuality.
11. For a fuller discussion, see his *Standard Edition* VIII: 33, 40 and 75.
12. Sarduy, "Escritura/travestismo," 44.
13. Maier, *Written on a Body,* 34.
14. MacAdam, "Writing/Transvestism," 31.
15. In an interesting discussion of how Kabuki theater and cosmetics are understood in the West, Sarduy points out that the colors of the make-up mean something very particular within their context; however, once the cosmetic act is taken out of context or "translated," something happens: "debilitación como función de *simulacro.*" [debilitation as function of the *simulacrum.*] *La simulación,* 69. Translation produces, then, a cosmetic weakening of the simulacrum; the signs of transvestism are rendered more visible, awkward, and the illusion of otherness is spoiled.
16. Sarduy, "Escritura/travestismo," 44–45.
17. Ibid., 45.
18. Paul de Man, "Semiology and Rhetoric," in *Allegories of Reading: Figural Language in Rousseau, Nietzsche, Rilke, and Proust* (New Haven and London: Yale University Press, 1979), 5.
19. For a clear discussion of the difference between American and French deconstructive readings, insofar as they relate (to) a distinction of "lan-

guage," "rhetoric," and "performance," see Shoshana Felman's introduction, "Écriture et folie: porquoi ce livre," *La folie et la chose littéraire* (Paris: Éditions du Seuil, 1978), esp. 21–27.
20. De Man, "Semiology and Rhetoric," 5–6.
21. To wit, this very tension is the one we notice currently in this country, as gay persons (really, gay academics) debate whether identity politics (denoted as "essentialist" by the opposition) or Lacanian psychoanalysis, Foucauldian genealogies, or other cultural studies (seen as "self-indulgent" and "unintelligible" by the other side) are better ways to figure their subjectivity. For a good discussion of the relationship between essentialist and constructionist discourses in the articulation of identity, see Diana Fuss, *Essentially Speaking* (New York: Routledge, 1990).
22. Derrida, "The Double Session," 205–206.
23. Jacques Lacan, "Le séminaire sur 'La Lettre volée'," *Écrits I* (Paris: Éditions du Seuil, 1966), 19–75.
24. Sarduy, "Escritura/travestismo," 48.
25. It is imperative to note that, at the time of writing his essay, Sarduy was highly involved with the Tel Quel group, and that he was very familiar with their debates. Appropriately, the citation comes from Jean-Louis Baudry, "Écriture, fiction, idéologie," *Tel Quel* 31 (1967): 15–30. Baudry states that "[c]ar s'il y a bien un masque, il n'y a rien derrière lui; surface que ne cache rien sinon elle-même, surface qui, en tant qu'elle suppose un derrière elle, empêche qu'on la considère comme surface. La masque laisse croire à une profondeur, mais qu'il masque, c'est lui-même: il simule la dissimulation pour dissimuler qu'il n'est que simulation" (20). I would argue that by giving us a "translation" of Baudry's text, Sarduy gives us an "inversion" of an idea. We might notice that Sarduy's rendering of Baudry's quote is quite literal; however, he does introduce a notion of "audience" in his translation, e.g., "[l]a masque laisse croire à une profondeur" [the mask makes believe there is depth] becomes "[l]a máscara *nos* hace creer que hay una profundidad." The "nos" ["nous" ("us")] is absent in the original. This translation "adjustment" can be seen as a sign of critical as well as cultural difference; after all Sarduy is giving a particularly Latin American twirl or turn of phrase to French criticism. The notion of "audience" introduced in Sarduy's translation is also important because his later works will emphasize the place of transvestism and performance—and without an "audience," there is no performance.

Another example of how Sarduy relates to other French theorists of the Tel Quel group can be seen earlier in "Escritura/travestismo"; Sarduy quotes Derrida's critique that the literality of writing is not the same thing as "the world around us": this belief of such a correspondence is a "[m]ito enraizado en el saber aristotélico, logocéntrico, en el saber del *origen,* de un algo primitivo y *verdadero* que el autor lleva al blanco de la página" (47).

[(m)yth rooted in Aristotelian knowledge, logocentric, in the quest for the *origin,* [myth] of a primitive and *true* thing that the author takes to the whiteness (or blankness or center) or the page.] Sarduy attributes this idea to Derrida *L'Écriture et la différence* (Paris: Éditions du Seuil, 1967) without any reference to a particular page or essay. I would like to suggest that, if indeed Sarduy did not give us the "place" of his quote by citing so liberally, it is because his quote is a reconstruction of Derrida, a rewriting that signifies on his entire project of transvestism; this, of course, reminds us of Carpentier's uses of quotations to re-present Woman. Sarduy's use of Derrida represents clear echoes of his readerly "recollection," and that Sarduy is recapitulating, rescuing his "revised" or "translated" version of Derrida's text. In other words, when Sarduy notes that this idea is from *L'Écriture* (*sans* page number), we should take this reference literally: his citation is a rewriting of the entire Derridean text. Sarduy writes (on) Derrida's body of writing metonymically. Another question to think about is whether Sarduy has turned Derrida into Paz's "Máscaras mexicanas" ["Mexican Masks"] in *El laberinto de la soledad* [*The Labyrinth of Solitude*].

In both Baudry and Derrida's cases, Sarduy shows how translation is a critical and, I would suggest, a cultural act of rewriting. Furthermore, it is of the essence to understand *how* Sarduy is reading and deploying other critics, rather than accept his understanding of those critics. There are moments in Sarduy's writing where he misunderstands and misuses Lacan, Derrida, and others; what is important to see in Sarduy's work is how he puts French criticism into motion.

26. Sarduy, "Escritura/travestismo," 48.
27. Edelman, "Homographesis," 194.
28. I have used the preceeding quote by Edelman and my analysis as part of my essay "The Swishing of Gender: Homographetic Marks in *Lazarillo de Tormes,*" *Hispanisms and Homosexualities,* ed. by Sylvia Molloy and Robert Irwin (Durham: Duke University Press, 1998), 134.
29. González Echevarría, "Prologue" to *Maitreya,* i-ii.
30. Writing about the "body" always happens from the space and perspective of race and culture. David Savran makes this point clearly by noting that " . . . a racialized category is not simply added to gender. For gender is always articulated *through* race, through possibilities opened up by particular racial identities"; see Savran, *Taking It Like a Man: White Masculinity, Masochism, and Contemporary American Culture* (Princeton: Princeton University Press, 1998), 8.
31. Sarduy, *La simulación,* 11.
32. Birds and feathers are classic metaphors for homosexuality in Latin America.
33. Sarduy, *La simulación,* 62.
34. Butler argues that "it would be a mistake to think that homosexuality is best explained through the performativity that is drag." See *Bodies That Matter,*

235. For a discussion of the cultural limitations of this perspective, refer to my discussion in chapter 1.
35. Along similar lines, Sedgwick makes a powerful critique of the use of the trope of "cross-dressing" in the "virtual erasure of the connection between transvestism and . . . homosexuality": "Critics may well feel that the rubric 'cross-dressing' gives them . . . a way of tapping into this shared knowingness [the idea that "everyone already knows" that transvestism generally alludes to homosexuality] without having to name its subject; without incurring many of the punitive risks of openly gay enunciation in a homophobic culture. . . ." Eve K. Sedgwick, *Tendencies* (Durham, Duke University Press, 1993), 221–222. For a fuller discussion of her argument as it relates to play and antiessentialist critiques of gender construction, see pp. 220–224.
36. Roberto González-Echevarría, *La ruta de Severo Sarduy* (Hanover: Ediciones del Norte, 1987).
37. Sarduy, *La simulación*, 13.
38. Ibid., 13.
39. Freud tells us that "the fetish is a substitute for the woman's (the mother's) penis that the little boy once believed in and—for reasons familiar to us— does not want to give up." "Fetishism," *Standard Edition* XXI: 152–153. The fetish—in its surrogate function—allows the boy to disavow the possibility of castration.
40. Jacques Lacan, "The mirror stage as formative of the function of the 'I' as revealed in psychoanalytic experience," *Écrits: A Selection*, trans. Alan Sheridan (New York: W. W. Norton and Co., 1977), 4.
41. Lacan, "The mirror stage," 5–6.
42. "La mujer no es el límite donde se detiene la simulación. [Los travestís] son hipertélicos: van más allá de su fin, hacia el absoluto de una imagen abstracta, religiosa incluso, icónica en todo caso, mortal. Las mujeres—vengan a verlo al *Carrousel* de París—los imitan." [Woman is not the limit where the simulation stops. [The transvestites] are hypertelic: they go beyond their end, toward the absolute of an abstract image, inclusively religious, iconic in every case, mortal. Women—come see it at the *Carrousel* in Paris—imitate them.] Sarduy, *La simulación*, 62.
43. Again, de Certeau's effort to relate Freudian writing as a mode of affect is an appropriate way to understand Sarduy's use of Freud. See de Certeau, "The Freudian Novel," 25–27.
44. From Slavoj Žižek's excellent work, *Looking Awry: An Introduction to Jacques Lacan through Popular Culture* (Cambridge: The MIT Press. 1991), 90.
45. Sarduy, *La simulación*, 25.
46. I would like to explain that this conceptualization would be quite different from Bakhtin's idea of the *grotesque* in *Rabelais and His World*, trans. Hélène Iswolsky (Bloomington: Indiana University Press, 1984), 1–30. The grotesque is a figure of fascination because, as spectators, we seek and find

ourselves in it *momentarily;* this obeys an instinct to "control" the horror. The transvestite's mirror (as a reification of the Symbolic) reflects our image, our self-figuration, our performativity, our horror; it is always there and cannot be broken.
47. I discuss Felman's reading of Lacan in fuller detail in chapter 3.
48. Melville beautifully conjures up this scene of misrecognition in *Moby Dick* (1851): "And still deeper the meaning of that story of Narcissus, who because he could not grasp the tormenting, mild image he saw in the fountain, plunged into it and was drowned. By that same image, we see ourselves in all rivers and oceans. It is the image of the ungraspable phantom of life." Herman Melville, *Moby Dick; or, The Whale,* ed. by Harold L. Beaver (Harmondsworth: Penguin Books, 1972), 95.
49. Again, refer to Sarduy's essay "El barroco y el neobarroco," where he provides a series of Baroque strategies—condensation, proliferation, anaphora, etc.—to point to the possible ways in which *la cubanidad* may be read; also, Gustavo Guerrero provides an insightful and nuanced reading of Sarduy's neo-Baroque in his narrative in his *La estrategia neobarroca: Estudio sobre el resurgimiento de la poética barroca en la obra narrativa de Severo Sarduy* (Barcelona: Edicions del Mall, 1987).
50. From the collection by the same name, in his *Poesía y teatro completos de Xavier Villaurrutia,* 2nd ed., ed. by Alí Chumacero (Mexico: Fondo de Cultura Económica. 1966), 27.
51. Sarduy, *La simulación,* 65.
52. José Lezama Lima, "Muerte de Narciso," *Obras completas,* vol. I, intro. Cintio Vitier (Mexico: Aguilar, 1975), 658.
53. Sarduy, *La simulación,* 67.
54. Ibid., 64; italics mine.
55. Severo Sarduy, "Las estructuras de la narración: Entrevista con Severo Sarduy," interview by Emir Rodríguez Monegal, in *Mundo Nuevo* 2 (1966): 16.
56. Severo Sarduy, *De donde son los cantantes,* ed. Roberto González-Echevarría (Madrid: Ediciones Cátedra, 1993). The novel has been translated as *From Cuba with a Song,* trans. Suzanne Jill Levine (Los Angeles: Sun & Moon Press, 1994). *De donde son los cantantes* marks Severo Sarduy's intervention in the "Boom" in Latin America. It is a work of enormous complexity; the most illuminating readings of the novel include: González-Echevarría, *La ruta,* especially the chapter entitled "Son de la loma." Gustavo Guerrero offers a deft reading of how the neo-Baroque emerges in the novel; see his *La estrategia neobarroca,* as well as Adriana Méndez Rodenas, *Severo Sarduy: El neobarroco de la transgresión* (Mexico: Universidad Nacional Autónoma de México, 1983); and Oscar Montero, *The Name Game: Writing/Fading Writer in De donde son los cantantes* (Chapel Hill: North Carolina Studies in the Romance Languages and Literatures, 1988).
57. Sarduy, *De donde son los cantantes,* 235.

58. Ibid., 235.
59. According to González-Echevarría, Sarduy "desmonta," "deslee," "deslie." *La ruta*, 99–100.
60. Sarduy, *De donde son los cantantes*, 100.
61. Ibid., 101.
62. Villaurrutia, 34–35.
63. Ibid., 62.
64. René Prieto argues that Sarduy "parodied Freud's and Lacan's theories but he could not avoid exploring their implications while mocking them at the same time." See his "The Degraded Body," 146. I agree that Sarduy parodies Freud, Lacan, and members of the Tel Quel group in his literary works; in his essays, however, Sarduy tries to be rigorous and engage with these critics. Sometimes his evaluations of Lacan and others are perfunctory, word-for-word, summaries; others are incorrect. These psychoanalytic "errors" could perhaps be fruitfully reformulated as "misreadings."
65. González-Echevarría offers the best reading of the complexity of the novel's title as *both* a question and an answer. *La ruta*, 102.

Chapter 5

1. Paul Celan, "Der Meridian," *Gesammelte Werke in 5 Bänden*, vol. III (Frankfurt: Sumrkamp Verlag, 1983), 195. [He who stands on his head, Ladies and Gentleman, he who stands on his head has Heaven as an abyss.]
2. It is important to remember that film has been an important textual form that has been adapted into Latin American literature. I am thinking about works by Carlos Fuentes, Gabriel García Márquez, or Juan Rulfo, where the authors incorporate the language and style of cinematic representation into their narratives. This practice culminates from the very beginning in Puig's work, especially *La traición de Rita Hayworth* (1968). In *Boquitas Pintadas* (1969), Puig will use the romance novel as a model; in *The Buenos Aires Affair* (1973), he uses the detective story as a structuring form. In every case, Puig is a master storyteller who samples other literary styles—both from high and popular cultures—and recycles them in his narratives.
3. Manuel Puig, "Entrevista con Manuel Puig: 'Soy tan macho que las mujeres me parecen maricas' [I'm so macho that women seem like fags]," interview by Manuel Osorio, *Cuadernos para el diálogo* 231 (1977): 53.
4. Manuel Puig, *El beso de la mujer araña* (Barcelona: Editorial Seix Barral, 1976). All citations from the novel will be from this edition. The novel has been translated as *Kiss of the Spider Woman*, trans. by Thomas Colchie (New York: Vintage Books, 1980). However, as noted before, all translations are mine.
5. Along those lines, Judith Butler states that "[a]lthough the claim of universal patriarchy no longer enjoys the kind of credibility it once did, the notion

of a generally shared conception of 'woman,' the corollary to that framework, has been much more difficult to displace." *Gender Trouble,* 4. I agree with Butler that the category of "woman" as the subject of feminism has been difficult to de-essentialize, primarily, because of political concerns. However, I am not so confident that the cancer of "universal patriarchy" has been excised altogether: insidious revisions of patriarchy have appeared in such unlikely groups as "conservative minorities"—namely, right-wing Blacks, gay republicans, etc.
6. Puig, "Soy tan macho," 53.
7. The introductory paragraphs of this section "Writing Sexual Culture" have been presented in an abridged form in my essay "National Fantasies," 295–296.
8. For a good analysis on the signature that the question of homosexuality brings to a text, see Sedgwick, *Epistemology of the Closet;* Edelman, "Homographesis"; and articles by Fuss and Butler in Fuss, *Inside/Out.*
9. For instance, Foster's *Gay and Lesbian Themes in Latin American Writing* (Austin: University of Texas Press, 1991) represents a clear example of scholarship that ignores a whole body of critical writing about gender and gay/lesbian studies, thus producing a limited discussion of Latin American gay and lesbian sexuality.
10. Some of the more interesting readings that take into account the relation between text and film(s) include the following: Michael Boccia (1986); Stephanie Merrim (1985); and Frances Wyers (Weber) (1981). These essays seek to establish some of the intertextual relations and differences between the novel and film; however, given their dates of publication, they do not consider that the production of Babenco's 1985 film—which, incidentally, uses for the "Hollywood production" a newly adapted screenplay by Leonard Schrader, and not by Puig, himself a very able screenwriter—problematizes the project of reading Puig's novel or play.
11. Merrim identifies the films Molina retells. Accordingly the six films in the novel, "three of which are based on real films, three which are composites of several films: (in order of their appearance in the novel) 'Cat People,' dir., Jacques Tourneur (1942); the invented Nazi propaganda film called 'Destino;' 'The Enchanted Cottage,' dir. John Cromwell (1946); what [Merrim] call[s] the 'Adventure' film; "I Walked with a Zombie,' dir., Jacques Tourneur (1943); what [she] call[s] the 'Mexican' film." See Merrim, "Through the Film Darkly: Grade 'B' Movies and Dreamwork in *Tres tristes tigres* and *El beso de la mujer araña,*" *Modern Language Studies* 15, 4 (1985): 311, note 9.
12. Puig, *El beso,* 33.
13. Puig, *El beso,* 33–34; italics mine.
14. Judith Butler, "Imitation and Gender Insubordination," *Inside/Out,* ed. by Diana Fuss, (New York: Routledge, 1991), 15–16.

15. For a fine discussion of the difficult relation between sexuality and Marxism, see Andrew Parker's "Unthinking Sex: Marx, Engels and the Scene of Writing," *Social Text* 29, 9, 4 (1991): 28–45.
16. Puig, *El beso*, 34.
17. See Freud's second essay, "Infantile Sexuality" of the *Three Essays on the Theory of Sexuality* (1905) in *Standard Edition* VII: 173–206. This work is certainly one of Freud's most radical, for therein he argues forcefully that children have a sexuality of their own, which is manifested in their early years through sublimation and other innocuous practices (thumb-sucking, anal eroticism, etc.) until puberty when more overt (sexual) manifestations are deemed "appropriate." In this section, I discuss the mechanics of anal eroticism and its relation to Valentín's obsessional neurosis; for further discussion of Freud's work on the subject, see "Character and Anal Erotism" (1908) in *Standard Edition* IX: 167–175, and his celebrated case history of the "Wolf Man," esp. part VII, "Anal Erotism and the Castration Complex," in *Standard Edition* XVII: 72–88.
18. Freud, *Three Essays*, 185.
19. Ibid., 185.
20. Ibid., 185–186.
21. Ibid., 186.
22. Ibid., 185–193.
23. Ibid., 186.
24. While suddenly introducing so much fresh material, Freud both manages to bring information that he has yet to work through as well as silently continue the polemic with his students Adler and Jung. It is important to know that by 1914 he had finished the analysis of the Wolf Man case.
25. Freud, *Three Essays*, 187, n.1.
26. Ibid., 187.
27. For an excellent discussion of Freud's attitude toward homosexuality, see Henry Abelove, "Freud, Male Homosexuality and the Americans," *Dissent* 33 (1986): 59–69.
28. Puig, *El beso*, 65–66.
29. Ibid., 101.
30. Ibid., 117.
31. Ibid., 25.
32. Seconal (or secobarbital) is a barbiturate. It is a highly addictive sedative-hypnotic drug.
33. Puig, *El beso*, 117.
34. Ibid., 123.
35. Johnson, *A World of Difference*, 16.
36. Puig, *El beso*, 125.
37. We could argue then that "voice" interrupts Valentín's indulgence in the oral and anal spheres, the pre-Oedipal.

38. Puig, *El beso,* 125–26.
39. Ibid., 126.
40. Ibid., 128–133.
41. Ibid., 128.
42. Ibid., 33.
43. Ibid., 49–50.
44. The comparison between Valentín's girlfriend's and "Jacqueline"'s notion of "feminism" that allows the performance as the "masculine" is ready-made here.
45. Puig, "Soy tan macho," 52.
46. Puig, *El beso,* 285.
47. The relationship between (or collapsing of) film and psychoanalysis has been criticized as a film theorist's misreading of psychoanalytic theory by David N. Rodowick. In his *The Difficulty of Difference* (New York: Routledge, 1991), Rodowick suggests that a theory of the "gaze" as related to "identification" has failed to account for the complexity of the Freudian phenomenon, thus, making the question of sexual difference more difficult to address within the given paradigm. He argues that "the most productive area for a turn to Freud in film theory is to derive a theory of signification from the Freudian theory of phantasy. This theory would first have to account for permutations in the signification of the look in relation to the variations and shiftings of the subject and object of enunciation as transactions of sexual difference. Secondly, I would caution that although this theory could describe *possibilities* of cinematic identification, its claims for the positions adopted by any spectator would be purely speculative" (11). I think that Rodowick's comments are important in this discussion of *Kiss of the Spider Woman* because, as I mentioned at the beginning, that "figure of contamination [which] provides for a messy set of circumstances in reading the novel," along with reading "transvestism" and other textual configurations, would be better addressed theorizing fantasy rather than deploying, say, an intertextual, Marxist, or any monotheoretical approach for these would only address part of the texture of the arachnid trap, the kiss of the spider woman.
48. For a good discussion of how Puig uses the footnotes to discuss different theories of homosexuality and also as a structuring element of the novel, see Daniel Balderston, "Sexualidad y revolución: en torno a las notas de *El beso de la mujer araña,*" *El deseo, enorme cicatriz luminosa* (Caracas: Ediciones eXcultura, 1999), 73–82.
49. Puig, *El beso,* notes dealing with Altman's work on 154–155; 170; and 199–200. Altman's *Homosexual: Oppression and Liberation* (1971) is considered a foundational text by many early activists in the gay and lesbian movements in Latin America.
50. For a discussion of how Puig refunctions popular culture as high culture through the figure of Rita Hayworth (in the role of Gilda) as the "Gio-

conda of the twentieth century," also how this shifter of "popular" and "high" relates to the broader questions of homosexuality and the Latin American literary canon, see my discussion in "National Fantasies," 296–300.
51. Sylvia Molloy, *At Face Value: Autobiographical Writing in Spanish America* (Cambridge: Cambridge University Press, 1991), 5.
52. Puig, *El beso*, 49.
53. In Puig's *El beso de la mujer araña: adaptación escénica realizada por el autor* (Barcelona: Seix Barral, 1983), 87.
54. Puig, "Soy tan macho," 51.
55. Molloy suggests the neologism "autobiographeme" to begin talking about autobiographical tropes in her article "At Face Value: Autobiographical Writing in Spanish America," *Dispositio* IX, 24–26 (1985): 3–4.
57. Michel Foucault, *The History of Sexuality, Volume I: An Introduction,* trans. by Robert Hurley (New York: Vintage Books, 1978), 53.
58. Ibid., 61–62.
59. Puig, *El beso*, 34.
60. Ibid., 34–35.
61. I have conflated "effeminacy" and "transvestism" here again because I have argued that this distinction between both categories is caused by the lack of critical language within a Latin American social and cultural context to address sexualities and genders. Furthermore, for women, "effeminacy" is a quality that is not only acceptable but encouraged; however, that same quality for men labels them as "homosexual." This immediate labeling of an effeminate man as a homosexual happens because the spectrum of gender and sexual signs is so severe, so dichotomized—and, even, so arbitrary. When I choose to confuse the terms "effeminacy" and "transvestism," in effect, I am following the rules prescribed: that is, to use a gender marker to designate sexual behavior, no matter how problematic this mislabeling might be. Transvestism—which both connotes defined, visual gender signs as well as hidden and uncertain sexual practices—might then be a convenient metaphor for understanding how homosexuality is understood within the discourse of repronarrativity.
62. Puig, *El beso*, 66–68, notes.
63. Ibid., 66.
64. Ibid., 66, notes; italics mine.
64. Paul de Man, "Autobiography as De-Facement," *The Rhetoric of Romanticism* (New York: Columbia University Press, 1984), 70; italics mine.
65. Puig, *El beso*, 75.
66. Ibid., 66.
67. Ibid., 69.
68. de Man, "Autobiography," 70.
69. Ibid., 267.

70. Ibid., 269–279.
71. Ibid., 269.
72. Ibid., 271.
73. Ibid., 272.
74. Ibid., 275.
75. Ibid., 277.
76. Ibid., 277.
77. Ibid., 279.
78. A publicity folio of the movie *Destino* in which Leni stars, is part of the text as a footnote. It is worthwhile reading the lavish language that is used to present the star: "The greatest diva of French music would be presented later that afternoon to the most conspicuous representatives of the free international press. [. . .] Leni had been identified with the most frivolous, *dernièrs cris de la mode française,* which had used of her beauty to give life to these voices, etc." (Puig, *El beso,* 88–89, note) The similarities with Jacqueline's own descriptions are certain and inescapable.
79. Ibid., 93, note.
80. Ibid., 63.
81. Of course, I am thinking about Borges's short story "Deutsches Requiem" when the Nazi is shot, he says that his body may be afraid to die, but that "he" (his subjectivity or "I") is not, in other words, his spirit continues. Jorge Luis Borges, "Deutsches Requiem," *El aleph* (Madrid: Alianza Editorial, 1971), 83–92.
82. Puig, *El beso,* 285.
83. Ibid., 266.
84. Ibid., 219–222.
85. Ibid., 222.

Bibliography

Bibliographical note: When I first began this project, I was concerned in studying "transvestism" as a radical figure through which I could look at questions of gender and sexuality in Latin America. I was deeply concerned in creating a *corpus* of Latin American texts that (re)presented transvestism. Certainly, such archival effort would be beneficial and interesting; however, I have become deeply aware that discussing "transvestism in Latin America" necessitates beforehand a thorough understanding of "sexuality" in Latin America, an understanding that has only begun to be fleshed out and articulated recently. Throughout my study and the development of a bibliography, I have borrowed from recent works in the burgeoning fields of gender, lesbian and gay studies, and queer theory; I hope to import some of the interesting critiques of "performativity" and "gender" to the study of sexuality in Latin America, as well as use the Latin American context as a "testing ground" for some of these theories. Establishing this dialogue should explain the presence of some of the texts below.

—BSJ
July 2001

1. Primary Sources (Works by authors studied)

Carpentier, Alejo [Jacqueline, pseudonym]. "De la moda femenina." In *Social* (La Habana) X (8): 51–52, 56; X (9): 51–53; X (10): 51–53; X (11): 49–51; and, X (12): 55–58. 1925.

———. "S. M. La Moda." In *Social* (La Habana) XI (1): 69–72; XI (2): 63–65; XI (3): 67–69; XI (4): 65–67; XI (5): 67–70; XI (6): 67–70; XI (7): 67–70; XI (8): 71–73; XI (9): 67–69; XI (10): 69–72; XI (11): 67–69; and, XI (12): 67–70. 1926.

———. "S. M. La Moda." In *Social* (La Habana) XII (1): 89–92; XII (2): 89–91; XII (3): 89–91; XII (4): 89–92; and, XII (5): 89–91. 1927.

Carpentier, Alejo. *Obras completas de Alejo Carpentier.* Mexico: Siglo XXI Editores, 1983.

———. *Los pasos perdidos.* Edited by Roberto González-Echevarría. Madrid: Ediciones Cátedra, 1985.

Castrejón, Eduardo A. *Los cuarenta y uno. Novela crítico-social.* Mexico: Fondo Rafael H. Valle, 1906.

Donoso, José. *El obsceno pájaro de la noche.* Barcelona: Seix Barral, 1970.

———. *Hell Has No Limits* in *Triple Cross.* Translated by Hallie D. Taylor and Suzanne Jill Levine. New York: E. P. Dutton & Co., Inc, 1972.

———. *El jardín de al lado.* Barcelona: Seix Barral, 1981.

———. *Historia personal del "boom."* Barcelona: Seix Barral, 1983.

———. *El lugar sin límites.* 4th Edition. Barcelona: Seix Barral, 1987.

Puig, Manuel. *La traición de Rita Hayworth.* Barcelona: Seix Barral, 1971.

———. *Boquitas pintadas.* Barcelona: Seix Barral, 1972.

———. *El beso de la mujer araña.* Barcelona: Seix Barral, 1976.

———. *The Buenos Aires Affair.* Barcelona: Seix Barral, 1977.

———. "Entrevista con Manuel Puig: 'Soy tan macho que las mujeres me parecen maricas'." Interview by Manuel Osorio. In *Cuadernos para el diálogo* 231 (1977): 51–53.

———. *Kiss of the Spider Woman.* Translated by Thomas Colchie. New York: Vintage Books, 1980.

———. *Bajo un manto de estrellas: pieza en dos actos; El beso de la mujer araña: adaptación escénica realizada por el autor.* Barcelona: Seix Barral, 1983.

Sarduy, Severo. *Gestos.* Barcelona: Seix Barral, 1963.

———. "Las estructuras de la narración: Entrevista con Severo Sarduy." Interview by Emir Rodríguez Monegal. In *Mundo Nuevo* 2 (1966): 15–26.

———. *De donde son los cantantes.* Mexico: Joaquin Mortiz, 1967.

———. "Escritura/Travestismo." In *Mundo Nuevo* 20 (1968): 72–74.

———. *Escrito sobre un cuerpo; ensayos de crítica.* Buenos Aires: Editorial Sudamericana, 1969.

———. "El barroco y el neo-barroco." In *América en su literatura.* Edited by César Fernández Moreno. Mexico-Paris: Siglo XXI-UNESCO, 1972. 167–184.

———. *Cobra.* Buenos Aires: Editorial Sudamericana, 1972.

———. "Writing/Transvestism." Translated by Alfred MacAdam. In *Review* 9 (1973): 31–33.

———. *Maitreya.* Barcelona: Seix Barral, 1978.

———. *La doublure.* Paris: Flammarion, 1981.

———. *La simulación.* Caracas: Monte Ávila Editores, 1982.

———. *Ensayos generales sobre el barroco.* Mexico: Fondo de Cultura Económica, 1987.

———. *Maitreya.* Translated by Suzanne Jill Levine. Prologue by Roberto González-Echevarría. Hanover: Ediciones del Norte, 1987.

———. *Written on a Body.* Translated by Carol Maier. New York: Lumen Books, 1991.

———. *From Cuba with a Song.* Translated by Suzanne Jill Levine. Los Angeles: Sun & Moon Press, 1994.

2. Works Cited and Secondary Sources

Abelove, Henry. "Freud, Male Homosexuality, and the Americans." In *Dissent* 33 (1986): 59–69.

Aching, Gerard. *The Politics of Spanish American Modernismo: By Exquisite Design.* Cambridge: Cambridge University Press, 1997.

Achugar, Hugo. *Ideología y estructuras narrativas en José Donoso, 1950–1970.* Caracas: Centro de Estudios Latinoamericanos Rómulo Gallegos, 1979.

Ackroyd, Peter. *Dressing up, Transvestism and Drag: The History of an Obsession.* New York: Simon and Schuster, 1979.

Altman, Dennis. *Homosexual: Oppression and Liberation.* New York: Dutton, 1971.

———. *The Homosexualization of America: The Americanization of the Homosexual.* New York: St. Martin's Press, 1982.

Auerbach, Erich. "Figura." In *Scenes from the Drama of European Literature.* Gloucester, MA: Peter Smith, 1973. 11–71.

Austin, J. L. *How to Do Things with Words.* 2nd Edition. Edited by J. O. Urmson and Marina Sbisà. Cambridge: Harvard University Press, 1975.

Bacarisse, Pamela. *The Necessary Dream: A Study of the Novels of Manuel Puig.* Cardiff: University of Wales Press, 1988.

———. "Manuel Puig and the Uses of Culture." In *Review of Contemporary Fiction* 11, 3 (1991): 197–207.

Bakhtin, Mikhail. *Rabelais and His World.* Cambridge: The MIT Press, 1968.

Balderston, Daniel. *El deseo, enorme cicatriz luminosa.* Caracas: Ediciones eXcultura, 1999.

Balderston, Daniel, and Donna Guy, eds. *Sex and Sexuality in Latin America.* New York: New York University Press, 1997.

Barradas, Efraín. "Notas sobre notas: *El beso de la mujer araña*." In *Revista de Estudios Hispánicos* 371 (1979): 177–182.

Barthes, Roland. *Système de la mode.* Paris: Éditions du Seuil, 1967.

———. "Sarduy: la faz barroca." *Mundo Nuevo* 14 (1967): 70–71.

———. *Le plaisir du texte.* Paris: Éditions du Seuil, 1973.

———. *Incidents.* Translated by Richard Howard. Berkeley: University of California Press, 1992.

Baudry, Jean-Louis. "Écriture, fiction, idéologie." In *Tel Quel* 31 (1967): 15–30.

Beaujour, Michel. *Miroirs d'encre: rhétorique de l'autoportrait.* Paris: Éditions du Seuil (Collections Poétique), 1980.

Beaver, Harold. "Homosexual Signs (in memory of Roland Barthes)." In *Critical Inquiry* 8, 1 (1981): 99–119.

Benjamin, Walter. *Illuminations.* Translated by H. Zohn. New York: Schocken Books, 1969.

Benstock, Shari. *Women of the Left Bank. Paris, 1900–1940.* Austin, University of Texas Press, 1986.

Bergmann, Emilie L., and Paul Julian Smith, eds. *¿Entiendes?: Queer Readings, Hispanic Writings.* Durham: Duke University Press, 1995.

Bersani, Leo. "Is the Rectum a Grave?" In *AIDS: Cultural Analysis, Cultural Activism.* Edited by Douglas Crimp. Cambridge: The MIT Press, 1988. 197–222.

Blanco, José Joaquin. *Funciones de medianoche: ensayos de literatura cotidiana.* Mexico: Ediciones Era, 1981.

———. *Las púberes canéforas.* Mexico: Ediciones Océano, 1983.

———. *Calles como incendios.* Mexico: Ediciones Océano, 1985.

Bloom, Harold. *The Anxiety of Influence.* Oxford: Oxford University Press, 1973.

Boccia, Michael. "Versions (Con-, In- and Per-) in Manuel Puig's and Hector Babenco's *Kiss of the Spider Woman.*" In *Modern Fiction Studies* 32, 2 (1986): 417–425.

Borges, Jorge Luis. "Deutsches Requiem." In *El aleph.* Madrid: Alianza Editorial, 1971. 83–92.

Brooks, Peter. *Reading for the Plot.* New York: Vintage Books, 1984.

Butler, Judith. *Gender Trouble: Feminism and the Subversion of Identity.* New York: Routledge, 1990.

———. "Performative Acts and Gender Construction: An Essay in Phenomenology and Feminist Theory." In *Performing Feminisms: Feminist Critical Theory and Theater.* Edited by Sue-Ellen Case. Baltimore: The Johns Hopkins University Press, 1990. 270–282.

———. "Imitation and Gender Insubordination." In *Inside/Out.* Edited by Diana Fuss. New York: Routledge, 1991.

———. *Bodies That Matter: On the Discursive Limits of "Sex."* New York: Routledge, 1993.

———. *Excitable Speech: A Politics of the Performative.* New York: Routledge, 1997.

Celan, Paul. "Der Meridian." In *Gesammelte Werke in 5 Bänden.* Frankfurt: Sumrkamp Verlag, 1983. 187–202.

Chambers, Ross. "Graffiti on the Prison Wall: Writing under Dictation." In *Room for Maneuver: Reading (the) Oppositional (in) Narrative.* Chicago: The University of Chicago Press, 1991. 175–233.

Christ, Ronald. "An Interview with Manuel Puig." In *Partisan Review* 44 (1977): 52–61.

Clark, David Draper. "Manuel Puig: Selected Bibliography." In *World Literature Today* 65, 4 (1991): 655–662.

Cosío Villegas, Daniel. *Historia moderna de México. Vol. IV, La vida social.* Mexico: Editorial Hermes, 1955.

de la Cruz, Sor Juana Inés. *Obras completas,* Vol. I. Edited by Alfonso Méndez Plancarte. Mexico: Fondo de Cultura Económica, 1951.

Darío, Rubén. *Azul* . . . 20th ed. Madrid: Colección Austral, Espasa-Calpe, 1984.

———. *Prosas profanas.* 11th ed. Mexico: Colección Austral, Espasa-Calpe, 1985.

de Certeau, Michel. *Heterologies: Discourse on the Other.* Translated by Brian Massumi. Minnesota: University of Minnesota Press, 1986.

de Man, Paul. *Allegories of Reading: Figural Language in Rousseau, Nietzsche, Rilke, and Proust.* New Haven: Yale University Press, 1979.

———. *Blindness and Insight: Essays in the Rhetoric of Contemporary Criticism.* 2nd Revised Edition. Introduction by Wlad Godzich. Minneapolis: University of Minnesota Press, 1983.

———. *The Rhetoric of Romanticism.* New York: Columbia University Press, 1984.

Dekker, Rudolf M. *Tradition of Female Transvestism in Early Modern Europe.* London: MacMillan Press, 1989.

Delarue Mardrus, Lucie. *Embellissez-vous! dessins de Lucie Delarue Mardrus.* Paris: Les Éditions de France, 1926.

Derrida, Jacques. *L'écriture et la différance.* Paris: Éditions du Seuil (Collection Tel Quel), 1967.

———. *Of Grammatology.* Translated by Gayatri C. Spivak. Baltimore: The Johns Hopkins University Press, 1974.

———. *Dissemination.* Translated by Barbara Johnson. Chicago: The University of Chicago Press, 1981.

Diamond, Elin, ed. *Performance and Cultural Politics.* New York: Routledge, 1996.

Echevarren Welker, Roberto, and Enrique Giordamo. *Manuel Puig, montage y alteridad del sujeto.* Santiago: Instituto Profesional del Pacífico, 1986.

Edelman, Lee. "Homographesis." In *The Yale Journal of Criticism* 3, 1 (1989): 189–207.

Felman, Shoshana. *La folie et la chose littéraire.* Paris: Éditions du Seuil, 1978.

———. "Rereading Femininity." In *Yale French Studies (Feminist Readings: French Texts/American Contexts)* 62 (1982): 19–44.

———. *The Literary Speech Act: Don Juan with J. L. Austin, or Seduction in Two Languages,* trans. Catherine Porter. Ithaca: Cornell University Press, 1983.

———. *Writing and Madness (Literature/Philosophy/Psycho-analysis).* Translated by M. N. Evans and the author. Ithaca: Cornell University Press, 1985.

———. "Postal Survival, or, the Question of the Navel." In *Yale French Studies* 69 (1985): 49–72.

———. *Jacques Lacan and the Adventure of Insight: Psychoanalysis and Contemporary Culture.* Cambridge: Harvard University Press, 1987.

Foster, David William. *Gay and Lesbian Themes in Latin American Writing.* Austin: University of Texas Press, 1991.

———. *Sexual Textualities: Essays in Queer/ing Latin American Writing.* Austin: University of Texas Press, 1997.

Foucault, Michel. *History of Sexuality. Volume 1: An Introduction*. Translated by Robert Hurley. New York: Vintage Books, 1978.

———. *Discipline and Punish: The Birth of the Prison*. Translated by Alan Sheridan. New York: Vintage Books, 1979.

Freud, Sigmund. *Standard Edition of the Complete Works of Sigmund Freud*. 24 Volumes. Translated and edited by James Strachey et al. London: The Hogarth Press, 1953–74.

Fusco, Coco. "Who's Doin' the Twist? Notes toward a Politics of Appropriation." In *English Is Broken Here: Notes on Cultural Fusion in the Americas*. New York: The New Press, 1995. 65–77.

Fuss, Diana. *Essentially Speaking: Feminism, Nature and Difference*. New York: Routledge, 1990.

———. *Identification Papers*. New York: Routledge, 1995.

Fuss, Diana, ed. *Inside/Out*. New York: Routledge, 1991.

Gaines, Jane, and Charlotte Herzog, eds. *Fabrications: Costume and the Female Body*. New York: Routledge, 1990.

Garber, Marjorie B. *Vested Interests: Transvestism and Cultural Anxiety*. New York: Routledge, 1991.

García Márquez, Gabriel. *Crónica de una muerte anunciada*. Buenos Aires: Sudamericana, 1981.

Gates, Henry Louis. *The Signifying Monkey: A Theory of African-American Literary Criticism*. Oxford: Oxford University Press, 1988.

Girard, René. *Deceit, Desire, and the Novel: Self and Other in Literary Structure*. Translated by Yvonne Freccero. Baltimore: The Johns Hopkins University Press, 1972.

Gómez Serrano, Jesús. *José Guadalupe Posada: Testigo y crítico de su tiempo*. Aguascalientes [Mexico]: Universidad Aútonoma de Aguascalientes, SEP, 1995.

González Castillo, José. *Los invertidos*. Buenos Aires: Argentores, Ediciones del Carro de Tespis, 1957.

González Echevarría, Roberto. "Interview/Severo Sarduy." In *Diacritics* 2, 2 (1972): 41–45.

———. *Relecturas: Estudios de literatura cubana*. Caracas: Monte Avila, 1976.

———. *Alejo Carpentier: The Pilgrim at Home*. Ithaca: Cornell University Press, 1976.

———. "El primer relato de Severo Sarduy." In *Isla a su vuelo fugitiva*. Madrid: José Porrúa Turanzas, S.A., 1983. 123–143.

———. *The Voice of the Masters*. Austin: University of Texas Press, 1985.

———. *La ruta de Severo Sarduy*. Hanover: Ediciones del Norte, 1987.

———. "Plain Song: Sarduy's *Cobra*." In *Contemporary Literature* 28, 4 (1987): 437–459.

———. *Myth and Archive: Toward a Theory of Latin American Narrative*. Cambridge: Cambridge University Press, 1990.

González Echevarría, Roberto, and Klaus Muller-Bergh. *Alejo Carpentier: Bibliographical Guide/Guía bibliográfica*. Westport: Greenwood, 1983.

Gosser, Mary Ann. "*Conversación en la Catedral* and *Cobra:* (Per)versions of French Narrative." Ph.D. Dissertation, Department of Comparative Literature, Yale University, 1990.

Goytisolo, Juan. "El lenguaje del cuerpo (sobre Octavio Paz y Severo Sarduy)." In *Disidencias*. Barcelona: Seix Barral, 1977.

Guerrero, Gustavo. *La estrategia neobarroca: estudio sobre el resurgimiento de la poética barroca en la obra narrativa de Severo Sarduy.* Barcelona: Ediciones del Mall, 1987.

Gutiérrez Mouat, Ricardo. *José Donoso, impostura e impostación: la modelización lúdica y carnavalesca de una producción literaria.* Gaithersburg: Hispamérica, 1983.

Gutmann, Matthew. *The Meanings of Macho: Being a Man in Mexico City.* Berkeley: University of California Press, 1996.

Hinojosa, Claudia. "Una perspectiva lesbiana del lesbianismo." In *fem.: 10 años de periodismo feminista*. Mexico: Fascículos Planeta, S.A. de C.V., 1988. 149–153.

———. "Confessiones de una mujer de costumbres raras." In *fem.: 10 años de periodismo feminista*. Mexico: Fascículos Planeta, S.A. de C.V., 1988. 215–217.

hooks, bell. "Is Paris Burning?" In *Reel to Real: Race, Sex, and Class at the Movies*. New York: Routledge, 1996. 214–226.

Hotchkiss, Valerie. *Clothes Make the Man: Female Cross Dressing in Medieval Europe.* New York: Garland, 1996.

Holland, Norman S. "Fashioning Cuba." In *Nationalisms and Sexualities*. Edited by Andrew Parker et al. New York: Routledge, 1992. 147–156.

Hwang, David Henry. *M. Butterfly*. New York: New American Library, 1986.

El Imparcial, 1 November-25 November 1901.

Irigaray, Luce. *Speculum of the Other Woman*. Translated by Gillian C. Gill. Ithaca: Cornell University Press, 1985.

Jameson, Frederic. "Third-World Literature in the Era of Multinational Capitalism." In *Social Text* 15 (1986): 65–88.

Jardine, Alice, and Paul Smith, eds. *Men in Feminism*. New York: Metheun, 1987.

Johnson, Barbara. *The Critical Difference*. Baltimore: The Johns Hopkins University Press, 1985.

———. *A World of Difference*. Paperback edition. Baltimore: The Johns Hopkins University Press, 1989.

Kerr, Lucille. *Suspended Fictions: Reading Novels by Manuel Puig.* Urbana: University of Illinois Press, 1987.

Kirkpatrick, Gwen. *The Dissonant Legacy of Modernismo: Lugones, Herrera y Reisig, and the Voices of Modern Spanish American Poetry.* Berkeley: University of California Press, 1989.

Kiss of the Spider Woman: The Screenplay. Adapted by Leonard Schrader. Boston: Faber & Faber, 1987.

Koestenbaum, Wayne. *Double Talk: The Erotics of Male Literary Collaboration*. New York and London: Routledge, 1989.

———. *The Queen's Throat: Opera, Homosexuality and the Mystery of Desire*. New York: Poseidon Press, 1993.

Krauze, Enrique. *Mexico: Biography of Power*. New York: Harper Collins Publishers, 1997.

Kunzle, David. "Dress Reform as Antifeminism: A Response to Helene E. Roberts's 'The Exquisite Slave: The Role of Clothes in the Making of the Victorian Woman'." In *Signs* 2, 3 (1977): 570–579.

Kushigian, Julia. *Orientalism in the Hispanic Literary Tradition: In Dialogue with Borges, Paz, and Sarduy*. Albuquerque: University of New Mexico Press, 1991.

Lacan, Jacques. *Écrits* I. Paris: Éditions du Seuil, 1966.

———. *Écrits: A Selection*. Translated by Alan Sheridan. New York: Norton, 1977.

———. *The Four Fundamental Concepts of Psycho-analysis*. Translated by Alan Sheridan. London: Hogarth, 1977.

———. *Feminine Sexuality: Jacques Lacan and the École Freudienne*. Translated by Jacqueline Rose. New York: W. W. Norton, 1985.

Lancaster, Roger. *Life is Hard: Machismo, Danger, and the Intimacy of Power in Nicaragua*. Berkeley: University of California Press, 1992.

Laqueur, Thomas, and Catherine Gallagher, eds. *The Making of the Modern Body: Sexuality and Society in the 19th Century*. Berkeley: University of California Press, 1987.

Levine, Suzanne Jill. "Discourse as Bricolage." In *Review* 74 (1974): 32–37.

Lezama Lima, José. *La expresión americana*. La Habana: Instituto Nacional de Cultura, 1957.

———. "Muerte de Narciso." In *Obras completas*. Volume I. Introduction by Cintio Vitier. Mexico: Aguilar, 1975. 651–58.

Limentani, Adam. *Between Freud and Klein: The Psychoanalytic Quest for Knowledge and Truth*. London: Free Association, 1989.

Lyotard, Jean-François. *La condition post-moderne: Rapport sur le savoir*. Paris: Éditions de Minuit, 1979.

MacAdam, Alfred. *Modern Latin American Narratives: The Dreams of Reason*. Chicago: The University of Chicago Press, 1977.

Macazaga, Ramirez de Arrellano. *Las calaveras vivientes de José Guadalupe Posada*. Mexico, D. F.: Editorial Cosmos, 1976.

Macchi, Yves. "Fonctions narratives des notes infrapaginales dans *El beso de la mujer araña*." In *Les Langues néo-latines* 76 (1982): 67–81.

Magnarelli, Sharon. *Understanding José Donoso*. Columbia: University of South Carolina Press, 1993.

Mallarmé, Stephane. "La musique et les lettres." In *Œuvres complètes*. Edited and annotated by Henri Mondor and G. Jean-Aubry. Paris: Éditions Gallimard, Bibliothéque de la Pléiade, 1945. 635–57.

———. *La dernière mode: gazette du monde et de la famille*. Paris: Ramsay, 1978.

Melville, Herman. *Moby Dick; or, The Whale*. Edited by Harold L. Beaver. Harmondsworth: Penguin Books, 1972.

Méndez Rodenas, Adriana. *Severo Sarduy: El neobarroco de la transgresión*. Mexico: Universidad Nacional Autónoma de México, 1983.

Merck, Mandy, ed. *The Sexual Subject: A Screen Reader in Sexuality.* New York and London: Routledge, 1992.

Merrim, Stephanie. "For a New (Psychological) Novel in the Works of Manuel Puig." In *Novel* 17, 2 (1984): 141–157.

———. "Through the Looking-Glass Darkly: Grade 'B' Movies and Dreamwork in *Tres Tristes Tigres* and *El beso de la mujer araña.*" In *Modern Language Studies* 15, 4 (1985): 300–312.

Miller, D. A. *The Novel and the Police.* Berkeley: University of California Press, 1988.

———. *Bringing Out Roland Barthes.* Berkeley: University of California Press, 1992.

Mitchell, Juliet. "Whatever Happened to Don Juan? Don Juan and Male Hysteria," In *Mitos* (Biblioteca peruana de psicoanálisis) 2–3, 5 (1990): 77–84.

———. "From King Lear to Anna O and Beyond: Some Speculative Theses on Hysteria and the Traditionless Subject." In *The Yale Journal of Criticism* 5, 2 (1992): 91–107.

La Moda, Gacetín semanal de música, de poesía, de literatura, de costumbres. Volumes 1–23. Reimpresión facsimilar publicado por la Academia Nacional de Historia. Prologue and notes by José A. Oría. Buenos Aires: Guillermo Kraft Ltda., S.A., 1938.

Molloy, Sylvia. "At Face Value: Autobiographical Writing in Spanish America." In *Dispostio* IX, 24–26 (1985): 1–18.

———. *At Face Value: Autobiographical Writing in Spanish America.* Cambridge: Cambridge University Press, 1991.

———. "Too Wilde for Comfort: Desire and Ideology in Fin-de-Siècle Spanish America." In *Social Text* 31/32 (1992): 187–201.

———. "Voice Snatching: *De sobremesa,* Hysteria, and the Impersonation of Marie Bashkirtseff." In *Latin American Literary Review* XXV, 50 (1997): 11–29.

———. "The Politics of Posing" In *Hispanisms and Homosexualities.* Edited by Sylvia Molloy and Robert Irwin. Durham: Duke University Press, 1998. 141–160.

Molloy, Sylvia and Robert Irwin, eds. *Hispanisms and Homosexualities.* Durham: Duke University Press, 1998.

Monsiváis, Carlos. "El mundo soslayado." Introduction to *La estatua de sal* by Salvador Novo. Mexico: Consejo Nacional para la Cultura y las Artes, 1998.

Montero, Oscar J. *The Name Game: Writing/Fading Writer in* De donde son los cantantes. Chapel Hill: University of North Carolina, Department of Romance Languages, 1988.

———. "Lipstick Vogue: The Politics of Drag." In *Radical America* 22, 1 (1988): 35–42.

Moon, Michael. *A Small Boy and Others: Imitation and Initiation in American Culture from Henry James to Andy Warhol.* Durham: Duke University Press, 1998.

Morell, Hortensia R. *Composición expresionista en* El lugar sin límites *de José Donoso.* Río Piedras: Editorial de la Universidad de Puerto Rico, 1986.

Muñoz, Elías Miguel. *El discurso utópico de la sexualidad en Manuel Puig*. Madrid: Pliegos, 1987.

Murray, Stephen O., ed. *Latin American Male Homosexualities*. Albuquerque: University of New Mexico Press, 1995.

Muyaes, Jaled. *La Revolución Mexicana vista por José Guadalupe Posada*. Mexico: Talleres "Policromia," 1960.

Newton, Esther. *Mother Camp: Female Impersonators in America*. Englewood Cliffs, N.J.: Prentice Hall, 1972.

Ovid. *Metamorphoses*. 2 Volumes. Translated by F. J. Miller (3rd. Rev. Edited by G. P. Goold). Cambridge: Harvard University Press (Loeb Classical Series), 1977.

Palaversich, Diana. "The Metaphor of Transvestism in *El lugar sin límites* by José Donoso." In *AUMLA: Journal of the Australian Universities Language and Literature Association* 73 (1990): 156–165.

Parker, Andrew. "Unthinking Sex: Marx, Engels and the Scene of Writing." In *Social Text* 29 (1991): 28–45.

Parker, Andrew et al., eds. *Nationalisms and Sexualities*. New York: Routledge, 1992.

Parker, Andrew and Eve K. Sedgwick, eds., *Performativity and Performance*. New York: Routledge, 1995.

Paz, Octavio. *El arco y la lira: el poema; la revolución poética; poesía e historia*. Mexico: Fondo de Cultura Económica, 1972.

———. *Los hijos del limo; del romanticismo a la vanguardia*. Barcelona: Seix Barral, 1974.

———. *El laberinto de la soledad*. Edited by Enrico Mario Santí. Madrid: Cátedra, 1993.

Pérez, Rolando. *Severo Sarduy and the Religion of the Text*. Lanham: University Press of America, 1988.

Phelan, Peggy. *Unmarked: The Politics of Performance*. New York: Routledge, 1993.

Prieto, René. "La ambivalencia en la obra de Severo Sarduy." In *Cuadernos Americanos* 258, 1 (1985): 241–253.

———. *Body of Writing: Figuring Desire in Spanish American Literature*. Durham: Duke University Press, 2000.

José Guadalupe Posada: Illustrador de la vida mexicana. Mexico: Fondo Editorial de la Plástica Mexicana, 1963.

Puig, Manuel. "Growing up at the Movies: A Chronology." In *Review* 72 (Winter 1971–Spring 1972): 49–51.

———. "Puig por Puig." In *Zona Franca* 51–54 (1977): 49–54.

Quiroga, José. *Tropics of Desire: Interventions from a Queer Latino America*. New York: New York University Press, 2000.

Ramírez, Rafael. *What It Means to Be a Man: Reflections on Puerto Rican Masculinity*. Translated by Rosa E. Casper. New Brunswick: Rutgers University Press, 1999.

Ramos, Julio. *Desencuentros de la modernidad en América Latina: Literatura y política en el siglo XIX*. Mexico: Fondo de Cultura Económica, 1989.

Rich, Adrienne. "Compulsory Heterosexuality and Lesbian Existence." In *Signs* 5, 4 (1980): 631–660.
Ríos Avila, Rubén. "Gaiety Burlesque: Homosexual Desire in Puerto Rican Literature." Manuscript of Lecture Delivered for the Second Annual Lesbian and Gay Studies Colloquium at Yale (LGSCY), 1988.
Ríos, Julián, ed. *Severo Sarduy*. Madrid: Editorial Fundamentos, 1976.
Rivière, Joan. "Womanliness as a Masquerade." In *International Journal of Psychoanalysis* 10 (1929): 303–313.
Roberts, Helene E. "The Exquisite Slave: The Role of Clothes in the Making of Victorian Women." In *Signs* 2, 3 (1977): 554–569.
Rodowick, David N. *The Difficulty of Difference*. New York: Routledge, 1991.
Rodríguez Monegal, Emir. "Conversación con Severo Sarduy." In *Revista de Occidente* 93 (1970): 315–343.
———. "El folletín recatado" (interview). In *Revista de la Universidad de México* 74 (1972): 25–35.
Ross, Andrew. "The Uses of Camp." In *No Respect: Intellectuals and Popular Culture*. New York: Routledge, 1989. 135–170.
Rubin, Gayle. "The Traffic in Women: Notes on the 'Political Economy' of Sex." In *Toward an Anthropology of Women*. Edited by Rayna R. Reiter. New York: Monthly Review Press, 1975. 157–210.
———. "Thinking Sex: Notes for a Radical Theory of the Politics of Sexuality." In *Pleasure and Danger: Exploring Female Sexuality*. Edited by Carole S. Vance. Boston: Routledge & Kegan Paul, 1984. 267–319.
Said, Edward. *Orientalism*. New York: Vintage Books, 1982.
———. "Travelling Theory." In *The World, the Text and the Critic*. Cambridge: Harvard University Press, 1983.
Salessi, Jorge. *Médicos, maleantes y maricas: higiene, criminología y homosexualidad en la construcción de la nación argentina (Buenos Aires, 1871–1914)*. Rosario: Beatriz Viterbo Editora, 1995.
Santi, Enrico Mario. "Textual Politics: Severo Sarduy." In *Latin American Literary Review* VIII, 16 (1980): 152–160.
Sarduy, Severo. "Notas a las notas a las notas . . . : A propósito de Manuel Puig." In *Revista Iberoamericana* 37 (1971): 76–77.
Savran, David. *Taking It Like a Man: White Masculinity, Masochism, and Contemporary American Culture*. Princeton: Princeton University Press, 1998.
Schneider, Luis Mario. *La novela mexicana entre el petróleo, la homosexualidad y la política*. Mexico: Nueva Imagen, 1997.
Schulz, Berhardt Roland. "La Manuela: Personaje homosexual y sometimiento." In *Discurso literario* VII, 1 (1990): 225–240.
Sedgwick, Eve Kosofsky. *Between Men: English Literature and Male Homosocial Desire*. New York: Columbia University Press, 1985.
———. "Privilege of Unknowing." In *Genders* 1 (1988): 102–124.

———. *The Epistemology of the Closet*. Los Angeles: University of California Press, 1991.

———. "Queer Performativity: Henry James's *The Art of the Novel*." In *GLQ: A Journal of Lesbian and Gay Studies* 1, 1 (1993): 1–16.

Sedgwick, Eve Kosofsky, and Michael Moon. "Divinity: A Dossier: A Performance Piece: A Little-Understood Emotion." In *Tendencies*. Durham: Duke University Press, 1993. 213–251.

Sifuentes-Jáuregui, Ben. "Gender without Limits: Transvestism and Subjectivity in *El lugar sin límites*." In *Sex and Sexuality in Latin America*. Edited by Daniel Balderston and Donna Guy. New York: New York University Press, 1997. 44–61.

———. "National Fantasies: Peeking into the Latin American Closet." In *Queer Representations: Reading Lives, Reading Cultures*. Edited by Martin B. Duberman. New York: New York University Press, 1997. 290–301.

———. "The Swishing of Gender: Homographetic Marks in *Lazarillo de Tormes*." In *Hispanisms and Homosexualities*. Edited by Sylvia Molloy and Robert Irwin. Durham: Duke University Press, 1998. 123–140.

Silverman, Kaja. *Male Subjectivity at the Margins*. New York: Routledge, 1992.

Smith, Paul Julian. *The Body Hispanic: Gender and Sexuality in Spanish and Spanish American Literature*. Oxford: Clarendon Press, 1989.

———. *Laws of Desire: Questions of Homosexuality in Spanish Writing and Film, 1960–1990*. Oxford: Clarendon Press, 1992.

———. *Representing the Other: "Race," Text, and Gender in Spanish and Spanish American Narrative*. Oxford: Clarendon Press, 1992.

Sollers, Philippe. "La boca obra." *Tel Quel* 42 (1970): 46–47.

Solotorevsky, Myrna. *José Donoso: incursiones en su producción novelesca*. Valparaíso: Ediciones Universitaria de Valparaíso, 1983.

Sommer, Doris. *Foundational Fictions: The National Romances of Latin America*. Berkeley: University of California Press, 1991.

Sontag, Susan. *Against Interpretation*. New York: Dell, 1967.

Spivak, Gayatri C. "Displacement and the Discourse of Woman." *Displacement: Derrida and After*. Edited by Mark Krupnick. Bloomington: Indiana University Press, 1983.

Suleiman, Susan R., ed. *The Female Body in Western Culture: Contemporary Perspectives*. Cambridge: Harvard University Press, 1986.

Taylor, Clark L. "Mexican Male Homosexual Interaction in Public Contexts." In *The Many Faces of Homosexuality*. Edited by Evelyn Blackwood. New York: Harrington Park Press, 1986. 117–136.

Tyler, Ron, ed. *Posada's México*. Washington D. C.: Library of Congress (in cooperation with the Amon Carter Museum of Western Art, Ft. Worth Texas), 1979.

Urbistondo, Vicente. "La metáfora don Alejo/Dios en *El lugar sin límites*." In *Texto Crítico* 7, 22–23 (1981): 280–291.

Urquizo, Francisco L. *Símbolos y números*. Mexico: B. Costa-Amic, 1965.

Vallejo, Catharina de. "Las estructuras significativas de *El lugar sin límites* de José Donoso." In *Revista Canadiense de Estudios Hispánicos* XV, 2 (1991): 283–294.

Vidal, Hernán, *José Donoso: Surrealismo y rebelión de los instintos*. Gerona: Ediciones Aubí, 1972.

Villaurrutia, Xavier. *Obras: poesía, teatro, prosas varias, críticas*. Prologue by Alí Chumacero. Mexico: Fondo de Cultura Económica, 1953.

Warner, Michael. "Introduction: Fear of a Queer Planet." In *Social Text* 29 (1991): 3–17.

Whitam, Frederick L., and Robin M. Mathy. *Male Homosexuality in Four Societies: Brazil, Guatemala, the Philippines, and the United States*. New York: Praeger, 1986.

Wicke, Jennifer. *Advertising Fictions: Literature, Advertisement and Social Reading*. New York: Columbia University Press, 1988.

Wyers (Weber), Frances. "Manuel Puig at the Movies." In *Hispanic Review* 49 (1981): 163–181.

Yúdice, George. "*El beso de la mujer araña* y *Pubis angelical:* Entre el placer y el saber." In *Literature and Popular Culture in the Hispanic World: A Symposium*. Edited by Rose S. Mine. Gaithersburg: Hispámerica, 1981. 43–57.

Zea, Leopoldo. *El positivismo en México: Nacimiento, apogeo y decadencia*. Mexico: Fondo de Cultura Económica, 1968.

Zeitlin, Israel [Clara Beter, pseudonym]. "Versos de una . . ." In *Poesías completas de César Tiempo*. Buenos Aires: Stilman Editores, 1979. 1–41.

Žižek, Slavoj. *Looking Awry: An Introduction to Jacques Lacan through Popular Culture*. Cambridge: The MIT Press, 1991.

Index

(illustration pages are indicated in **boldface** type)

Ahuizote, El (newspaper), 28
Altman, Dennis, 174
anal eroticism
   as *écriture*, 164–69
   Sigmund Freud on, 160–62, 162–63, 169
   masculine men and, 159–64
anamorphosis, 137–38
Austin, J. L., 23
autobiography
   sexuality and, 183–85

Bakhtin, Mikhail, 85
Barthes, Roland, 67, 85
Benjamin, Walter, 53
Beter, Clara (César Tiempo), 12
body
   in Latin American literature, uses of, 7, 194–95
Boom, novels of, 145
Butler, Judith, 133
   on cross-dressing representing homosexuality, 46–47
   on injury traced to a specifiable act, 15, 22
   on originality of heterosexuality, 105–6

camp
   see transvestism and camp
Carpentier, Alejo ("Jacqueline"), 11, 55–73, 133, 141
   "De la moda femenina," 55–62
   on Paris, 58–62
   Los pasos perdidos [*The Lost Steps*], 57
   "S.M. La Moda," 73–81
   sadomasochism in, 83–85
   third-person "woman," using, 81–83
   transvestism and *différance* in, 85–86
   transvestite narrative and racial other in, 11
Casal, Julián, 133
Castro, Fidel, 145
Castrejón, Eduardo
   Los cuarenta y uno. Novela crítico-social, [*The Forty-one. A Social-Critical Novel*], 16, 35, 41–51
   colonization, 60–61
Cosío Villegas, Daniel, 17–18, 28, 40
"41" (*cuarenta y uno*) scandal, 11, 16–22
   Castrejón on, 16, 35, 41–48, 48–51
   El Imparcial newspaper on, 24–26, 34–35, 37–38
   media on, 18–19, 24–40

"41" (cuarenta y uno) scandal (continued)
Posada's engravings, **27, 29, 32–33,
35, 36, 39, 40**
straight interests and, 48–51
Urquizo on, 19–21, 24
Cosío Villegas on, 17, 24
zoological scale, 28

Darío, Rubén, 13, 65
de Certeau, Michel, 121
de Man, Paul, 120, 178
  on fiction and autobiography, 183
  on Romanticism, 82–83
Delarue Mardus, Lucie, 76, 80, 80–81
Derrida, Jacques, 13, 119–120, 141
Díaz, Porfirio, 38
Diablito rojo, El (newspaper), 28
Donoso, José, 1, 4, 12, 87
  El lugar sin límites [Hell Has No
    Limits], 88–97, 106–31: sex scene
    between la Japonesa Grande and
    la Manuela, 97–105

écriture, 164–69
Edelman, Lee, 131
effeminacy
  homosexuality and, 19–20

Felman, Shoshana, 35, 72
  on the referent, 22–24
  The "41" (forty-one)
    see under "41" (cuarenta y uno) scandal
Foucault, Michel, 18, 178–79
Fresa y chocolate [*Strawberry and
  Chocolate*] (film), 5–6
Freud, Sigmund
  on anal eroticism, 160–63, 169
  on jokes and inversion, 121–22

Garber, Marjorie , 7–9
  on the "third term," 8
García Lorca, Federico, 6
García Márquez, Gabriel

Cien años de soledad [*One Hundred
  Years of Solitude*], 114, 145
*Crónica de una muerte anunciada
  *[*Chronicle of a Death Foretold*],
  6–7
gender signs, reading, 53–55
Gide, André, 6
González Castillo, José, 38
González-Echevarría, Roberto, 60, 121,
  131–34
Goytisolo, Juan, 6
Guacamaya, La (newspaper), 28

heterosexual panic, 170–74
heterosexuality
  originality of, 105–6
  Manuel Puig on, 172–73
  as symptom of pornography,
    105
Hinojosa, Claudia, 38
homographesis, 131
homosexuality
  cross-dressing representing,
    46–47
  and effeminacy, 19–20

Imparcial, El (newspaper), 18–19
  on the "41" scandal, 24–26, 34–35,
    37–38

"Jacqueline"
  see under Carpentier, Alejo
Johnson, Barbara
  on ignorance, 53
Joyce, James, 59

Koestenbaum, Wayne, 45

Lacan, Jacques, 13, 141, 149
  on the mirror-stage, 135–36
"Los Lagartijos" (lithograph), **30**
Lam, Wilfredo, 133
Lemebel, Pedro, 5

Index 239

lesbianism
  as a fantasy of male heterosexuality, 105
Lezama Lima, José, 5, 133
  "Muerte de Narciso," ["The Death of Narcissus"], 141–43

Martí, José, 5
masculinity, *machismo*
  and anal eroticism, 159–64
  as parody, 105–9
  as transvestism, 112–18
Molloy, Sylvia, 7, 18, 64
  on cultural imposition and hierarchy, 9
  on the politics of posing, 19–22
  on self-figuration and national identity, 176–78
Monsiváis, Carlos, 19–20, 46
Moon, Michael, 51

national identity, nationalism
  self-figuration and, 176–77, 178
  sexuality and, 6–10

Paz, Octavio, 7, 48, 151
  penetration paradigm, 7
performance
  and transvestism, 2–4
politics of posing, 7, 18, 9–22
pornography
  heterosexuality as symptom of, 105
Posada, José Guadalupe, 11, 16, 26, 28, 31, 34–35, 38, 40
  "Aquí están los Maricones" (corrido), 31, 32
  calaveras (skulls), 28
  "Calavera de un lagartijo," 28, **29**
  "Catrina Calavera," 28, **29**
  "El feminismo se impone," 38–40, **39, 40**, 46
  "El gran viaje de los 41 maricones para Yucatán," 35–38, **36**

engravings and etchings, 29, 32–33, 35, 36, 39, 40
  "Los 41 maricones encontrados en un baile de Calle de la Paz el 20 de Noviembre, 1901," 31–35, **32–33**
Puig, Manuel, 4–5, 12–13, 38, 140, 177
  El beso de la mujer araña [*Kiss of the Spider Woman*]: anal eroticism as *écriture*, 164–69; creating the super man, 152–55; heterosexual panic, 170–74; homosexuality, notes on, 174–83; kissing, 190–91; masculine men and anal eroticism, 159–64; Molina, politicization of, 185–90; the prison of narration, 155–59; sexuality and autobiography, 183–85; success of, 151–52
  Buenos Aires Affair, 177
  on heterosexuality, 172–73

Rodríguez, Jesusa, 5
Rodríguez Monegal, Emir, 143
Rulfo, Juan
  Pedro Páramo, 145

sadomasochism
  and fashion, 83–85
Sarduy, Severo, 4, 12–13, 67, 70, 72, 131–133, 138–41, 148–49
  Cobra, 119
  cubanidad in, 143–48
  De donde son los cantantes [*From Cuba with a Song*], 119, 144–48
  Escrito sobre un cuerpo, 119–120
  "Escritura/travestismo" ["Writing/Transvestism"], 119, 120–31
  La simulación, 54–55, 119, 131–38, 145
Sedgwick, Eve Kosofsky, 24

self-figuration and national identity, 176–78
sexuality
   and autobiography, 183–85
   and nationalism, 6–10
Social (magazine), 11, 55–81
   see also Carpentier, Alejo ("Jacqueline")
Sontag, Susan
   "Notes on 'Camp'," 62–63
Stoller, Robert J.
   fetish, definition of, 67

Tarántula, La (newspaper), 28
transvestism
   and camp, 62–63
   and *différance*, 85–86
   and madness, 71–73
   and performance, 2–4

Urquizo, Francisco L.
   on the "41," 19–21

Vanegas Arroyo, Antonio, 26, 28
Vargas Llosa, Mario
   Conversación en la Catedral, 6
Vasconcelos, Tito, 5, 50
Villaurrutia, Xavier, 140, 148–49
   "Nocturno en que nada se oye" ["Nocturne where nothing can be heard"], 148–49
   "Reflejos" ["Reflections"], 140

Wilde, Oscar, 6, 144

Yeguas del apocalípsis, Las, 5

Zeitlin, Israel, 12
Žižek, Slavoj 137–38